eight meditations on architecture

eight meditations on architecture

JUHANI PALLASMAA

Edited by MATTEO ZAMBELLI

Alberto Campo Baeza Essays, translated from Spanish by Penelope Eades

WILEY

This edition first published 2026.

Registered Offices
John Wiley & Sons, Inc., 111 River Street, Hoboken, NJ 07030, USA
John Wiley & Sons Ltd, New Era House, 8 Oldlands Way, Bognor Regis, West Sussex, PO22 9NQ, UK

For details of our global editorial offices, customer services, and more information about Wiley products visit us at www.wiley.com.

The manufacturer's authorized representative according to the EU General Product Safety Regulation is Wiley-VCH GmbH, Boschstr. 12, 69469 Weinheim, Germany, e-mail: Product_Safety@wiley.com.

Wiley also publishes its books in a variety of electronic formats and by print-on-demand. Some content that appears in standard print versions of this book may not be available in other formats.

Library of Congress Cataloging-in-Publication Data:

Names: Pallasmaa, Juhani, 1936- author. | Campo Baeza, Alberto, 1946- author. |
Zambelli, Matteo, 1968- author.
Title: Eight meditations on architecture / Juhani Pallasmaa, Helsinki,
Finland, Alberto Campo Baeza, Madrid
Spain, Matteo Zambelli, Belluno, Italy.
Description: Hoboken, NJ : Wiley, 2026. | Includes bibliographical
references and index.
Identifiers: LCCN 2025026283 (print) | LCCN 2025026284 (ebook) | ISBN
9781394369805 (cloth) | ISBN 9781394369812 (adobe pdf) | ISBN
9781394369829 (epub)
Subjects: LCSH: Architecture—Philosophy. | Architecture—Aesthetics. |
Architectural design. | LCGFT: Essays.
Classification: LCC NA2500 .P3478 2025 (print) | LCC NA2500 (ebook) | DDC
720.1—dc23/eng/20250625
LC record available at https://lccn.loc.gov/2025026283
LC ebook record available at https://lccn.loc.gov/2025026284

Cover Design: Wiley
Cover Images: Courtesy of Alberto Campo Baeza and Juhani Pallasmaa

Set in 11/13 pts and ITC New Baskerville Std by Straive, Chennai, India

Printed and bound in Great Britain by Bell & Bain Ltd, Glasgow
BB136601-220126

CONTENTS

Foreword / Eight Meditations on Architecture
Matteo Zambelli **vii**

1 **THE ETHICAL AND EXISTENTIAL MEANING OF BEAUTY** 1

2 **THE TOUCH OF LIGHT** / Materiality and Tactility of Illumination 13

3 **THE SPACE OF TIME** / Mental Time in Architecture 35

4 **SELFHOOD, MEMORY, AND IMAGINATION** / Landscapes of Remembrance and Dream 55

5 **NEWNESS, TRADITION, AND IDENTITY** / Existential Content and Meaning in Architecture 75

6 **WISDOM AND MODESTY** 92

7 **SPIRITUALITY IN ARCHITECTURE** / Architecture, Art, and Existential Sacredness 99

8 **THE COMPLEXITY OF SIMPLICITY** / The Inner Structure of the Artistic Image 129

Bibliography **147**

Index **153**

FOREWORD

Eight Meditations on Architecture

Matteo Zambelli

For years, I had been trying to publish a collection of essays by my dear friend Juhani Pallasmaa on topics that I consider foundational to the education of a good architect. I had chosen the essays from the thousands, meticulously catalogued, that populate his archive, to which he had given me access in 2016 while Juhani and Hannele, his wife, hosted me at their home in Helsinki and at the summer house on the lake in Sammatti where I slept in the very same *cabanon*, where he often wrote his books. I needed the collected essays to complete *Inseminations: Seeds for Architectural Thoughts*,[1] the updated and expanded English version of the book, *Lampi di pensiero. Fenomenologia della percezione in architettura*[2], which I had conceived and translated a few years earlier, collecting Juhani Pallasmaa's thoughts broken down into self-contained fragments, organized alphabetically in the style of an encyclopaedia.

For a series of conjunctural reasons, we had never managed to realize the collection I longed to publish in Italian. Then one day, as I regularly do because of my passion for Alberto Campo Baeza's architecture and writings, I went to visit his website; among the news, a book I did not know was highlighted. It had been published recently, in 2023, and was entitled *Siete lecciones de arquitectura.*[3] The lectures were dedicated to seven fundamental topics of architecture. In football, as in other sports, the word "fundamentals," used as a noun, means the basic techniques that every player must possess to make a career; therefore, *mutatis mutandis*, the fundamentals are the basic knowledge that architects must possess, and against which they must measure themselves, if they aspire to become a good architect.

The themes of the seven lectures were "Wisdom," "Beauty," "Time," "Memory," "Light," "Intellectual Enjoyment," and "Universality."

1 Pallasmaa, Juhani and Zambelli, Matteo (2020). *Inseminations: Seeds for Architectural Thoughts*. Oxford: Wiley.

2 Pallasmaa, Juhani (2011). *Lampi di pensiero. Fenomenologia della percezione in architettura* (Flashes of Thought: Phenomenology of Perception in Architecture). Bologne: Pendragon.

3 Alberto Campo Baeza's *Siete lecciones de arquitectura* (Seven Lessons of Architecture) is a self-published book available at: https://www.campobaeza.com/books/siete-lecciones-de-arquitectura/ (accessed March 2025).

Serendipity would have it that six of the seven themes were the same as some of the essays I had collected from Pallasmaa's archive. At that point, satisfied and fired up, I went back to Juhani and proposed to publish and translate them into Italian alongside those of Alberto Campo Baeza. What I envisioned was a confrontation between two great architects/thinkers on the same topics, an even more exciting idea than the initial one. Pallasmaa's response was not long in coming; he was stimulated by the idea, because he knew Alberto personally and held him in high esteem – they had lectured together on several occasions – also having read some of his writings, but, fatefully, not the ones I proposed publishing in conjunction with his,[4] and Juhani called him "a well-read and poetic writer."

4 Pallasmaa was amazed and delighted to learn that Campo Baeza and he had written about the same topics each without each other's knowledge.

There was another "serendipitous" occurrence. Pallasmaa was the president of a jury that had recently awarded Alberto Campo Baeza the prestigious and munificent "The Daylight Award", which would be presented to him in Copenhagen on 16 May 2024.

It was now a question of involving Alberto, whom I did not know personally. He immediately responded to my proposal with a "Thank you very much" and immediately afterwards, in another e-mail, with a triple "Thank you, thank you, thank you." So, we arranged to meet in Copenhagen to address together, face-to-face, a few issues concerning the book.

First, we removed the essay on "Intellectual Enjoyment," because Pallasmaa had written nothing about it; in its place, we inserted one on "Essentiality." Then we increased the number of essays to eight, despite Alberto's reluctance and his preference to keep "only" seven, because he considered seven a "nice" number; I asked to add the topic on the religious and sacral dimension of space.

We then decided to include images wherever they could be functional to the text. In the case of *Siete lecciones de arquitectura* by Campo Baeza, as in his other books – with specific reference to those published in Italian: *L'idea costruita*,[5] *Principia architectonica*,[6] and *Palinsesto architettonico*[7] – the images were already present; they were a selection of photos of historical buildings and works of art, referenced by Alberto in his texts, and sketches and images of some of his own projects, which he did not always necessarily talk about, but which made explicit the topics he dealt with; they represented the interpretation and translation of the concepts he

5 Baeza, Alberto Campo (2012). *L'idea costruita*. Syracuse: Lettera Ventidue. The English version of the book is: Campo Baeza, Alberto (2015). *The Built Idea*. Beijing: Oscar Riera Ojeda Publishers.

6 Baeza, Alberto Campo (2018). *Principia architectonica*. Milan: Christian Marinotti Edizioni.

7 Baeza, Alberto Campo (2022). *Palinsesto architettonico* (Architectural Palimpsest). Syracuse: Lettera Ventidue.

expressed in words into the metalanguage of architecture. This was a way to make his readers understand the unity of thought and action, the unity of *theoresis* and *poiesis* that characterizes him as a thinker-architect.

Pallasmaa's essays were without illustrations. The reason is easily explained: most of his essays are written for conferences, which he attends, all over the world, for which he normally prepares a slide-show of images looped during the reading of the text of his speech. Aside from this, his words are so evocative that they generally do not need any iconographic apparatus, also because, in my opinion, Pallasmaa uses words precisely with the intention of stimulating the reader to associate his text with his/her own baggage of images. Some of his most popular books, such as *The Eyes of the Skin: Architecture and the Senses,*[8] *The Thinking Hand: Existential and Embodied Wisdom in Architecture,*[9] *The Embodied Image: Imagination and Imagery in Architecture,*[10] have practically no images.

Regarding the evocative role of the word, Pallasmaa told me that, "During the past twenty years, I have aspired for literary, emotional qualities in my writing; a logical argument rarely moves you, whereas a poetic formulation has the chance of engaging the reader emotionally. Beauty, signification and truth are related. In my younger age, precision was my ideal, but later I have learned that an expression that evokes associations or even doubt, or counter-argument, has its value, too. I have learned the value of uncertainty and insecurity from the writings of Joseph Brodsky. I wish to relate assurance and doubt in my writings."[11]

The last decision concerned the book as an artefact, namely the cover and the layout, the appearance of which should have been functional to express the dialogue of the two authors on the same themes. For the Italian version,[12] I proposed to Campo Baeza and Pallasmaa a book with a double cover, thus without a back cover, so that it could be read by starting from one side or the other, simply by flipping it over 180 degrees. The reason for this choice is, trivially, that I did not want one author to come before the other, although, in order not to upset anyone, I could have resorted to alphabetical order (of course!). The two overturned texts, actually, stand for two different but consonant points of view on the underlying topics and, often, the approach.

8
Pallasmaa, Juhani (2008). *The Eyes of the Skin: Architecture and the Senses*. Oxford: Wiley.

9
Pallasmaa, Juhani (2009). *The Thinking Hand: Existential and Embodied Wisdom in Architecture*. Oxford: Wiley.

10
Pallasmaa, Juhani (2011). *The Embodied Image: Imagination and Imagery in Architecture*. Oxford: Wiley.

11
Pallasmaa, Juhani (2012). *Frammenti. Collage e discontinuità nell'immaginario Architettonico / Fragments. Collage and Discontinuity in Architectural Imagery*, 125–126. Pordenone: Giavedoni Editore.

12
Pallasmaa, Juhani and Campo Baeza, Alberto (2024). *Otto meditazioni di architettura*. Florence: Firenze University Press.

Let us see the differences and consonances.

The first difference concerns the approach. The architect Juhani Pallasmaa – his practice grew to about 50 employees and was among the largest in Finland – is nowadays best known as a successful essayist – so much so that his books have been translated into 38 languages – starting, in particular, with two books: *Questions of Perception: Phenomenology of Architecture* and *The Eyes of the Skin*. Pallasmaa's point of view is that of the phenomenology of perception applied to architecture; a point of view and approach that he developed after a teaching period in Ethiopia that led him to abandon the refined abstractions of Mies van der Rohe, which generated architecture labeled in Finland as constructivist, due to an apparent similarity to the experiments of Russian constructivism. As he revealed to me in an interview,[13] his thinking developed from quasi-scientific rationalism, through anthropological interests, social psychiatry, psychoanalysis, and environmental psychology, to phenomenology, when he was dazzled by reading Maurice Merleau-Ponty, and, more recently, to neuroscience, which could help architects design buildings capable of supporting both mind and body.

13 Pallasmaa, *Frammenti / Fragments*, op. cit., p. 128.

For Pallasmaa, what he calls the "neglected senses" – i.e. touch, hearing, smell, and taste – are important in the perception of architecture. Neglected because they have taken a secondary role compared to sight, the sense that dominates in the perception and conception of architecture. The author writes, in this regard: "Frammenti / Fragments."[14] Pallasmaa is convinced of "the role of the body as the locus of perception, thought and consciousness, and of the significance of the senses in articulating, storing and processing sensory responses and thoughts."[15] According to the Finnish author, in the conception and perception of architecture, we must be guided by the four neglected senses, the atmospheric senses, the senses of blurred vision and peripheral vision, namely those that, through the flesh of which we are made allow us to perceive the "roundness" of the situation, its *gestalt* dimension, and make us become flesh of the same flesh of the world, leading to the fusion between subject and object, between self and world.

14 Pallasmaa, *The Eyes of the Skin*, op. cit., p. 10.

15 Ibid.

For Pallasmaa, touch is the most important sense because "All the senses, including vision, are extensions of the tactile sense; the senses are specializations of skin tissue, and all sensory experiences are modes of touching and thus related to tactility. Our contact with the world takes place at the boundary line of the self through specialized parts of our enveloping membrane."[16] Our body, Pallasmaa reminds us, is "the navel of the world," that is, "the very locus of reference, memory, imagination and integration."[17]

16 Ibid., p. 4–11.

17 Ibid., p. 11.

Alberto Campo Baeza gave the *Siete lecciones de arquitectura* between 8 February and 21 March 2023 at the Real Academia de Bellas Artes de San Fernando (RABASF), Calle Alcalá 13 in Madrid, on the occasion of the awarding of the RABASF Medal of Honor to the Madrid School of Architecture ETSAM (Escuela Técnica Superior de Arquitectura de Madrid). The lectures are a rewriting of texts written and published on other occasions, in particular for the courses in which he taught as a full professor at ETSAM, on certain topics that he considered central, fundamental for the architect. Campo Baeza reveals that "I initially had doubts about taking the decision to rewrite my texts, thinking how complicated the whole process would be. But I must confess that, to my surprise, quite the opposite has occurred. Tidying and fine-tuning my texts by rewriting them has turned out to be a most enjoyable experience, an unexpected gift."[18] Rewriting them for him was "like perfecting a poem, where each finely tuned stanza and word can tell us much more and sound much clearer. Like tuning a musical instrument, which, while remaining the same, acquires the ability to sound much better after tuning."[19]

18 Campo Baeza, Alberto (2020). *Re-writing about Architecture*, 10. Madrid: Estudio Arquitectura Campo Baeza.

19 Ibid., p. 9.

His approach to writing seems to me that of someone who tries to explain his way of seeing architecture and at the same time shed light on the genesis of his projects. In Campo Baeza, writing and doing are deeply intertwined, they are consubstantial. Writing is indispensable to his role as a teacher, because it allows him to rationalize his intuitions so that he can explain them clearly and intelligibly, because it allows him to give substance to his thoughts with the language of materials and space that are specific to architecture. It is no coincidence that the title of one of his very stimulating books is precisely *L'idea costruita* (The Built Idea).[20] In the "Introduction to the Italian edition," Campo Baeza states: "Words in architecture are always expressions of those ideas whose construction is proper to architecture. Without ideas, architecture is vain, empty. *Architectura sine idea, vana architectura est.*"[21]

20 Campo Baeza, *L'idea costruita*. op. cit.

21 Ibid., op. cit., p. 9.

He then adds: "The transmission of architecture is done through the universality of the built works, the keys that generate it and with which this architecture develops are often hidden, reserved. Showing these keys, offering them, discovering the reasons with which these ideas were conceived and illuminated, whose construction is the architecture we make, is what we propose today through the Italian version of these writings."[22] These two quotations, together with the next one, explain the possible key to understanding the meaning of the essays contained in this book: "Architecture, beyond the forms with which it appears to us, is an idea that expresses itself with such forms. It is idea materialized with measures that relate to man, the center of Architecture. It is constructed idea. The History of Architecture, far from being only a history of forms, is fundamentally a History of Constructed Ideas. Forms disintegrate with time but ideas remain, they are eternal."[23]

Regarding the intertwining of writing and design, when I asked whether his writing and his theoretical approach had influenced and still influence his design practice and vice versa, or whether they are autonomous realities, devoid of mutual influence, Juhani Pallasmaa replied: "For me, writing (theorizing) and designing are two parallel but independent approaches to architecture. I can even say that my intense writing career has made design work increasingly difficult for me as it has raised my level of critical and intellectual awareness. But my interest in thinking and writing has had an indirect impact; it has made me more observant and, hopefully, a bit wiser. Most importantly, theorizing and writing have humbled me. As Joseph Brodsky argues, 'Poetry – writing it as well as reading it – will teach you humility and rather quickly at that. Especially if you are both writing and reading it.'"[24]

In addition to their approach and the meaning of their writing, another difference, which Juhani pointed out to us when we met, are their respective bibliographical references from which they have drawn the numerous quotations that characterize their texts and their argumentative proceeding. Most of the books referred to by Alberto Campo Baeza are Latin classics – the beloved Marcus Aurelius[25] with his *Meditations*, Cicero, and Quintilian – and Greek – Aristotle of the *Protrepticus* and Plato – Saint Augustine, one of the four Fathers of the Western Church, who, I am not sure if just by chance, was one of the authors Mies van der Rohe often liked to quote,[26] and finally the Book of Books, the Holy Bible, a sort of red thread that is sewn through all the essays.

22 Ibid., p. 10.

23 Ibid., p. 11.

24 Pallasmaa, *Frammenti / Fragments*, op. cit.

25 In Copenhagen, Alberto Campo Baeza revealed to me that he has dozens of translations of Marcus Aurelius' *Meditations* and that it is a book he always has within reach in his study.

26 According to Reyner Banham, more because of his German training, which included the study of the classics. In Beam, Alex (ed.) (2020). *Broken Glass: Mies van der Rohe, Edith Farnsworth, and the Fight over a Modernist Masterpiece*, 33. New York: Random House Publishing Group. Kindle edition.

If the Spanish architect's bibliographical references are classics that take us far back in time, those of Juhani Pallasmaa are predominantly contemporary, and refer to philosophy – John Dewey, Ludwing Wittgenstein, Gaston Bachelard, Jean-Paul Sartre, Maurice Merleau-Ponty are cited – to psychology – Sigmund Freud, Carl Gustav Jung, and Anton Ehrenzweig – to poetry – Paul Valéry, Rainer Maria Rilke and his beloved Joseph Brodsky, his polar star – and to literature – Marcel Proust – and finally (so to speak) two authors he never fails to refer to in his books: Igor Stravinsky and his *Poetics of Music in the Form of Six Lessons*, and Andrei Tarkovsky and his *Sculpting in Time*.

T.S. Eliot is the only author shared by Campo Baeza and Pallasmaa, both of whom cite the two fundamental essays "What Is a Classic?" and "Tradition and Individual Talent," and the *Four Quartets*; for the rest, there are no other books in common in their bibliography (with the exception of Paul Dirac and André Wogenscky).

Given the differences, let us now come to the consonances. The first is certainly an unrestrained passion for books. Campo Baeza reveals: "I love books. My house is full of books everywhere. So full that I have sometimes thought that if they get together, the day I least expect it, they will throw me out of the house. At the moment, being together for so long, they talk to each other, who knows what they will say to each other! I used and still use books to prepare my lessons, and I always recommend them."[27] And Juhani Pallasmaa remarks, in open polemic with the frequent and almost exclusive access to the internet as the source of knowledge: "I have a distrust of this placeless and usually nameless source of information. I trust and love books, and I appreciate that this is a type of information that is placed (I have a physical image of most of the nine thousand volumes in my library), and a named individual usually guarantees the truth value of the printed information. There is also a sense of historicity and layering of knowledge in books whereas the internet is immaterially out there somewhere, without causality and inherent logic. The search media of today fragment knowledge into isolated bits of information. Information is meaningful only when it is contextualized; that is, when information turns into knowledge. And knowledge turns into wisdom through the context of individual life experience."[28]

27
"Introducción." In: Campo Baeza, *Siete lecciones*, op. cit., p. 9.

28
Pallasmaa, *Frammenti / Fragments*, op. cit., pp. 130–131.

One aspect that Campo Baeza and Pallasmaa have in common, in addition to the rich apparatus of citations, is the almost total absence of bibliographical references in the field, namely of "architectural literature". At a time when (also out of academic necessity) much is written about architecture, it seems to me that for the two authors the current flood of publications is almost irrelevant and there are no significant texts to which the authors refer for their arguments. The polar stars Frank Lloyd Wright, Le Corbusier, Alvar Aalto, Louis Kahn, and Jørn Utzon are mentioned *en passant*, then there remains – really – little else, Steen Elier Rasmussen and Peter Zumthor. It is as if for both authors, writing about architecture is done without the need to resort to literature of and about architecture, so much so, that both write about architecture mostly relying on other disciplines, heteronomous (one could perhaps say), on which their reasoning about architecture seems to be based and dependent. In 2012, Pallasmaa revealed to me that when he was designing and looking for inspiration, he never consulted architecture publications, but rather art books; I believe the same applies to his writing.

Another characteristic that I think Campo Baeza and Pallasmaa share is the awareness that today, in the age of postmodernity and weak thinking and in the society of fragmentation, plurality, and exception, there is no possibility of normative theoretical constructions, strong and all-encompassing (i.e. from which to derive the organization of the whole of architectural reality) typical of classical modernity – whose last attempts in this sense were probably, right at the end of the 1960s but before 1968, those of Aldo Rossi with *The Architecture of the City*[29] (1st Italian edition 1966) and Robert Venturi with *Complexity and Contradiction in Architecture*[30] (1st English edition 1966). After that, I cannot identify any normative texts in the discipline of architecture. I do not believe that texts such as *The Language of Post-Modern Architecture*[31] (1st English edition 1971) and *The Architecture of the Jumping Universe*[32] (1st English edition 1995) by Charles Jencks, nor *After Modern Architecture*[33] (1st Italian edition) by Paolo Portoghesi, nor even *Deconstructivist Architecture*[34], the catalogue of the 1988 Exhibition of the same name at the MoMA in New York, nor Bernard Tschumi's collection of essays entitled, *Architecture and Disjunction*[35] (1st English edition), nor the reference texts on digital architecture, such as *Folding in Architecture*, the issue of *Architectural Design* magazine n. 102, 1993, edited by Greg Lynn, *Folds, Bodies & Blobs: Collected Essays*[36] (1998) and *Animate Form*[37] (1999) by Greg Lynn or *Diagram Diaries*[38] (1999) by Peter Eisenman, or the text by James Wines, founder of the SITE group, *Green Architecture: The Art of*

29
Rossi, Aldo (1984). *The Architecture of the City*. Cambridge, MA: The MIT Press.

30
Venturi, Robert (1984). *Complexity and Contradiction in Architecture*. New York, NY: The Museum of Modern Art.

31
Jencks, Charles (1971). *The Language of Post-Modern Architecture*. London: Academy Editions.

32
Jencks, Charles (1997). *The Architecture of the Jumping Universe*. London: Academy Editions.

33
Portoghesi, Paolo (1982). *After Modern Architecture*. New York: Rizzoli.

34
Wigley, Mark and Johnson, Philip (ed.) (1988). *Deconstructivist Architecture*. New York, NY: MoMA.

35
Tschumi, Bernard (2000). *Architecture and Disjunction*. Cambridge. MA: The MIT Press.

36
Lynn, Greg (1988). *Folds, bodies & blobs: Collected essays*. Bruxelles: La Lettre Volée.

37
Lynn, Greg (1999). *Animate Form*. New York, NY: Princeton Architectural Press.

38
Eisenman, Peter (1999). *Diagram Diaries*. London: Thames & Hudson.

Architecture in the Age of Ecology[39] (2000), however important they may have been, can aspire to be normative and refounding texts in the discipline of architecture (and perhaps it was not even their intention to do so).

39 Wines, James (2000). *Green Architecture: The Art of Architecture in the Age of Ecology*. Cologne: Taschen.

Perhaps the answer to this impossibility, even if it does not refer to writing, but to architecture, is to be found in Bernard Tschumi's remark in his essay, "Abstract mediation and strategy": "When the philosopher Jean-François Lyotard speaks about the crisis of the grand narratives of modernity ('progress,' the 'liberation of humanity,' etc.), it only prefigures the crisis of any narrative, any discourse, any mode of representation. The crisis of these grand narratives, their coherent totality, is also the crisis of limits. As with the contemporary city, there are no boundaries delineating a coherent and homogeneous whole. On the contrary, we inhabit a fractured space, made of accidents, where figures are disintegrated, dis-integrated. From a sensibility developed during centuries around the 'appearance of a stable image' ('balance,' 'equilibrium,' 'harmony'), today we favor a sensibility of the disappearance of unstable images: first. movies (24 images per seconds), then television, then computer-generated images, and recently (among few architects) disjunction, dislocations, deconstructions . . . The city and its architecture lose their symbols – no more monuments, no more axes, no more anthropomorphic symmetries, but instead fragmentation, parcellization, atomization, as well as random superimposition of images that bear no relationship to one another, except through their collision. No wonder that some architectural projects sublimate the idea of explosion . . . No more certainties, no more continuities. We hear that energy, as well as matter, is a discontinuous structure of points: punctum, quantum. Question: could the only certainty be the point?"[40]

40 Tschumi, Bernard (1994). Abstract mediation and strategy. In: *Architecture and Disjunction* op. cit,. p. 194.

The texts by Alberto Campo Baeza and Juhani Pallasmaa – not only those published here – are indeed fragmentary, weak, peripheral, devoid of normative and refoundational intentions, they are thoughts, meditations on fundamental architectural themes, topics with which every student and architect must constantly be confronted. In Pallasmaa's case, it was he himself who confirmed this in an e-mail dated 23 March 2006, when, regarding my idea from which *Lampi di pensiero. Fenomenologia della percezione in architettura* was born and, later, *Inseminations: Seeds for Architectural Thoughts*, namely to fragment his essays, so as to obtain the monads of his thought, he wrote to me: "You have understood my approach very well, indeed; I never aspire for a comprehensive, closed theoretical formulation.

I like open-endedness, associations and recollections, a certain degree of obscurity, and the idea of collage or assemblage. I simply cast my eyes on phenomena related to the subject matter given to me, and report on what I see. I would consider it pretentious on my part to aspire for definite and final statements; what you see and grasp at each given moment in your life depends on your life situation, and how you are focused. As a consequence of this situationality, one is bound to contradict with one's earlier views every now and then."

Happy reading!

THE ETHICAL AND EXISTENTIAL MEANING OF BEAUTY 1

Art is realistic when it strives to express an ethical idea. Realism is a striving for the truth, and truth is always beautiful. Here esthetic coincides with the ethical.

—Andrei Tarkovsky[1]

Art is not only a selective sampling of the world; art implies transforming the world, an endless modification toward the good.

—Rainer Maria Rilke[2]

BEAUTY, ESTHETICIZATION, AND NEWNESS

Beauty and ethics, as well as their hidden relationships are, no doubt, unfashionable subjects in today's artistic and architectural discourse. In the era that reveres newness, appealing images, and formal inventions, the ethical perspective has been pushed aside, and the ethical dimension has rarely entered recent writings on art and architecture. *The Ethical Function of Architecture* (1998) by philosopher Karsten Harries is a rare example in our time of the interest in the ethical dimension of architecture.[3] Artistic quality is generally seen as a subjective and unique expression, and instead of suggesting an ethical resonance, it is expected to exhibit unforeseen imageries and experiences. In fact, beauty and ethics have been problematic concepts in the arts for a century and a half, and artists themselves have usually questioned or dismissed both notions. In our obsessively consumerist culture, beauty has turned into a deliberate esthetic manipulation and seduction; everything from products to environments, personality to behavior, and politics to war, is now manipulatively estheticized. We have entered the era of "aesthetic capitalism" in accordance with the title of a book by the late Gernot Böhme, German philosopher and a friend of mine, who has also pioneered in the philosophical analysis of atmospheres.[4] This new mode of Capitalism implies a distinct calculated manipulation of

1
Tarkovsky, Andrei (1986). *Sculpting in Time*, 113. Austin, TX: University of Texas Press.

2
Rainer Maria Rilke, "Letter to Jacob Baron Uexkull," Paris, dated August 19, 1909. Rainer Maria Rilke, *Hiljainen taiteen sisin: kirjeitä vuosilta 1900–1926* (The Silent Innermost Core of Art: Letters 1900–1926), edited by Liisa Envald (Helsinki: TAI-teos, 1997), p. 41.

3
Harries, Karsten (1998). *The Ethical Function of Architecture*. Cambridge, MA: The MIT Press.

4
Böhme, Gernot (2017). *Critique of Aesthetic Capitalism*. Milan: Mimesis International. Kindle edition.

Eight Meditations on Architecture, First Edition. Juhani Pallasmaa. Edited by Matteo Zambelli.

appearances, planned aging, and the loss of sincerity. We used to have two seasons of fashion, summer and winter, then four seasons, and, now, eight seasons. Have architectural fashions accelerated similarly, we can ask? Besides, today's formalist and rhetorically dramatized architecture hardly aspires to beauty and serenity, as experiences of the unforeseen, stunning, and the *unheimlich*, or of outright imbalance and threat, are frequently more apparent in its imagery. In the culture of attention, anything goes as long as it is noticed.

During the modern era, the requirement for beauty has been replaced by the obsession with newness. Paradoxically, however, even newness turns into repetitiousness. "As the new is searched only because of its newness, everything becomes identical, because it has no other properties but its newness," the Norwegian philosopher Lars Svendsen points out in his book, *A Philosophy of Boredom*.[5] However, beauty is always connected with timelessness, as it turns our consciousness to permanence and eternity. "The language of beauty is essentially the language of timeless reality," philosopher Karsten Harries claims.[6] "Beauty connects us with the eternal," Jorge Luis Borges, the poet and writer, formulated this thought.[7]

5

Svendsen, Lars (2012). *A Philosophy of Boredom*. London: Reaktion Books.

6

Harries, Karsten (1982). Building and the terror of time. *Perspecta: The Yale Architectural Journal* 19: 58–62.

7

Borges, Jorge Luis (2000). *The Craft of Verse*, 115. Cambridge, MA: Harvard University Press.

What is the meaning of this forceful distancing of art and architecture from beauty, ethics, and life? In his book, *The Dehumanization of Art and Other Essays on Art, Culture and Literature* (1925), José Ortega y Gasset, the Spanish philosopher, suggests that the subject matter of art has gradually shifted from "things" to "sensations" and, finally, to "ideas."[8] In Ortega's view, this development has gradually weakened the human content in art. Regardless of whether we agree with Ortega's analysis or not, it opens a thought-provoking view into the transformation of the essence of art. This is a shift from concrete and sensory representations of things that exist to fabricated and cognitive expressions. At the same time, artistic expressions have moved toward the realms of conceptual ideas and scientific imagery. In this development, the role of beauty has changed accordingly, and it is difficult to relate sensory representation and phenomenal experience of beauty with the cerebral and instrumentalized ideas in today's artistic expressions. Art and architecture have frequently turned to being autonomous and self-conscious of their means and ends. Also the sense of a temporal continuum has been lost. Instead of mediating between different realities, such as life and ideals, ideas and feelings, time and timelessness, art has turned into an autonomous reality. In this development, the role of beauty has changed

8

Ortega y Casset, José (1968). *The Dehumanization of Art and Other Essays on Art, Culture, and Literature*. Princeton, NJ: Princeton University Press.

accordingly, and it is not possible to relate sensory representation and phenomenal experience of beauty with the cerebral and instrumentalized ideas in today's artistic expressions of RIPETIZIONE. Not surprisingly, these fundamental changes in artistic thinking and focus also apply in architecture.

THE ETHICS OF LIMITS

Sublime beauty was the highest aspiration of art until the end of the nineteenth century, but the quasi-rational and materialist consumer culture of today regards art as a cultural deviation, entertainment, and a cultural as well as a monetary investment. However, an interest in the connections of ethics and esthetics, truth and beauty, seems to be re-emerging. The haunting environmental and ecological problems and the consequences of uncritical technological development, such as excessive digitalization, artificial intelligence, and genetic manipulation, are also awakening wider ethical concerns. The dramatic psychological influence on pre-school children has been revealed. For instance, chioldren who have used smartphones since early childhood fail to identify human faces and to recognize emotions in the faces.

At the same time, however, the attention is beginning to shift from the forced and noisy, but mentally empty architecture of abundance to the ways of building that are emerging in the developing world. This architecture of necessity is bound to be based on real needs, scarcities, and necessities. In these ways of building, architectural form still arises from the materials and ways of constructing, not from detached estheticized ideas and meaningless compositional complexities. While the deep existential meaning is disappearing from the constructions of the world of surreal wealth, the severely restricted constructions in the realities of need still mediate existential and ethical values. This architecture of limits expresses the beauty of necessity as opposed to the limitless esthetics and swiftly changing fashions of abundance. Leonardo da Vinci's wise advice on the meaning of limits, "Strength is born from constraints and it dies in freedom," has regrettably been forgotten.[9]

9 Leonardo da Vinci, as quoted in Stravinsky, Igor (1947). *Poetics of Music: In the Form of Six Lessons*. Cambridge, MA: Harvard University Press.

The perspective of approaching ecological, political, and moral catastrophes calls for a reintegration of the esthetic and ethical sensibilities. At the same time, our focus needs to shift from the subjective, exclusive, and exceptional back to the universal, mental, and existential concerns. *The Ethical Function of Architecture* of Karsten Harries, as well as several other significant philosophical books of the past decades, such as Elaine Scarry's *On Beauty and Being Just*,[10] and Martha Nussbaum's *Poetic Justice*,[11] exemplify these concerns. Joseph Brodsky, the Nobel Laureate poet, wrote frequently about the interactions of these two mental dimensions and gave the esthetic perception primacy: "Man is first an aesthetic creature before he is an ethical one."[12] He considers our esthetic instinct as the origin of ethics: "Every new aesthetic reality makes man's ethical reality more exact, because aesthetics is the mother of ethics."[13] But for the poet, esthetics means something more universal and autonomous than today's commercialized and manipulated beauty, serving the purposes of desire, convention, consumption, and forced change. Brodsky's book on Venice, *Watermark*, contains thought-provoking reflections on the meaning of beauty and its loss.

BEAUTY IN SCIENCE

Beauty, reason, and truth are usually seen as exclusive and independent properties and notions, but they can well share the same mental and emotive grounding. Beauty and reason seem to be equally valid approaches and criteria of judgment in both science and art. Erich Fromm, the philosopher and social psychiatrist, provides a striking expression of the fusion of beauty and truth: "Beauty is not the opposite of the "*ugly*," but of the "*false*.""[14] This view points directly at the interconnection of the esthetic and ethic criteria.

Esthetic aspirations are primarily related to the world of the arts, architecture, design and styles, but beauty and elegance of thought are essential criteria also in mathematics, physics, and other sciences. Beauty represents comprehensive and synthetic qualities and integrities, which cannot be formalized and expressed through any other means. The experience of convincing and disarming beauty is a proof of the correctness, coherence, and inner harmony of the phenomenon also outside of art. The pure and selfless beauty of a Piero della Francesca or Johannes Vermeer painting is likely to be beyond analyses and explanations, as it penetrates every cell of the viewer. "Be like me," is the authoritative demand of great poetry, according to Joseph Brodsky, and this command applies to all art.[15]

Beauty is also a quality in mathematics and sciences. The theoretical physicist Paul A.M. Dirac argued that the theories of physics, which project beauty, are probably also the correct ones.[16] Physicist Hermann Weyl, who completed the quantum and probability theories, made an even more outspoken confession: "My work has always

10 Scarry, Elaine (1999). *On Beauty and Being Just*. Princeton, NJ: Princeton University Press.

11 Nussbaum, Martha (1995). *Poetic Justice: The Literary Imagination and Public Life*. Boston, MA: Beacon Press.

12 Brodsky, Joseph (1997). An immodest proposal. In: *On Grief and Reason* (ed. Joseph Brodsky), 208. New York, NY: Farrar, Straus & Giroux.

13 Ibid.

14 Fromm, Eric (1968). *The Revolution of Hope: Toward a Humanized Technology*, 75, New York: Harper & Row. Available at: https://archive.org/details/revolutionofhope00from.

15 Brodsky, op. cit., p. 206.

16 Dirac, Paul (1963). The evolution of the physicist's picture of nature. *Scientific American* 208 (5): 45–53.

attempted to combine truth with beauty, but when I have been obliged to choose one of the two, I have chosen the beautiful."[17] Today, mathematicians use the notion "dirty proof" (in the sense of "ugly") of a mathematical proof, which has been attained through immense computing power, beyond the capabilities of human perception and intellectual grasp.[18] I feel the same "dirtiness" in architectural projects generated by computers or algorithms and texts produced by artificial intelligence.

17 "In meinen Arbeit habe ich immer versucht, das Wahre mit den Schönen zu vereinen; wenn ich über das Eine oder das Andere entscheiden musste, habe ich stets das Schöne gewählt." The quotation appears above the bust of Hermann Weyl in the Herman Weyl Zimmer at the ETH in Zürich.

18 The notion was used by several of the mathematician presenters at the conference, Simplicity in Arts and Mathematics: Ideals of Practice in Mathematics & the Arts, at the City University of New York, Graduate Center, 2013.

THE HOLISTIC ESSENCE OF BEAUTY

Beauty is not an added surface value on top of the essence of things, as it expresses the coherence, integrity, wholeness and completeness of the thing or phenomenon. There is no esthetic reality separate from the reality of things, as beauty arises from the perfect integration and balance of this reality. Our current culture prioritizes power, cerebral capacity, and quantification, although emotive reactions and intuitions are often our most synthetic modes of understanding, and beauty arises from the experience of a complex entity as an integrated singularity. The "understanding" of atmospheres is an example of our capacity to grasp even unfocused, shapeless, and diffuse phenomena experienced simultaneously through all our senses. Altogether, we tend to regard perceptions, skills, and understanding as processes that advance from details and parts toward entities. This simplistic idea of the dynamics of understanding is regrettably also the prevailing method in education. However, neuroscience has established that we grasp entities first and they give meaning to the parts. This fact of neuroscience shakes the accepted elementarist pedagogical foundations in a fundamental manner. Students of art, architecture, and design, for instance, should first be made to encounter real and complete works of art, and only later given detailed intellectual analyses of the artistic phenomena in question. The individual sensory experience of the work has to proceed its conceptual analyses and cognitive understanding. "According to the right hemisphere, understanding is derived from the whole, since it is only in the light of the whole that one can truly understand the nature of the parts," Iain McGilchrist, therapist and philosopher, argues in his thorough book on the human mind.[19]

19 McGilchrist, Iain (2009). *The Master and His Emissary: The Divided Brain and the Making of the Western World*, 142. New Haven, CT: Yale University Press.

Beauty is a complete judgment of a thing in the same way that we grasp the characteristics of places and vast environmental situations through our unfocused atmospheric sense. We grasp the meanings of the world as integrated entities, not as a flood of unrelated stimuli. We grasp entities before we understand details. As I enter a place, the place simultaneously enters me, my sense of self and the place fuse into each other. "I enter a building, see a room, and – in the fraction of a second – have this feeling about it," Peter Zumthor confesses.[20] Beauty is an immaterial experiential and mental quality, which suggests a distinct "thingness" – the sensuous and mental thingness of beauty. At the same time that beauty arises from the integration of things, it appears to have its independent existence. As the light artist James Turrell has argued, also light can project a "thingness" in our experience.[21] Beauty, like atmosphere, is a complex experiential quality, which is encountered and grasped in a synthetic, embodied, multi-sensory, and emotional manner, rather than understood through intellectual and analytic reading. As we experience beauty, it does not remain outside of us, but becomes part of our very being. "Be like me," is the command of poetry in accordance with Joseph Brodsky.[22]

20 Zumthor, Peter (2006). *Atmosphere: Architectural Environments Surrounding Objects*, 13. Basel: Birkhäuser.

21 Turrell, James (2000). The thingness of light. In: *Light as Experience and Imagination from Medieval to Modern Times* (ed. Scott Poole), 1–2. Blacksburg, VA: Architecture Edition.

22 Brodsky, op. cit., p. 206.

We usually experience phenomena and creatures of nature as beautiful. As products of timeless evolution, they are complete, integrated, and self-sufficient entities. They are all part of the secret narrative of life. As biological beings, we are also products of the same laws and processes of nature, and consequently appreciation of nature as beautiful is in our very constitution. The time dimension of reality is surprisingly little understood outside of mere historical chronology. We are usually totally unaware of the signs of our biological evolution in our bodies even today, the remains of gills in our lungs, the tail in our backbone, and the pink triangles in our eye corners, which are the spots where our horizontally moving eyelids were attached when we were lizards. Altogether, we should finally acknowledge that emotions and experiences of beauty are part of the domain of "existential intelligence," implying a comprehensive judgment of the perceived phenomenon. By this notion I refer to the powerful expression of Merleau-Ponty, "the flesh of the world."[23] We exist in the flesh of the world, as the heart exists in our body, not outside of it as onlookers. Mark Johnson, the philosopher, makes the significant remark: "There is no cognition without emotion, even though we are often unaware of the emotional aspect of our thinking."[24] In his view, emotions are the source of primordial meaning: "Emotions are not second-rate cognitions; rather they are affective patterns of our encounter with our world, by which we take the meaning of things at a primordial level."[25] As architects, we should also sense the primordial dimensions and meanings of buildings and dwelling. Emotions unify ethical and esthetic qualities and give

23 Merleau-Ponty, Maurice (1992). The Intertwining - The Chiasm. In: *The Visible and the Invisible* (ed. Claude Lefort). Evanston, IL: Northwestern University Press.

24 Johnson, Mark (2007). *The Meaning of the Body: Aesthetics of Human Understanding*, 9. Chicago: University of Chicago Press.

25 Ibid., p. 18.

them their lived existential meanings. "It is only with the heart that one can see right. What is essential is invisible to the eye," Antoine de Saint-Exupéry, the legendary pilot, asserts in his best-known book, *The Little Prince*.[26]

26

de Saint-Exupéry, Antoine (1943). *The Little Prince*, Chapter 21. Paris: Gallimard.

INTELLIGENCE AND EXPERIENCE

In his book, *Intelligence Reframed*, psychologist Howard Gardner identifies 10 categories of intelligence beyond the characteristics measured by the standard IQ test: linguistic, logical-mathematical, musical, bodily-kinesthetic, spatial, interpersonal, intrapersonal, naturalistic, spiritual, and existential intelligence.[27] Based on my personal experiences and intuitions, I wish to add five further categories – esthetic, emotional, atmospheric, imaginative, and existential – intelligences to this already thought-provoking list of the psychologist. All these categories of intelligence are seminal in architecture, and a wise teacher of architecture uses this entire range of intelligences in her teaching method. It is evident that even in the creative fields and their education, the complexities of human intelligence, embodied and emotional capacities, and the essences of the phenomena of beauty and ethical judgment are barely understood, to say nothing of the complex, emotive, and largely unconscious nature of the creative process.

27

Gardner, Howard (1999). *Intelligence Reframed: Multiple Intelligencies for the Twenty-First Century*, Chapters 3 and 4. New York, NY: Basic Books.

The poetic and artistic reality of a work of art is not in the material and physical object, but in its internalization through individual experience and identification; beauty has to be experienced and felt. "Nothing ever becomes real till experienced," as the poet John Keats wrote.[28] This is also the seminal view of John Dewey's book, *Art as Experience* of 1934: "In common conception, the work of art is often identified with the building, book, painting, or statue in its existence apart from human experience. Since the actual work of art is what the product does with and in experience, the result is not favorable to understanding . . . When artistic objects are separated from both conditions of origin and operation in experience, a wall is built around them that renders almost opaque their general significance, with which esthetic theory deals."[29]

28

John Keats, Keats' quote is available at: https://www.goodreads.com/quotes/622634-nothing-ever-becomes-real-till-experienced-even-a-proverb (accessed December 2025).

29

Dewey, John (1980). *Art as Experience*, 3. New York, NY: The Berkley Publishing Company.

Art articulates and expresses the world of lived experiences, and it mediates the human mental essence of these very encounters and so does architecture. A true artist or designer is not depicting an isolated detail or aspect of the world. Every real artistic work is a microcosm, a complete world of its own, or in the words of Andrei Tarkovsky, the film director, "a whole world as reflected in a drop of water."[30] Every true work of art, including architecture, projects an entire world. This existential sense of the world, and its interaction with the self, are the most difficult and significant areas of learning for a creative person. However, this seminal inclusivity and relatedness of architecture have been almost entirely lost.

ART AND THE WORLD

I wish to argue firmly that art is not merely estheticization, as it is a form of genuine existential thinking about the world and our being in that very world, through embodied and poeticized images and means characteristic to the art form in question. "How would the poet or the painter express anything other than his encounter with the world?" Maurice Merleau-Ponty asks, pointing out the existential focus of art.[31] How could the architect express anything else, we need to ask accordingly. Significantly, like Dewey, Merleau-Ponty does not regard the material or performed work itself as the objective of art. "We come to see not the work of art, but the world according to the work," he states.[32] This view turns art into a mediating act; it tells primarily of something else than itself; the meaning of art is always behind and beyond the work itself. This position also rejects the common idea of art as the artist's self-expression. Indeed, art is a relational medium, which tells us about the essences of the lived world, or perhaps more precisely, about being a human in this world; art expresses the human existence in the world, not the theretical world of physics or other sciences. Balthus (Balthazar Klossowsky de Rola), one of the finest realist painters of the last century, points out the significance of the world as the artist's true subject: "If a work only expresses the person who created it, it wasn't worth doing . . . Expressing the world, understanding it, that is what seems interesting to me."[33] In another context the painter articulates his position further: "Great painting has to have universal meaning. This is no longer so today and that is why I want to give painting back its lost universality and anonymity, because the more anonymous a painting is, the more real it is."[34] This is a thought-provoking argument against the understanding of art as self-expression or conscious estheticization.

ART AND ITS PAST

Here again, the ethical perspective enters the domain of art and architecture. Like all art, the art of building is simultaneously about the lived world and the layered histories and meanings of the artform itself. All arts carry their timeless traditions along their route

30

Tarkovsky, Andrei (1986). *Sculpting in Time: Reflections on the Cinema*, 110. London: The Bodley Head.

31

Maurice Merleau-Ponty, quoted in Kearney, Richard (1994). Maurice Merleau-Ponty. In: *Modern Movements in European Philosophy* (ed. Richard Kearney), 82. New York, NY: Manchester University Press.

32

Merleau-Ponty, Maurice, quoted in Iain McGilchrist, *The Master and His Emissary*, op. cit., 409.

33

Roy, Claude (1996). *Balthus*, 18. Boston, MA: Little, Brown and Company.

34

Ibid.

toward the future. Meaningful works are conversations across time, and truly radical works open up new ways of reading and experiencing historical works of art. Picasso has opened our eyes to see the 25,000-year-old cave paintings. All great artists reveal the existential essence of art through the layers of recorded history of art. Aldo van Eyck, the structuralist architect, refused to give his inaugural professorial lecture at the University of Delft on the suggested topic of the influence of Giotto on Cézanne, and gave the lecture on the influence of Cézanne on Giotto.[35] This example opens up the simultaneity of the world of art. One of my closest friends was the legendary Finnish designer and artist Tapio Wirkkala. He told me that his most important teacher was Piero della Francesca, but Piero died 423 years before Tapio was born. It is this amazing simultaneity of the world of art that gives us the opportunity to select our teachers from the entire history of art. I have personally been taught by the artists of the Sienna School and the Cubists.

35
Aldo van Eyck in private conversation with the author in 1982.

As a consequence of this multiple time perspective, also architecture needs to have a double focus; the lived world and the mythical traditions of constructing. The highly refined technologies of today tend to weaken the deep unconscious meanings and the essential, but hidden mythical and unconscious contents of building, which are echoed in all great architectural works. All meaningful works are timeless and they are always simultaneously about the past, the present, and the future.

A BIOLOGICAL PERSPECTIVE

The esthetic reality has also been extended to biological phenomena. It is well known that certain selective criteria, that could be regarded as esthetic choices, such as symmetry and signs of health and strength, are essential factors in mate selection among animals. Certain "esthetic" gestures, rituals, and deliberate constructions are also used to attract a mate, such as the empty silk balloon of the Balloon fly (Hilara sartor), presented to the female, the huge staged and decorated nests of the bowerbirds (*Ptilonorhynchidae*); in constructing the decorations in front of the entrance to the bower, the bird uses false or reversed perspective to exaggerate his own experiential size in the eyes of the potential mate. Another remarkable example of the role of esthetics in the animal world is the co-ordinated group singing and dancing by male Blue manakins (*Chiroxipia caudata*) in front of the potential mate. The male birds practice this crucial opera performance all their lives.[36]

36
For decoration in animal constructions, see Pallasmaa, Juhani (ed.) (1995). *Animal Architecture*. Helsinki: Museum of Finnish Architecture.

A recent book, *The Evolution of Beauty* by Richard O. Prum,[37] reintroduces Charles Darwin's second book on evolution entitled, *The Descent of Man, and Selection in Relation to Sex*, published in 1871,[38] published 13years after his celebrated *On the Origin of Species* of 1858.[39] Darwin published his second book after becoming convinced that the selective principles in his first theory did not explain all the variations among animal species, including the proverbial case of the peacock's tail, which had caused Darwin nightmares at the time of writing *The Origin of Species*. In the Victorian era, a book that suggested autonomous esthetic choice as a sexual motif, practiced by the female sex, could not even be discussed. However, scientists have recently shown through mathematical modeling that, indeed, combining the two theories of Darwin fully explains all the varieties among animal species, including the peacock's tail. Surprisingly, individual esthetic judgment is a fundamental principle of choice also in the animal world. The notion of Biophilia, "the science and ethics of life," introduced and articulated by the biologist Edward O. Wilson, expands the ethical responsility beyond the realm of human interaction all the way to our duty in maintaining bio-diversity.[40] Semir Zeki, a pioneering neurobiologist, also connects esthetics with biological evolution, as he suggests the feasibility of "a theory of aesthetics that is biologically based," in his book, *Inner Vision: An Exploration of Art and the Brain*.[41] With the intuition and courage of a poet, Joseph Brodsky supports the scientist's view: "The purpose of evolution, believe it or not, is beauty, which survives it all and generates truth simply by being a fusion of the mental and the sensual."[42]

37 Prum, Richard O. (2018). *The Evolution of Beauty: How Darwin's Forgotten Theory of Mate Choise Shapes the Animal World - and Us*, 20. New York, NY: Anchor Books.

38 Darwin, Charles (1871). *The Descent of Man, and Selection in Relation to Sex*. London: John Murray.

39 Darwin, Charles (1859). *On the Origin of Species*. London: John Murray.

40 Wilson, Edward O. (1984). *Biophilia: The Human Bond with Other Species*. Cambridge, MA: Harvard University Press.

41 Zeki, Semir (1999). *Inner Vision: An Exploration of Art and the Brain*, 1–2. Oxford: Oxford University Press.

42 Brodsky, op. cit., p. 207.

BEAUTY, EMPATHY, AND INTEGRITY

We have an unconscious capacity to identify ourselves with other living creatures and even with objects and phenomena of our perceptions, such as human and spatial situations, and to project ourselves and emotions onto them. We fuse countless aspects of every situation and place into an atmospheric experience, on which our mood and expectations are grounded. "Be like me," is the imperative of the poem in Joseph Brodsky's view.[43] We even simulate the individual characters of great novels and momentarily share their fates, lives, life situations, and emotions. Experiencing a work of art is an exchange, the work lends us its authority and magic, and we lend the work our emotions. Neuroscience has associated this act of unconscious mirroring and exchange with our "mirror neurons."[44]

43 Ibid., p. 206.

44 Mirror-neurons were discovered by the research group of Giacomo Rizzolatti and Vittorio Gallese at the University of Parma over 30 years ago.

Recent research on the mental worlds, and capabilities of a number of animals from chicken to dogs and rats, as well as whales and squid have already revealed unexpected intelligence, imagination, sense of time, and emotive reactions. Somewhat unexpectedly, empathy is a capacity that also animals possess, as Frans de Waal's book, *The Age of Empathy* argues.[45] The recent research on the chemical communication and collaboration of trees and mushrooms extends the realm of purposeful communication far beyond our own mental worlds.[46]

The great ethical value and human equality of art are that we are able to experience our own emotions mirrored by the most profound and sensitive minds in human history. We not only reflect the thoughts, feelings, and experiences of the living, as our empathic imagination can also bring the dead back to life. We can sense through the skin, muscles, and emotions of Michelangelo, see through the eyes of Piero della Francesca, hear through the ears of Johann Sebastian Bach, and feel through the heart of Rainer Maria Rilke. As the master poet Rilke suggests in the motto of my lecture, art and beauty are not only nouns, they constitute the very core of a humane and dignified life.

Beauty is a synthetic and integrated character and quality of a phenomenon, akin to the human ethical quality of integrity. The notion of integrity also refers to the singularity, inner coherence, and autonomy of a thing, behavior, or phenomenon. In 1954, at the age of 85, Frank Lloyd Wright formulated the mental task of architecture as follows: "What is needed most in architecture today is the very thing that is most needed in life – integrity. Just as it is in a human being, so integrity is the deepest quality in a building . . . If we succeed, we will have done a great service to our moral nature – the psyche – of our democratic society . . . Stand up for integrity in your building and you stand for integrity not only in the life of those who did the buildings but socially a reciprocal relationship in inevitable."[47]

These words of the master architect are even more valid today, 70 years later. We need to seek integrity, and integrity is expressed through beauty.

45

de Waal, Frans (2010). *The Age of Empathy: Nature's Lessons for a Kinder Society*. New York, NY: Broadway Books.

46

Wohlleben, Peter (2016). *The Hidden Life of Trees: What They Feel, How They Communicate – Discoveries from A Secret World*. Vancouver: Greystone Books.

47

Lloyd Wright, Frank (1954). Integrity. In: *The Natural House*. Published in Edgar Kaufman and Ben Raeburn, *Frank Lloyd Wright: Writings and Buildings* (New York, NY: Horizon Press, 1960), pp. 292–293.

THE TOUCH OF LIGHT 2

Materiality and Tactility of Illumination

Georges de la Tour, Boy Blowing Into a Lamp, around 1640.
Wikimedia Commons: © Yelkrokoyade (Creative Commons Attribution-Share Alike 4.0 International license) https://commons.wikimedia.org/wiki/File:Le_souffleur_%C3%A0_la_lampe_Georges_de_la_Tour.jpg

We were born of light. The seasons are felt through light. We only know the world as it is evoked by light, and from this comes the thought that material is spent light. To me natural light is the only light, because it has mood – it provides a ground of common agreement for man – it puts us in touch with the eternal. Natural light is the only light that makes architecture architecture. . .

—Louis Kahn[1]

Through its light alone, the house becomes human. It sees like a man. It is an eye open to night.

—Gaston Bachelard[2]

EXPERIENCING SPACE

As Louis Kahn declares in the motto of my lecture, the experiences of space and light are inseparable, and there is no true architectural experience of space without light, except the limited and specific experiences of spatiality grasped in complete darkness solely through hearing, touch, or smell. Even in those cases, the spatial experience usually refers to the characteristics of space acquired through vision and light. In his seminal book, *Experiencing Architecture*,[3] Steen Eiler Rasmussen recalls the powerful acoustic percept of the underground tunnels in Vienna, the memorable settings in Carol Reed's (1949) film, *The Third Man*, with Orson Welles as the protagonist: "Your ear receives the impact of both the length and the cylindrical form of the tunnel."[4] Significantly, the last chapter of Rasmussen's book is entitled "Hearing architecture."

We can similarly hear the specific shapes of Romanesque cloisters and Gothic cathedrals by means of their powerful and evocative

1 As quoted in Plummer, Henry (1987). *Poetics of Light*, 135. Tokyo: A + U Architecture and Urbanism, Extra Edition.

2 Bachelard, Gaston (1969). *The Poetics of Space*, 35. Boston, MA: Beacon Press.

3 Rasmussen, Steen Eiler (1993). *Experiencing Architecture*. Cambridge, MA: The MIT Press.

4 Ibid., p. 225.

Eight Meditations on Architecture, First Edition. Juhani Pallasmaa. Edited by Matteo Zambelli.

echoes. The dying notes of a Gregorian chant mark the depth and height of the cathedral, and the ascension of a fugue theme by the organ heightens the weave of the Baroque vaults and ornaments. In the silent darkness of the night, the echo of our footsteps on the paved streets of an old town, reflected back by the weathered walls, creates a pleasurable spatial experience and a deep sense of belonging.

In his famous series of paintings of the cathedral of Rouen, Claude Monet transforms stone into an atmospheric vibration of light that addresses the skin with sensations of moisture and temperature just as forcefully as it speaks to the retina.

THE MULTI-SENSORY TOUCH

All sensory experiences are fundamentally experiences of touch; we touch with our eyes, ears, nose and tongue as much as we do by our skin. In addition to the five Aristotelian senses, we measure and touch the world with our senses of gravity, balance, temporal continuum, and self. As Merleau-Ponty notes of the paintings of Paul Cézanne, they make us experience "how the world touches us."[5] We touch the world most fundamentally by our existential sense.

All real experiences of architecture are embodied and multi-sensory. Maurice Merleau-Ponty gives this simultaneous multi-sensory essence of experience a poetic description: "My perception is [therefore] not a sum of visual, tactile, and audible givens: I perceive in a total way with my whole being: I grasp a unique structure of the thing, a unique way of being, which speaks to all my senses at once."[6]

5

Merleau-Ponty, Maurice (1964). Cézanne's doubt. In: *Sense and Non-Sense* (ed. Hubert L. Dreyfus and Patricia Allen Dreyfus), 19. Evanston, IL: Northwestern University Press.

6

Merleau-Ponty, Maurice (1964). The film and the new psychology. In: *Sense and Non-Sense*, op. cit., p, 48.

LIGHT AND PLACE

Every distinct space and place has its characteristic light, and light is often the quality that most directly conditions our mood. Light is the strongest conditioner of the atmosphere of a place, the most comprehensive criterion of the character of space, place, and setting. Just think of the joy and revitalizing energy of the morning light, or the romantic but weary light of the evening, the cool light of a moonlit night, and the emotive colored light of sunrise and sunset. Our senses and body rhythms are tuned and calibrated to the daily and seasonal cycles of light, as with all life on this planet. Light can even characterize entire geographic regions, such as the dramatic differences between the burning vertical light of equatorial areas, and the melancholic horizontal light of the polar regions. The nightless summer light of the North is magical and intoxicating, whereas the scant light in the continuous darkness of the polar winter night seems to emanate from below as snow reflects the slightest light of the firmament and makes it mysteriously visible. One of the most sublime experiences of light that we can experience anywhere is the Aurora Borealis, the Northern Lights, whose fluorescent or colored electronic curtains may rise to the dizzying height of 200 miles.

Light controls the processes of life and even certain essential hormonal activities depend on light. It has a deep effect on our mood, activity, and energy level. In the Nordic countries, special bright artificial lights are nowadays occasionally used during the darkest months of winter in both private homes and cafés to compensate for the lack of daylight, and to stimulate our crucial hormonal activities.

LIGHT AND SHADOW

Light and its accompanying shadow give volumes, spaces, and surfaces their character and expressive power, and they reveal the shapes, weight, hardness, texture, moistness, smoothness, and temperature of materials. The interplay of light and shadow also connects architectural spaces with the dynamics of the physical and natural worlds, seasons, and the hours of the day. "What is there more mysterious than clarity? . . . What more capricious than the way in which light and shade are distributed over hours and over men?," Paul Valéry asks.[7] Natural light brings life into architecture and connects the material world with cosmic dimensions. Light is the cosmic breathing of space and the universe.

7

Valéry, Paul (1956). Eupalinos, or the Architect. In: *Dialogucs*, 107. New York, NY: Pantheon Books.

Light has its own atmospheres, ambiences, and expressions; it is surely the most subtle and emotive of the means of architectural expression. No other medium in the art of building – spatial configuration, form, geometry, proportion, color, or detail – can express equally deep and subtle extremes of emotion, ranging from melancholy to joy, grief to ecstasy, sorrow to bliss. The occasional and happy mixing of the cool light of the northern half of the sky and the warm light of the southern sky in a single space can give rise to an experience of ecstatic happiness. As a young architect,

I understood light merely as a quantitative phenomenon, but I have learned to understand that, in fact, it expresses the most subtle, metaphysical, and emotive of qualities. Nowadays, I try to bring natural light into the darkest areas of my buildings, where it is experienced as a special gift and indication of the architect's generosity.

Light and shadow articulate space into sub-spaces and places, and their interplay gives space its rhythm, sense of scale, and intimacy. As Brancusi said, "Art must give suddenly, all at once, the shock of life, the sensation of breathing."[8] In architecture, this sensation of breathing is mediated by light. Light directs movement and attention, creating hierarchies and points of importance and foci. The paintings of Rembrandt and Caravaggio demonstrate the power of light to define hierarchy and a point of dominance. In these paintings, human figures and objects are wrapped in a soothing embrace of soft light and merciful shadow. In the paintings of Georges de la Tour and Louis Le Nain, the light of a single candle suffices to create an intimate enclosing space and a forceful sense of focus. Due to its fluttering character, candlelight is especially tactile; it seems to finger objects and surfaces like a gentle massage. Candlelight creates an entire universe of intimacy. No wonder Gaston Bachelard wrote an entire book on the light of the candle.[9]

8

As quoted in Shanes, Eric (1989). *Constantin Brancusi*, 57. New York, NY: Abbeville Press.

9

Bachelard, Gaston (1984). *The Flame of a Candle*. Dallas, TX: The Dallas Institute Publications.

A few months ago I experienced one of the most beautiful works of art I have ever seen. This was Johannes Vermeer's *Woman Holding a Balance* (c. 1664) in the Alte Pinakothek in Munich. I had seen the painting perhaps 12 years earlier at the National Gallery of Art in Washington, D.C., but it did not hit my soul quite as forcefully and nobly as it did now. The light enters behind the curtain from the upper left corner, embraces the room very gently, lights the white parts of the woman's dress into a sacred glow, and picks up the objects and pearls on the table just as one would pick berries in a meadow. This is not only light for the eyes; this soothing light penetrates directly into one's heart.

ARCHITECTURAL LIGHT

In architectural contexts, light has dramatically varying characteristics as exemplified by the singular metaphysical disc of illumination sliding across the coffered walls of the Pantheon, the immaterial foliage of form, ornamentation, and light in the Bavarian Baroque churches, the symphonic ensemble of colored perforations through the thick south wall of Le Corbusier's Ronchamp Chapel, the softly

Johannes Vermeer, Woman Holding a Balance, c. 1664.
Johannes Vermeer / Wikimedia Commons / Public domain. https://garystockbridge617.getarchive.net/media/woman-with-a-balance-by-vermeer-2856ea

embracing and therapeutic light of Alvar Aalto's Church of the Three Crosses. The rhythmically vibrating and musical light of Juha Leiviskä's churches in Finland feels as if Mozart himself were playing these lights. Leiviskä's use of reflected color adds yet another dimension of vibrating sensuality. The finest examples in architectural light turn architectural constructions into delicate instruments to play the music of light.

CONTAINED LIGHT, LIQUIFIED LIGHT

Light tends to be experientially and emotionally absent – we see the object rather than light – light is contained by space, or concretized by the surface that it illuminates. "Sun never knows how great it is until it hits the side of a building or shines inside a room," Louis Kahn suggests, echoing Wallace Stevens, the American poet.[10] Through a mediating matter, such as fog, mist, smoke, rain, snow, or frost, light turns into an illuminating virtual substance. The emotive impact of light is remarkably intensified when light is perceived as a substance; the liquefied light feels like a moist veil on the skin and it even seems to penetrate into the pores of our skin.

10 Kahn, Louis, paraphrasing Stevens, Wallace (1991). Harmony between man and architecture. In: *Louis I. Kahn Writings: Lectures, Interviews* (ed. Alessandra Latour), 343. New York, NY: Rizzoli International Publications.

The paintings of J.M.W.Turner and Claude Monet exemplify this embracing atmospheric light made tangible by moisture of the air. Alvar Aalto's daylight arrangements frequently reflect light by means of a curved white surface. The *chiaroscuro* created by Aalto's rounded surfaces gives light an experiential materiality, plasticity, and heightened presence. This light has a specific weight, temperature, touch, and feel. This is a molded light that feels like matter.

Also pleasurable fixtures for artificial light, such as those designed by Poul Henningsen and Alvar Aalto, articulate and mold light, as if slowing down the speed of light and making it reflect playfully back and forth between the curved surfaces and edges of the lighting device. The narrow roof slits of Tadao Ando's and Peter Zumthor's buildings force light into thin directional sheets that cut through the darkness of space, like immaterial veils or blades. In Luis Barragán's buildings, such as the Chapel for Capuchinas Sacramentarias in Mexico City, light turns into a warm colored liquid, that even suggests sonorous qualities, invoking an imaginary humming sound – the architect himself writes about "the interior placid murmur of silence."[11] The lights, colors, and reflections in Barragán's Gilardi House create a true visual miracle, an architectural abstraction that does not seem to be part of our earthly reality; this light is an Annunciation.

11 Official address, 1980 Pritzker Architectural Prize. Reprinted in Barragán, Luis (1995). *Barragán: The Complete Works* (ed. Raul Rispa), 205. London: Thames and Hudson.

Luis Barragán, Gilardi House, Mexico City, Mexico, 1975–1977. Alamy Foto Stock: © Yueqi Li. https://www.alamy.com/casa-gilardi-by-luis-barragan-in-mexico-city-image475609417.html

↑ Tadao Ando, Church of Light, Ibaraki, Osaka, Japan, 1989.
Mith Huang / Flickr / CC BY 2.0
https://www.flickr.com/photos/mith17/6212766739

← Helander Leiviskä Architects, Juha Leiviskä, Church of the Good Shepherd, Western Pakila, Helsinki, Finland, 2003.
Htm / Wikimedia Commons / CC BY-SA 3.0
https://commons.wikimedia.org/wiki/File:Interior_of_Church_of_the_Good_Shepherd_Helsinki_01.jpg

The atmospheric installations of the Islandic-Danish artist Olafur Eliasson, such as his *Weather Project* at the Tate Modern in London 2003, and Eduardo Chillida's sculptures, carved in white translucent alabaster, are further examples of the magic of light in contemporary art that provides inspiration for architecture.

Light can also mediate sensations of weight or weightlessness. In the St Halvard's Church by Kjell Lund in Oslo, the darkness and weight of the space, under the hanging spherical roof of concrete, are heightened by the scarce sources of illumination, and we feel the threatening weight of deluge. The air of Renzo Piano's Menil Museum in Houston, Texas, bathes in a directionless light that seems to eliminate the force of gravity entirely.

LIGHT AND COLOR

Yet, even more unexpected transformations, materializations, and miracles of light take place in artistic works. The colored windows of the Matisse Chapel in Vence and many of James Turrell's light works turn light into colored air, invoking delicate sensations of skin contact, temperature, and oscillation; these spaces make one feel as if we are submerged in a transparent, colored substance that turns light and color into a haptic sensation. We can float in color in the way we float in water. Our eyes are a local specialization of skin tissue, and, indeed, we can all easily learn to distinguish half a dozen colors by the skin of our back. Steven Holl's use of reflected light and color creates the sensation of a pulsating mixture of color and light, a condition that paradoxically heightens both the immateriality and concreteness of light. This is a caressing, breathing, and healing light that connects us with the constantly changing nature of daylight, and it projects a cosmic ambience.

BLACK LIGHT

Artists have created yet another paradox of illumination: black light. Certain paintings of Ad Reinhardt appear as black rectangles until our prolonged stare acknowledges a minute shade of light in the darkness of the painting, and a most subtle image appears. Yet, we cannot quite decide whether the cross shape, that our eyes barely depict, really exists in the painting itself or whether it is a mere optical illusion on our retina. Similarly Mark Rothko's nearly black paintings in the Rothko Chapel in Houston invite us to an experiential limit phenomenon; this time, we feel that we are witnessing the border line between life and death, existence and non-existence.

⬆ Juhani Pallasmaa, Plaza at Cranbrook Academy, Bloomfield Hills, Michigan, 1994. Courtesy of Juhani Pallasmaa.

⬅ Olafur Eliasson, The Weather Project, Tate Modern, London, United Kingdom, 2003. Wonderferret / Flickr / CC BY 2.0 https://www.flickr.com/photos/wonderferret/1430970635

Juhani Pallasmaa (in collaboration with Roland Schweitzer), Finnish Institute in Paris, Paris, France, 1986–1991. Courtesy of Juhani Pallasmaa.

Isn't this dark light the same harbinger of the other world that we see in the darkness of Arnold Böcklin's painting *Isle of the Dead*? "I see dark light," were the last words of Victor Hugo, the French writer.

In addition to paintings, cinema offers inspiring examples of atmospheric light that creates a specific ambience, as well as of the threat of shadow and darkness. The sequence in Andrei Tarkovsky's *Nostalghia* (1983) in which the protagonist, the Russian poet Andrei Gorchakov enters his hotel room in Bagno Vignoni and absentmindedly and unintentionally creates an extraordinary chamber music of light by simply turning various sources of light on and off. It is useless to ask for the "meaning" of this cinematic sequence; it is simply breathtakingly beautiful and metaphysical, as if we were seeing the lights of the universe being turned off and on. One may read echoes of the poet's nostalgia for his home in Russia, his alienation from the world and his self, and of his weakening health, but all this has little value in relation to the sheer existential ambience and aura of this music of light.

ALIENATING LIGHT

In today's ordinary architectural practices, light is regrettably often treated merely as a quantitative phenomenon; design regulations and standards usually specify required minimum levels of illumination and window sizes, but they do not define maximum levels of luminance, or desired qualities of light, such as its orientation, temperature, color, or reflectedness. Besides, our buildings tend to permit too much light and distribute it too evenly, weakening thus the sense of place, intimacy, and secrecy. An evenly lit, shadowless space has a nauseating and alienating effect. No wonder, a powerful means of breaking the defenses of self in political and criminal interrogation and torture is the use of mercilessly bright light. Through millions of years, our system of vision has been adjusted to light coming from above, not from below. In the final section of Stanley Kubrick's *2001: A Space Odyssey* (1968), the room, decorated in quasi-Rococo style, and lit from below through the glass floor, is truly disturbing as it reverses the natural direction of light; it feels like the light of death and the end of the world.

Ever since the mid-nineteenth century, modernity has been obsessed with large surfaces of glass and consequently excessively high levels of illumination. No wonder, Luis Barragán, the alchemist of modern architecture, argued that most modern buildings would be more pleasant with only half of their window surface. "The use of enormous plate windows . . . deprives our buildings of intimacy, the effect of shadow and atmosphere. Architects all over the world have been mistaken in the proportions which they have assigned to large plate windows or spaces opening to the outside . . . We have lost our sense of intimate life, and have become forced to live public lives, essentially away from home."[12]

12
Ugarte, Alejandro Ramirez (1989). Interview with Luis Barragán. In: *Luis Barragán: Clásico del Silencio*, (ed. Enrique X. de Anda Alanis), 242. Bogotá, Colombia: Escala.

➔ Arnold Böcklin, Isle of the Dead, 3rd version, 1883. Sailko / Wikimedia Commons / CC BY 3.0 https://commons.wikimedia.org/wiki/File:Arnold_b%C3%B6cklin,_l%27isola_dei_morti,_1883,_02.jpg

➔ Sigurd Lewerentz, The Church of St Peter, Klippan, Sweden, 1962–1966. seier+seier / Flickr / CC BY 2.0 https://www.flickr.com/photos/seier/2356005438

IN PRAISE OF SHADOWS

The irreplaceable value of darkness and shadow is the lesson of Jun'ichirō Tanizaki's inspiring book, *In Praise of Shadows.* The writer points out that even Japanese cooking depends upon shadows, and that it is inseparable from darkness: "And when *Yōkan* is served in a lacquer dish within whose dark recesses its color is scarcely distinguishable, it is as if the darkness of the room were melting on your tongue."[13] This is yet another sensory metamorphoses; darkness turns into taste and fragrance.

13 Tanizaki, Jun'ichirō (1977). *In Praise of Shadows*, 16. New Haven, CT: Leete's Island Books.

Light acquires a heightened value and emotive power in relation to shadow and darkness. In the pitch black primordial smoke hut of the Finnish peasant, the light of a single tiny window feels like a shining jewel, a gracious gift presented to the inhabitant in the form of a radiant diamond of light, set on a dark mat background blackened by decades of smoke. In comparison, the excessive light of a contemporary glass wall is usually a source of sensory irritation and often causes a defensive repression of vision due to the painfully excessive illumination level.

Light and whiteness are associated with health and vitality, and the modern era has aspired to an abundance of light. Contrary to the prevailing modernist aspiration, the Council Chamber of Alvar Aalto's Säynätsalo Town Hall and the ecclesiastic spaces of Sigurd Lewerentz create a soothing darkness that facilitates the experience of concentration and meditation. In both cases, darkness is emphasized by dark, rough brick surfaces that seem to absorb all reflected light. In Lewerentz's St. Peter's Church, the deep crack in the brick floor, with water dripping slowly from a gigantic white sea cell into the darkness of the earth, echoes and emphasizes the darkness and dizzying depth of the space of the universe, the space of nothingness and eternity. The darkness in the floor is an open grave and endless fall. But it is also a window to eternity.

Deep shadows and darkness are essential, because they dim the sharpness of vision, make depth and distance ambiguous, and invite unconscious peripheral visions and tactile fantasies. "Shadow itself is of the light," as Frank Lloyd Wright observed.[14] We are not normally aware of the strong haptic and embodied ingredients in

14 As quoted in McCarter, Robert (1991). *Frank Lloyd Wright: A Primer on Architectural Principles*, 284. New York, NY: Princeton Architectural Press.

our visual perceptions but twilight reveals these forgotten sensibilities. Although we are not conscious of it, our skin has maintained a capacity to sense and identify light and color, and these normally suppressed sensory capabilities seem to be activated in the case of lost or weakened eyesight. Darkness also releases our sense of fantasy and imagination.

Sight is activated and sharpened in twilight. As James Turrell points out, the evolutionary process has tuned the human eye for twilight rather than bright daylight. Normal illumination levels today are so high that the full capacity of vision is suppressed as the pupil automatically closes. Paradoxically, our culture reveres vision and visibility, but at the same time weakens our capacities of vision through the use of excessive light.

THE THINGNESS OF LIGHT

Light is understood as a purely optical phenomenon, but it is essentially also connected with haptic perception. James Turrell, the light artist, speaks consequently about "the thingness of light."[15] "I basically make spaces that capture light and hold it for your physical sensing . . . It is . . . a realization that the eyes touch, that the eyes feel. And when the eyes are open and you allow for this sensation, touch goes out of the eyes like feel."[16] Turrell's light works are completely based on the experiential qualities of light and the characteristics of our perceptual mechanism, but they also give rise to spatial experiences that re-orient our judgment of figure and ground, near and far, horizon and verticality. These works turn light into a substance that seems to have its own haptic qualities and sense of materiality, pressure, and weight. Turrell also concretizes the age of light. We tend to think of light as a phenomenon of the present tense, the very definition of nowness. Yet, Turrell's light devices sometimes select light from the firmament that may be enormously old; he speaks appropriately of "old light." This can be light that has traveled through the bottomless darkness of the universe for thousands of years. In this context, we could appropriately speak of "an archaeology of light."

15

Turrell, James (2000). The thingness of light. In: *Light as Experience and Imagination from Medieval to Modern Times* (ed. Scott Poole), 1–2. Blacksburg, VA: Architecture Edition.

16

Ibid.

James Carpenter, another light artist, makes a similar claim about the tactility of light: "There is a tactility to something, which is immaterial, that I find rather extraordinary. With light you are dealing with a purely electromagnetic wavelength coming in through the retina, yet it is tactile. But it is not a tactility that fundamentally involves something that you can pick up or hold on to . . . Your eye tends to interpret light and bring to it some sort of substance, which, in reality, is not there."[17]

We inhabit simultaneously two domiciles: the physical world of matter and sensory experience, on the one hand, and the mental world of mental realities, imaginations, ideas, and intentions, on the other. These two worlds constitute a continuum, an existential singularity. In addition to its utilitarian purposes, the profound task of architecture is to "make visible how the world touches us," as Merleau-Ponty writes of the paintings of Paul Cézanne.[18] The world touches us, and we touch the world, primarily through the medium of light. "Through vision, we touch the stars and the sun."[19]

■ ■ ■

> *Light and shade are the loudspeakers of this architecture of truth, tranquillity and strength. Nothing further could add to it.*
>
> —Le Corbusier[20]

> *The worship of light is woven into the whole of human existence . . . even today, often unconsciously, we are dominated by it. Out of the half-death of sleep the light of day awakens us to life: 'to see the light', 'to behold the light of the sun', 'to be in the light', mean to live; 'to see the light' means to be born, 'to depart from the light' means to die. . .*
>
> —Hermann Usener[21]

17 Carpenter, James, Mason, Lawrence, Poole, Scott, and Sarpaneva, Pia (ed.) (2000). *James Carpenter*, 5. Blacksburg, VA: Architecture Edition.

18 Merleau-Ponty, "Cezanne's doubt," op. cit., p. 19.

19 As quoted in Levin, David Michael (1993). *Modernity and the Hegemony of Vision*, 14. Berkeley, CA: University of California Press.

20 Le Corbusier on the Abbey of Le Thoronet (near Lorgues, Var, France), quoted in Plummer, Henry (1987). *Poetics of Light*, 67. Tokyo: A+U Architecture and Urbanism, Extra Edition.

21 Hermann Usener, *Götternamen*, as quoted in ibid., p. 195.

➔ Peter Zumthor, Bruder Klaus Field Chapel, Mechernich, Cologne, Germany, 2005–2007. seier+seier / Wikimedia Commons / CC BY 2.0 https://commons.wikimedia.org/wiki/File:Dark_side_of_the_moon_-_peter_zumthor_-_Flickr_-_seier-seier.jpg

THE SPACE OF TIME 3

Mental Time in Architecture

It is as though space, cognizant . . . of its inferiority to time, answers it with the only property time doesn't possess: with beauty.

—Joseph Brodsky[1]

Time present and time past
Are both perhaps present in time future,
And time future contained in time past.
If all time is eternally present
All time is unredeemable.

—T.S. Eliot[2]

1 Brodsky, Joseph (1997). *Watermark*, 44. London: Penguin Books.

2 Eliot, T. S. (1988). Burnt Norton. In: *Four Quartets*, 13. New York, NY: Harcourt Brace Jovanovich.

TIME IN SCIENCE AND FICTION

Time is the most mysterious dimension of the physical reality and human consciousness. It appears self-evident in the context of everyday life, but beyond comprehension in deeper scientific and philosophical analyzes. St Augustine made an appropriate remark on the fundamental mystery of time: "What is time? If people do not ask me what time is, I know. If they ask me what it is, then I do not know."[3]

3 As quoted in Borges, Jorge Luis (2000). *This Craft of Verse*, 19. Cambridge, MA: Harvard University Press.

Time is the object of fascination for both the writer and the scientist, and, indeed, today the dreams of the fiction writer and the scientist can hardly be distinguished from one another; both suggest multiple realities of time. In his delightful little book about the multiple faces of time, entitled *Einstein's Dreams*,[4] the physics teacher and writer Alan Lightman fancies two dozen different realities of time: circular time, time that flows irregularly in rivulets and eddies like a stream, reversed time, time as a quality instead of quantity, and time that takes the form of a nightingale, for instance. On the other hand, today's astrophysicists theorize the feasibility of time travel through

4 Lightman, Alan (1993). *Einstein's Dreams*. New York, NY: Pantheon Books.

Eight Meditations on Architecture, First Edition. Juhani Pallasmaa. Edited by Matteo Zambelli.

"traversable wormholes" and "warp drives." They speak seriously of "chronology protection" and "time-machines." Looked at closely enough, quantum gravity theorists say, even ordinary space and time dissolve into a boiling mess that they call "space-time foam."[5]

5 Dennis Overbye, "Remembrance of Things Future: The Mystery of Time." *New York Times*, June 28, 2005.

Some quantum gravity theorists even argue that space and time are most likely a sort of illusion, or an approximation to be replaced by some more fundamental idea in the future. Regardless of the dizzying leaps of fantasy in today's physics, Stephen Hawking confesses modestly in his recent book, *The Universe in a Nutshell*: "Even if it turns out that time travel is impossible, it is important that we understand why it is impossible."[6]

6 Hawking, Stephen (2001). *The Universe in a Nutshell*, 147. London: Bantam Press.

Our common understanding of time seems to have evaporated under the scrutinity of science, and there are, indeed, several very different theories about time in physics today. And there are also vastly different scales of time, such as cosmic time, geological time, evolutionary time, cultural time, and human experiential time. And we all know how flexible and varied experiential time may be depending on the human situation, or horizon, that happens to provide the measure for the passing of time.

MODERN SPACE–TIME

Space and time, as well as the space–time continuum, have been central issues in theories of art and architecture since the early years of the last century. The new space–time concept is the focus in, for instance, Sigfried Giedion's seminal book, *Space, Time and Architecture*, originally published in 1941. "Space in modern physics is conceived as relative to a moving point of reference not as the absolute and static entity of the baroque system of Newton. And in modern art, for the first time since the Renaissance, a new conception of space leads to a self-conscious enlargement of the ways of perceiving space. It was in Cubism that this was most fully achieved," Giedion argues.[7] The masterpieces of Cubism exemplify the novel integration of space and time through movement and fragmentation of images. In Giedion's view, this new conception was first formulated by the mathematician Hermann Minkowski who claimed in 1908: "Henceforth, space alone or time alone is doomed to fade into a mere shadow: only a kind of union of both will preserve their existence."[8] Cubism did, indeed, historically emerge soon after this

7 Giedion, Sigfried (1952). *Space, Time and Architecture: The Growth of a New Tradition*, 368. Cambridge, MA: Harward University Press.

8 Ibid., p. 376.

mathematician's proclamation, and laid the foundation for the modern artistic consciousness.

In the early years of the nineteenth century, progressive writers, poets, painters, sculptors, and architects alike abandoned the idea of an objectified and static external world as exemplified by perspectival representation, and entered the dynamic experiential reality of human perception and consciousness that fuses reality and dream, actuality and memory.

My intention, however, is not to write here of the physical or philosophical speculations on the essence of time, or the dimension of time understood in terms of the mobile observer synthetizing his/her dynamic mosaic of observations. I am rather going to make some remarks on the significance of time as a mental dimension in artistic phenomena and architecture. I could characterize my subject matter as the "psyche and poetics of time." Marcel Proust claims: "As there is a geometry in space, so there is a psychology in time."[9]

9
Proust, Marcel (1996). *In Search of Lost Time*, Vol. 5: *The Captive, the Fugitive*, 637. London: Random House.

THE COLLAPSE OF TIME

Philosophers of postmodernity, such as David Harvey, have identified distinct changes that have taken place in our perception and understanding of space and time. They have, for instance, pointed out a curious reversal, or exchange of the two physical dimensions: the spatialization of time. In my view, the other reversal has also taken place: the temporalization of space. These reversals are exemplified by the fact that nowadays we commonly measure space through units of time and vice versa. Daniel Bell points out that space has taken over time also as the central concern of esthetics: "Space has become the primary aesthetic problem of mid-twentieth century culture as the problem of time (in Bergson, Proust and Joyce) was the primary aesthetic problem of the first decades of this century."[10]

10
Bell, Daniel. Statement: The cultural condition of capitalism. *Journal of Aesthetic Education* 6 (1/2): 11–38. As quoted in David Harvey, *The Condition of Postmodernity* (Oxford: Blackwell Publishers, 1992), p. 201.

The postmodern era has also brought about a curious new phenomenon: the collapse or implosion of the time horizon altogether onto the flat screen of the present. We can today appropriately speak of the simultaneity of the world. David Harvey writes in 1989 about the "time-space compression" and argues: "I want to suggest that we have been experiencing, these last two decades, an intense phase of time-space compression that has had a disorienting and disruptive impact upon political-economic practice, the balance of class power, as well as upon cultural and social life."[11]

In this process of time–space compression, time has lost its experiential depth, its plasticity, as it were. This collapse is brought about by an incredible acceleration of time in the contemporary world. Speed is the most seminal product of the current phase of industrial culture. This development has given rise to a "philosophy of speed," as exemplified by the writings of Paul Virilio;[12] Virilio calls his science of speed "dromology." In his view, contemporary architecture does not express spacelessness and timelessness but rather a concept of temporal space dominates our lives. The esthetics of speed, however, was introduced already in the first decades of the last century. "The world's magnificence has been enriched by a new beauty; the beauty of speed," Marinetti declared in his Manifesto.[13]

Coop Himmelb(l)au declares an "architecture of desolation," an architectural esthetics of speed, compression, fragmentation, and death "The aesthetics of the architecture of death in white sheets. Death in tiled hospital rooms. The architecture of sudden death on the pavement. Death from a rib-cage pierced by a steering shaft. The path of the bullet through a dealer's head on 42nd Street. The aesthetics of the architecture of the surgeon's razor-sharp scalpel. The aesthetics of the peep-show sex in washable plastic boxes. Of the broken tongues and the dried-up eyes."[14]

The dizzying acceleration of experiential time during the past few decades is rather easy for anyone to recognize in comparison with the slow and patient time projected by the great Russian, German, and French classical novels of the nineteenth century. It suffices here to mention the painfully slow description of Hans Castorp's seven-year stay in the Berghof Sanatorium in Thomas Mann's novel *The Magic Mountain*, or the 3500 pages of Marcel Proust's *In Search of Lost Time.*

Italo Calvino comments interestingly on this acceleration of time during the past century: "Long novels written today are perhaps a contradiction: the dimension of time has been shattered, we cannot live or think except in fragments of time, each of which goes off along its trajectory and immediately disappears. We can re-discover the continuity of time only in the novels of that period

11
Harvey, op. cit., p. 284.

12
For example, Virilio, Paul (1994). *Katoamisen Estetiikka* (The Esthetics of Disappearance). Tampere: Gaudeamus.

13
As quoted in Mayne, Thom (2006). Statement. In: *Ligang Qiu* (ed. Peter Pran), 4. Beijing, China: DUT Press.

14
Coop Himmelb(l)au, Die Fascination der Stadt, as quoted in Vidler, Anthony (1999). *The Architectural Uncanny*, 76. Cambridge, MA: The MIT Press.

when time no longer seemed stopped and did not yet seem to have exploded."[15]

It is quite astonishing to find the lament of Abbé Lamennais about the disappearance of time written already in 1819: "Man does not read any longer. There is no time for it. The spirit is called upon from all directions simultaneously; it has to be addressed quickly or else it disappears. But there are things, which cannot be said or comprehended quickly, and exactly these are most important for man. This rushing of movement, which does not allow man to concentrate on anything, finally shatters the entire human reason."[16] I give this piece of literary evidence, dating back two centuries, to assure you that the problem of the acceleration of time has its roots deep in the history of modern culture. Our loss of time is the consequence of a historical process.

Marcel Proust makes an interesting comment on the alteration of our consciousness of time since the Roman era: "Since railways came into existence, the necessity of not missing trains has taught us to take account of minutes, whereas among the ancient Romans, who not only had a more cursory acquaintance with astronomy but led less hurried lives, the notion of not only of minutes but even of fixed hours barely existed."[17]

I wish to point out a fundamental change that has recently occurred in a minute and commonplace detail: the difference in the reading of time by means of a traditional watch and a digital watch (my quote derives from a book entitled, *Conversations About the End of Time*, published at the turn of the Millennium): "When you look at a watch dial for the time, that is situated within the circle of time, you immediately recall what you have done in the course of the day, where you were this morning, what time it was when you bumped into your friend, you remember when dusk is going to fall, and you see the time that's left before bedtime, when you'll go to bed sure in the knowledge of another day well spent, and with the certainty also that on the following day, time will resume its daily course around your watch. If all you've got is a little rectangle, you have to live life as a series of moments, and you lose all true measure of time."[18] This is the fundamental experiential difference between analogical and digital measuring. What is essentially lost with the digital watch is the cyclical nature of natural time.

15

Calvino, Italo (1981). *If on a Winter's Night a Traveler*, 8. New York, NY: Harcourt Brace & Company.

16

As quoted in Huyghe, René (1955). *Dialogue avec le visible: Connaissance de la peinture*. Paris: Flammarion. page number unidentified.

17

Marcel Proust, op. cit., Vol. 4: *Sodom and Gomorrah*, p. 258.

18

David, Catherine, Lenoir, Frédéric, and de Tonnac, Jean-Philippe (2000). *Conversations About the End of Time*, 139. London: Penguin Books.

Significantly, we have even changed our bodily position in relation to the flow of time. The Greeks understood that the future came from behind their backs and the past receded away in front of their eyes. We have turned our faces toward the future and past is disappearing behind our backs.[19]

Most dramatically, however, we even seem to lose our memories. Milan Kundera makes a remark to that effect: "The degree of slowness is directly proportional to the intensity of memory; the degree of speed is directly proportional to the intensity of forgetting."[20] My chapter is essentially about the virtues and benefits of slowness, or the "chemistry of time,"[21] to use a notion of Proust.

We all have reason to be frightened by the disappearance and abstraction of time and the curiously related phenomenon: the expansion of boredom. I am not going to enter this subject matter, however, beyond simply referring to a recent book on the philosophy of boredom by the Norwegian philosopher Lars Svendsen.[22] I would like to suggest that we have lost our capacity to dwell in time, or inhabit time. We have been pushed outside of time, the experiential space of time. Time has turned into a vacuum in opposition to the "tactile sense of [time]"[23] in Proust's writings, for instance. We live increasingly outside of the continuum of time; we dwell solely in space. It is tragic, indeed, that as we have entered the age of four-dimensional, or multi-dimensional, space in our scientific thinking, we are experientially thrown back to Eucledian space restricted to its three spatial dimensions. The substance of time seems to exist nowadays only as archeological remains in the literary, artistic, and architectural works of past eras. Similarly, the originary silence of the world exists only in fragments, but as Max Picard, the philosopher of silence, suggests, we are frightened by all fragments.[24] We are equally frightened by fragments of silence and time.

MUSEUMS OF TIME

In the same way that we can encounter an amazing presence of time, almost as a still and heavy liquid, when reading Anton Chekhov's short story (in fact, it is more like a novel in its length), *The Steppe*, we experience a slow and thick time when entering a Romanesque cloister or a medieval cathedral, or walking on the streets of an old town. In his legendary novel, Proust describes the gradually released time dimension by the Combray Church: "all this made of the church for me something entirely different from the rest of the town – an edifice occupying, so to

19 Robert M. Pirsig, An Author and Father Looks Ahead at the Past. *The New York Times Book Review*. Date unidentified.

20 Kundera, Milan (1966). *Slowness*, 39. New York, NY: HarperCollins.

21 Proust, op. cit., Vol. 6: *Time Regained*, p. 331.

22 Svendsen, Lars (2012). *A Philosophy of Boredom*. London: Reaktion Books.

23 Carrière, Jean-Claude (2000). Answering the Sphinx. In: *Conversations About the End of Time*, op. cit., p. 95.

24 Picard, Max (1988). *The World of Silence*, 212. Washington, D.C.: Gateway Editions.

speak, a four-dimensional space – the name of the fourth being Time – extending through the centuries its ancient nave, which, bay after bay, chapel after chapel, seemed to stretch across and conquer not merely a few yards of soil – but each successive epoch from which it emerged."[25]

25

Proust, op. cit., Vol. 1: *Swann's Way*, p. 71.

We can experience a gradual quickening of time in the modernist masterpieces, and a further acceleration of velocity in today's deconstructionist buildings. The celebrated buildings of our time often appear to be rushing as if time were just about to disappear altogether. Every age and every building have their characteristic speed, sense of time, and silence. There are slow and patient spaces as well as fast and hurried buildings. There are also mute, silent, and garrulous spaces and buildings.

Every truly moving experience of art – ancient, modern, or contemporary – seems to suspend time and open the curtains of experience onto a calm, tranquil duration. I wish to suggest that a distinct slowness and silencing of experience belong to profound artistic greatness in general. When visiting the Great Peristyle of the Karnak temple in Luxor, I felt that my entire personality, my sense of separate self, evaporated as I became fused with the space, time, and matter of the age of the Pharaohs. As Paul Valéry makes Socrates remark in one of his dialogues: "Did it not seem to you that . . . time itself surrounded you on all sides?"[26] I experienced a similar vanishing of the temporal reality – the separate categories of past, present, and future – when standing in front of Mark Rothko's magnificent dark monochrome paintings in the Rothko Chapel in Houston, Texas. These painted spaces invite the viewer into a deep timeless space at the threshold of being and non-being. They bring the viewer to the ultimate shore of time.

26

Valéry, Paul (1956). *Dialogues*, 94. New York, NY: Pantheon Books.

The American artist and professor Sanda Iliescu writes perceptively of the peculiar perceptual and mental essence of poeticized time: "In aesthetic experiences, time seems to slow down, allowing our memories and perceptions to mingle. Unlike chronological time, which is concerned with actions and consequences, aesthetic time is a layered surface in which present (what is seen, touched, smelled, tasted, heard) and past (what is remembered or re-considered) are embedded. The past and present overlap in fluid ways, neither one serving or being summoned for the sake of the other. Time becomes less a singular journey we travel on than a richly marked and textured surface we touch."[27]

27

Sanda Iliescu, "Eight Aesthetic Propositions," unpublished manuscript, 2006, p. 23. Constantin Brancusi's *Sculpture for the Blind*, 1920, was first exhibited inside an opaque cloth sack with sleeves through which visitors could touch the primordial egg shape of the sculpture. Iliescu, ibid., p. 11.

← Karnak Temple, Luxor, Egypt, nineteenth century BCE.
Diego Delso / Wikimedia Commons / CC BY-SA 4.0 https://commons.wikimedia.org/wiki/File:Templo_de_Karnak,_Luxor,_Egipto,_2022-04-03,_DD_161.jpg

TIME-FREE PERCEPTION

Regardless of its ephemeral and mystical nature, time is the crucial fluid of our mental lives. We do not live in a fixed, objective reality; we live in a mental reality that perpetually keeps flowing back and forth between reality, dream, and imagination. Our mental reality has no fixed boundaries, no fixed temporal order or categories. In his seminal, but sadly forgotten book, *The Psychoanalysis of Artistic Vision and Hearing: An Introduction to a Theory of Unconscious Perception*, first published in 1953, Anton Ehrenzweig speaks of a "time-free" consciousness, or mode of perception, as a necessary condition for creative thought.[28] Time-free association, remembrance, and dreaming, in fact, also seem to be the condition of our normal daydreaming and concentrated thought; in these mental states we detach ourselves from the progression of time.

28 Ehrenzweig, Anton (1975). *The Psychoanalysis of Artistic Vision and Hearing: An Introduction to a Theory of Unconscious Perception*. London: Sheldon Press.

Ehrenzweig quotes a letter of Wolfgang Amadeus Mozart as an impressive example of time-free hearing. The composer describes the gradual disintegration of linear time in his creative process: "I spread it [the composition] out broader and clearer, and at last it gets almost finished in my head, even when it is a long piece, so that I can see the whole of it at a single glance in my mind, as if it were a beautiful painting or a handsome human being; in which way I do not hear it in my imagination at all as a succession – that way it must come later – but all at once, as it were. It is a rare feast! All the inventing and making goes on in me as in a beautiful dream. But the best of all is *the hearing of it all at once*."[29] Just try to imagine hearing the entire *Magic Flute* or *Requiem* all at once, an entire musical composition compressed into a singular volume of sound! This description of Mozart makes one think of the unimaginable compression of the entire Universe at the very moment of the Big Bang.

29 Ibid., pp. 107–108. Italics in original.

PERFECTION AND IMPERFECTION

Time has a seminal mental importance also because of our unconscious fear of death. We do not only live in space and place, we also inhabit time. Karsten Harries, the philosopher, points out the essential mental reality of time in the art of architecture: "Architecture is not only about domesticating space, it is also a deep defence against the terror of time. The language of beauty is essentially the language of the timeless reality."[30] Our longing and quest for beauty are an unconscious attempt to temporarily eliminate the reality of erosion, entropy, and death. Beauty is a promise; an experience of beauty gives a promise of the existence of permanent qualities and values. Jorge Luis Borges makes a strong remark to this effect: "There is

30 Harries, Karsten (1982). Building and the terror of time. *Perspecta, Yale Architectural Journal* 19: 59–69.

an eternity in beauty."[31] But Paul Válery gives a warning through the words of Phaedrus in his dialogue, "Eupalinos, or the Architect": "What is most beautiful is of necessity tyrannical."[32] Besides, Valéry disagrees with Borges in the permanence of beauty, as he writes: "What is most beautiful finds no place in the eternal."[33] This fundamental disagreement between two master poets is thought-provoking, indeed.

31 Borges, op. cit., p. 115.

32 Valery, *Dialogues*, op. cit., p. 86.

33 Ibid., p. 76.

At the same time that we dream of eternal life through images of timeless beauty and perfection, we need experiences that mark and measure the course of time; we need to be convinced of the depth and availability of time. Traces of erosion and wear remind us of the ultimate fate of the physical and biological world, "horizontal death"[34] – to use a notion of Gaston Bachelard – but they also situate us concretely in the flow of time. Time turns into a haptic sensation; time becomes a perception of the skin. Matter expresses time, whereas shape, particularly geometric form, expresses space. A pebble held on the palm conveys the experience of materialized time. We cannot mentally live in a placeless space, but we cannot exist in a timeless duration, either. Our contemporary, highly technological environments, built of man-made materials, do not usually mediate traces of time and history. Instead of promoting rootedness and a sense of belonging, they evoke an air of alienation, detachment, and lack of empathy. When comparing a contemporary cityscape with historical towns, we can distinguish a flat time from a thick time, time as absence from time as a comforting presence.

34 Bachelard, Gaston (1982). *Water and Dreams: An Essay on the Imagination of Matter*, 6. Dallas, TX: The Pegasus Foundation.

The human consciousness is balanced between Eros and Thanatos, and it is one of the mental tasks of architecture to mediate between the two polarities. Paul Válery argues: "Two dangers never cease threatening the world: order and disorder."[35] The quest for perfection has to be balanced by traces of imperfection. John Ruskin advises us: "Imperfection is in some way essential to all that we know of life. It is the sign of life in a mortal body, that is to say, of a state of process and change. Nothing that lives is, or can be, rigidly perfect; part of it is decaying, part nascent . . . And in all things that live, there are certain irregularities and deficiencies, which are not only signs of life but sources of beauty."[36]

35 Valery, Paul (1919). The Crisis of the Mind. In (1962) *History and Politics*, 29. New York, NY: Bellingen Foundation. Available at: https://ia802901.us.archive.org/3/items/in.ernet.dli.2015.137329/2015.137329.The-Collected-Works-Of-Paul-Valery-Vol-10.pdf.

36 Ruskin, John (1980). *The Lamp of Beauty: Writings on Art by John Ruskin* (ed. Joan Evans), 238. Ithaca, NY: Cornell University Press.

Architecture needs deliberate devices to express duration and time. The eighteenth century's fascination with artificial ruins is an example of the attempt to expand the scale of architectural time. An element that somewhat unexpectedly evokes time in juxtaposition with architecture is water.

Frank Lloyd Wright, Fallingwater (also known as the Kaufmann House), Mill Run, Stewart Township, Fayette County, Pennsylvania, 1936–1939.

Carlo Scarpa, Sculpture Garden, Venice Biennale, Venice, Italy, 1952.
Jean-Pierre Dalbéra / Wikimedia Commons / CC BY 2.0
https://commons.wikimedia.org/wiki/File:Carlo_Scarpa_%28Giardini,_Venise%29.jpg

WATER AND TIME

Joseph Brodsky gives a surprising meaning to time: "I always adhered to the idea that God is time, or at least that his spirit is."[37] He makes other intriguing associations: "I simply think that water is the image of time,"[38] and: "Water equals time and provides beauty with its double."[39] In the poet's imagination, God, time, water, and beauty are connected to create a mysterious cycle, or Mandala of sorts. These associations are not, however, Brodsky's alone; Gaston Bachelard, and Adrian Stokes, for instance, make similar suggestions. Water is also a frequent image in various art forms. Think of the fusion of images of water and the extraordinary sense of time, spirituality, and melancholy in the films of Andrei Tarkovsky, or the gentle

37 Brodsky, *Watermark*, op. cit., p. 42.

38 Ibid., p. 43.

39 Ibid., p. 134.

Juhani Pallasmaa, Summer Atelier for the Painter Tor Arne, Vänö Island, Finland, 1970. © Juhani Pallasmaa

and hypnotic slowness of the paintings of water by Claude Monet, or the architecture of water by Sigurd Lewerentz, Carlo Scarpa, and Luis Barragán. Water dripping from a giant seashell into the dark wound in the brick floor at the Klippan Church of Lewerentz, the underwater architecture of the Brion-Vega Chapel of Scarpa, and the reflecting veils of water, as well as images of rushing water in Luis Barragán's buildings, all evoke a hightened and sensitized experience of duration. The reflective surface of water hides its depth, as the present conceals the past and future. The life-supporting image of water also contains the mortal images of deluge and drought. We are suspended between the opposites of birth and death, utopia and oblivion.

Images of water turn into instruments of concretizing the passing and persistence of time. The dialogue of architecture and water is truly erotic. There is a special fascination in all towns that are in dialogue with water. As Stokes remarks: "The hesitancy of water reveals architectural immobility."[40] The sound of the waterfall at Frank Lloyd Wright's Fallingwater House creates a dense sensuous weave, almost like a textile of visual and audible ingredients, with architecture and the enveloping forest; one dwells comfortingly in a natural duration next to the beating heart of reality itself.

40 Stokes, Adrian (1978). Prolog: At Venice. In: *The Critical Writings of Adrian Stokes*, Vol. II, 88. Plymouth: Thames and Hudson.

SYMBOL AND REALITY

The two ideas that have given rise to fundamental misconceptions about the essence of artistic phenomena are: art understood as a symbol, and art seen as novelty.

Artistic and architectural works do not just symbolize something outside themselves; they create a reality and they *are* this other reality. "[A] poem . . . is not a paraphrase or a metaphor for reality, but a reality itself," as Brodsky argues.[41] A work of art or architecture is not a symbol that represents, or indirectly portrays something outside itself. It is an *image reality*, or *ideated reality* that places itself directly in our existential sphere and consciousness. It becomes part of us and we become part of it.

41 Brodsky, Joseph (1997). *On Grief and Reason*, 386. New York, NY: Farrar, Straus & Giroux.

Architecture, also, creates its own altered reality, in which perceptions and experiences of space, duration, and gravity are transformed. Architecture projects specific horizons of perception and understanding. Buildings condition our reading of time; like the cinematic or literary arts, they can speed up, slow down, halt and reverse time. Great buildings are not temporal symbols or metaphors, they are museums and stores of time. As we enter a great building, its particular silence and mode of time guide our experiences and emotions. In fact, the depth of the entire cultural time is measured and expressed primarily by architectural constructions. Just imagine how shallow and scaleless our sense of history would be without the image of the Egyptian pyramids in our minds. This is true regardless of whether we have ever seen a pyramid in reality or not. Architectural structures have seminal functions as externalized mental structures, and as extensions of our individual and collective memories and consciousnesses. They constitute instruments for grasping and sustaining history and time, as well as understanding social and cultural reality and human institutions.

ART AND NOVELTY

In his intriguing book, *The Philosophy of No: A Philosophy of the New Scientific Mind*,[42] Gaston Bachelard explains the development of scientific thought as a transition from animism through realism, positivism, rationalism, and complex rationalism to dialectical rationalism.[43] This is the closed orbit of scientific thought, in his view. "The philosophical evolution of a special piece of scientific knowledge is a movement through all these doctrines in the order indicated,"[44] the philosopher argues.

Significantly, artistic thinking aspires to develop in the opposite direction. An artistic image works its way from the realist, rational, and analytic understanding back toward a mythical and animistic grasp of the world. Science and art, therefore, seem to move past each other in opposite directions along the same continuum. Whereas scientific thought progresses and differentiates, artistic thought seeks to return back to a de-differentiated and experientially singular oceanic understanding of the world. Artistic imagination seeks expressions that are capable of mediating the entire complexity of human existential experience through singular images. In that sense, art is a perpetual tautology. It keeps repeating one and the same message: the experience of being a human being in this world. The paradoxical task of uniting singularity and universality is achieved through poeticized images that are experienced and lived rather than analyzed and understood.

Our time is obsessed by ideas of uniqueness and novelty, and art – particularly of our own time – is usually appreciated and judged primarily through its unforeseen novelty. I cannot think of a single profound artist, however, who would have written about this kind of

42 Bachelard, Gaston (1968). *The Philosophy of No: A Philosophy of the New Scientific Mind*. New York, NY: The Orion Press.

43 Ibid., p. 15.

44 Ibid., p. 16.

a futuristic interest, excluding the futurists, for whom the interest in the future was a semi-religious motive. "No real writer ever tried to be contemporary," Borges appropriately argues.[45] No real artist or architect is interested in such shallow and meaningless notions as contemporaneity and freedom. Whenever someone begins to speak enthusiastically about freedom in an artistic endeavor, the question arises; freedom from what, and freedom for what? "Strength . . . is born of constraints and and dies in freedom," Leonardo da Vinci already taught us.[46]

45

Borges, Jorge Luis (1994). *On Writing* (ed. Norman Thomas di Giovanni, Daniel Halpern, and Frank Mac Shane), 53. Hopewell, NJ: The Ecco Press.

46

As quoted by Stravinsky, Igor (1947). *Poetics of Music: In the Form of Six Lessons*, 76. Cambridge, MA: Harvard University Press.

REVERSED TIME

"[W]hen one writes verse, one's most immediate audience is not one's own contemporaries, let alone posterity, but one's predecessors," Brodsky confesses.[47] No authentic creative work takes place in a cultural or mental zero point or vacuum: creative work takes place in the continuum and traditions of culture, in a constant dialogue with one's great predecessors. The profound artist seeks advice and approval among the dead, not the contemporaries, not to speak of seeking to please the future reader, viewer, or inhabitant. Consequently, the past, the very depth of time is the real mental dimension of artistic work. "In its desire to acquire great perfection, each work of art must from the moment of its finalization descend into the darkness of millennia with great patience and extreme caution and return, if possible, into the immemorial night in which the dead will recognize themselves in this work," writes Jean Genet.[48] Instead of aspiring to futuristic fantasies, the artist seeks to recapture the undifferentiated consciousness of the child and the singularity of human existence. The artist defends the historicity of the human being and desires to fuse again with the world.

47

Brodsky, Joseph, Letter to Horace. In: Brodsky, *On Grief and Reason*, op. cit., p. 439.

48

Genet, Jean (1987). *Giacomettin ateljeessa* (In Giacometti's Atelier), 15. Helsinki: Kustannusosakeyhtiö Taide. Translation Juhani Pallasmaa.

The magical quality of art is exactly in its disregard for the element of progressive, causal, or linear time. All great works of art overcome the abyss of time and speak to us in present tense. "An artist is worth a thousand centuries," as Valéry writes.[49] A Stone Age cave painting confronts our eyes and mind with the same force of life and actuality as any work of our own day. This is exactly because time as a chronology or causality is meaningless in art. Art is fundamentally an existential expression that makes the observer confront his/her own existence with sensitized senses and heightened bravery.

49

Valéry, *Dialogues*, op. cit., p. XIII.

Instead of being interested in contemporaneity, art is driven by an aspiration for an ideal, an ideal mode of consciousness and being. This desire for the ideal is not a sentimental yearning; it is a search for an experientially singular world where the opposition of object and subject disappears, and this is the realm of beauty. This quest of the artist is the source of profound humility and uncertainty. As Brodsky wisely writes: "Uncertainty, you see, is the mother of beauty, one of whose definitions is that it's something which isn't yours."[50] Beauty cannot be possessed; it can only be encountered. Similarly, artistic meaning cannot be invented; it can only be re-discovered, re-identified, and re-articulated.

50 Brodsky, Joseph (1986). 'On September 1, 1939', by W. H. Auden. In: *Less than One* (ed. Joseph Brodsky), 309. New York, NY: Farrar, Straus & Giroux.

BIOLOGICAL TIME IN ARCHITECTURE

We are primarily biological and historical beings whose genetic programming extends millions of years back into the past of the human race. Our instinctive reactions to spatial situations and qualities are grounded in the living conditions of countless past generations of our predecessors. The human sensations of directions, above and below, darkness and light, safety and threat, pleasure and discomfort, horizontality and verticality, nearness and distance, etc., are all grounded in our collectively shared unconscious. We may live in a city and be deeply engaged in the technological and digital realities of today, but our embodied reactions continue to be grounded in our timeless past; there is still a hunter-gatherer, fisherman, and farmer concealed in the genes of each one of us, and architecture needs to acknowledge this deep historicity of humankind. This biocultural historicity poses a critical perspective to today's preference for novelty and uncritical enthusiasm for digital and virtual realities. Scientific research in the biological and evolutionary essence of esthetics and beauty has hardly begun,[51] but the poet and artist already know the depth of these phenomena. "Believe it or not, but the purpose of evolution is beauty," Joseph Brodsky declares with the assurance of a great poet.[52]

51 See, for instance, Rentschler, Ingo, Herzberger, Barbara, and Epstein, David (1988). *Beauty and the Brain: Biological Aspects of Esthetics*. Berlin: Birkäuser Verlag.

52 Brodsky, An immodest proposal. In: Brodsky, *On Grief and Reason*, op. cit., p. 207.

The historical grounding of architecture, also, is likely to be found decisively deeper than our current understanding of the few thousand years of architectural history suggests. It is evident that the origins of architecture are beyond history and verbal accounts in the deep anthropological past of humankind. In my view, the ethical task of architecture is to defend our biological essence and historicity in order to root us in the essential mental realities of life. This, I believe, is the most important time perspective for the art of architecture.

■ ■ ■

As the consequence of the annihilation of time, the public space is replaced by the public image.

—Paul Virilio[53]

Language is a diluted aspect of matter . . . By manipulating it into a harmony or, for that matter, disharmony, a poet . . . negotiates himself into the domain of pure matter – or, if you will, of pure time – faster than can be done in any other line of work.

—Joseph Brodsky[54]

To be conscious is not to be in time
But only in time can the moment in the rose-garden,
The moment in the arbour where the rain beat,
The moment in the draughty church at smokefall.
Be remembered; involved with past and future,
Only through time time is conquered.

—T.S. Eliot[55]

53 Paul Virilio, as quoted by Mika Määttänen. In: Virilio, *Katoamisen estetiikka*, op. cit., p. 127.

54 Brodsky, Profile of Clio. In: Brodsky, *On Grief and Reason*, op. cit., p. 311.

55 T.S. Eliot, Burnt Norton. In: Eliot, *Four Quartets*, op. cit., p. 16.

➔ John Soane, Sir John Soane Museum, Lincoln's Inn Field 13, London, United Kingdom, 1808–1809 and 1812. Archimage / Alamy Stock Photo https://www.alamy.com/stock-photo-interior-of-the-sir-john-soane-museum-in-lincolns-inn-london-78769677.html?imageid=3F036F01-148E-4B02-BCAC-4C1552B9FF82&p=52966&pn=1&searchId=aa0b149c2ea63ca1ca8c64a344a3533a&searchtype=0

SELFHOOD, MEMORY, AND IMAGINATION 4

Landscapes of Remembrance and Dream

THE TIME PERSPECTIVE IN ARCHITECTURE

Architecture is usually seen in futuristic terms; novel buildings are understood to probe and project an unforeseen reality, and architectural quality is directly associated with its degree of novelty and uniqueness. Modernity at large has been dominated by this futuristic bias. Yet, the appreciation of newness has probably never been as obsessive as in today's cult of spectacular architectural imagery. In our globalized world, newness is not only an esthetic and artistic value, it is a strategic necessity of the culture of consumption, and consequently, an inseparable ingredient of our surreal materialist culture.

However, human constructions also have the task of preserving the past, and enable us to experience and grasp the continuum of culture and tradition. We not only exist in a spatial and material reality, we also inhabit cultural, mental, and temporal realities. Our existential and lived reality is a thick, layered, and constantly oscillating condition. Architecture is essentially an art form of reconciliation and mediation, and, in addition to settling us in space and place, landscapes and buildings articulate our experiences of duration and time between the polarities of past and future. In fact, along with the entire corpus of literature and the arts, landscapes and buildings constitute the most important externalization of human memory. We understand and remember who we are through our constructions, both material and mental. We also judge alien and past cultures through the evidence provided by the architectural structures they have produced. Buildings project epic narratives.

In addition to practical purposes, architectural structures have a significant existential and mental task; they domesticate space for human occupation by turning anonymous, uniform and limitless

Eight Meditations on Architecture, First Edition. Juhani Pallasmaa. Edited by Matteo Zambelli.

space into distinct places of human significance, and, equally importantly, they make endless time tolerable by giving duration its human measure. As Karsten Harries, the philosopher, argues, "Architecture helps to replace meaningless reality with a theatrically, or rather architecturally, transformed reality, which draws us in and, as we surrender to it, grants us an illusion of meaning . . . we cannot live with chaos. Chaos must be transformed into cosmos . . ."[1] "Architecture is not only about domesticating space. It is also a deep defence against the terror of time," he states in another context.[2]

Altogether, environments and buildings not only serve practical and utilitarian purposes; they also structure our understanding of the world. "[The house] is an instrument with which to confront the cosmos," as Gaston Bachelard states.[3] The abstract and indefinable notion of the cosmos is always present and represented in our immediate landscape. Every landscape and every building are a condensed world, a microcosmic representation.

ARCHITECTURE AND MEMORY

We all remember the way architectural images were utilized as mnemonic devices by the orators of antiquity. Actual architectural structures, as well as mere remembered architectural images and metaphors serve as significant memory devices in three different ways: first, they materialize and preserve the course of time and make it visible; second, they concretize remembrance by containing and projecting memories, and; third, they stimulate and inspire us to reminisce and imagine. Memory and fantasy, recollection and imagination are related and they have always a situational and specific content. Someone who cannot remember can hardly imagine, because memory is the soil of imagination. Memory is also the ground of self-identity; we are what we remember.

Buildings are storage houses and museums of time and silence. Architectural structures have the capacity to transform, speeding up, slowing down, and halting time. They can also create and protect silence, following Kierkegaard's request: "Create silence!"[4] In the view of Max Picard, the philosopher of silence, "Nothing has changed the nature of man so much as the loss of silence."[5] "Silence no longer exists as a *world*, but only in fragments, as the remains of a world."[6] Architecture has to preserve the memory of the world of silence and to protect the existing fragments of this fundamental ontological state. When we enter a Romanesque monastery, we can still experience the benevolent silence of the universe.

1

Harries, Karsten (1993). Thoughts on a non-arbitrary architecture. In: *Dwelling, Seeing and Designing: Toward a Phenomenological Ecology* (ed. David Seamon), 47. Albany, NY: State University of New York Press.

2

Harries, Karsten (1982). Building and the terror of time. *Perspecta: The Yale Architectural Journal* 19: 59–69. As quoted in: David Harvey, *The Condition of Postmodernity* (Oxford: Blackwell, 1992), p. 206.

3

Bachelard, Gaston (1969). *The Poetics of Space*, 46. Boston, MA: Beacon Press.

4

As quoted in Picard, Max (1988). *The World of Silence*, 231. Washington, DC: Begnery Gateway. Kierkegaard writes: "The present state of the world and the whole of life is diseased. If I were a doctor and were asked for my advice, I should say: Create Silence! Bring men to silence."

5

Ibid., p. 221.

6

Ibid., p. 212.

There are, of course, particular building types, such as memorials, tombs, and museums that are deliberately conceived and built for the purpose of preserving and evoking memories and specific emotions; buildings can maintain feelings of grief and ecstasy, melancholy and joy, as well as fear and hope. All buildings maintain our perception of temporal duration and depth, and they record and suggest cultural and human narratives. We cannot conceive or remember time as a mere physical dimension; we can only grasp time through its actualizations; the traces, places, and events of temporal occurrence. Joseph Brodsky points out another deficiency of human memory as he writes about the composite images of cities in human memory and finds these cities always empty: "[The city of memory] is empty because for an imagination it is easier to conjure architecture than human beings."[7] Is this the inherent reason why we architects tend to think of architecture more in terms of its material existence than the life and human situations that take place in the spaces we have designed?

7 Brodsky, Joseph (1997). A place as good as any. In: *On Grief and Reason* (ed. Joseph Brodsky), 43. New York, NY: Farrar, Straus & Giroux.

Architectural structures facilitate memory; our understanding of the depth of time would be decisively weaker, for instance, without the image of the pyramids in our minds. The mere image of a pyramid marks and concretizes time. We also remember our own childhood largely through the houses and places that we have lived in. We have projected and hidden parts of our lives in lived landscapes and houses, exactly as the orators placed themes of their speeches in the context of imagined buildings. The recollection of places and rooms generates the recall of events and people. "I was a child of that house, filled with the memory of its smells, filled with the coolness of its hallways, filled with the voices that had given it life. There was even the song of the frogs in the pools; they came to be with me here," reminisces Antoine de Saint-Exupéry, the legendary pilot and writer, after having crash-landed his plane in a sand desert in North Africa.[8]

8 de Saint-Exupéry, Antoine (1991). *Wind, Sand and Stars*, 39. London: Penguin Books.

THE MENTAL POWER OF FRAGMENTS

In his novel, *The Notebooks of Malte Laurids Brigge*, Rainer Maria Rilke gives a similarly moving record of a distant memory of home and self, arising from fragments of the grandfather's house in the protagonist's memory: "As I recover it in recalling my child-wrought memories, it is no complete building: it is all broken up inside me; here a room, there a room, and here a piece of hallway that does not connect these two rooms but is preserved, as a fragment, by itself. In this way it is all dispersed within me . . . all that is still in me and will never cease to be in me. It is as though the picture of this house had fallen into me from an infinite height and had shattered against my very ground."[9] The remembered image arises gradually, piece by piece, from fragments of memory as a painted Cubist picture emerges from detached visual motifs.

9 Rilke, Rainer Maria (1992). *The Notebooks of Malte Laurids Brigge*. 30–31. New York, NY: W.W. Norton & Co.

I have written about my own memories of my grandfather's humble farmhouse, and pointed out that the memory house of my early childhood is a collage of fragments, smells, conditions of light, specific feelings of enclosure and intimacy, but rarely precise and complete visual recollections. My eyes have forgotten what they once saw, but my body still remembers.

Buildings and their remains suggest stories of human fate, both real and imaginary. Ruins stimulate us to think of lives that have already disappeared, and to imagine the fate of their deceased occupants. Ruins and eroded settings have a special evocative and emotional power; they force us to reminisce and imagine. Incompleteness and fragmentation possess a special evocative power. In medieval illustrations and Renaissance paintings, architectural settings are often depicted as a mere edge of a wall or a window opening, but the isolated fragment suffices to conjure up the experience of a complete constructed setting. This is the secret of the art of collage but also some architects, such as John Soane and Alvar Aalto, have taken advantage of this emotional power of the architectural fragment. Rilke's description of the images of life lived in a demolished house triggered by the remains and stains left on the end wall of the neighboring house, is a stunning record of the ways of human memory: "But most forgettable of all were the walls themselves. The stubborn life of these rooms had not let itself be trampled out. It was still there; it clung to the nails that had been left there, it stood on the remaining hand-breadth of flooring, it crouched under the corner joints where there was still a little bit of interior. One could see that it was in the paint which, year by year, had slowly altered: blue into moldy green, green into gray, and yellow into an old, stale rotting white."[10]

10 Ibid., pp. 47–48.

➔ Gustave Eiffel, Eiffel Tower, Paris, France, 1887–1889. Thorsten technoman / Pexels / Public Domain https://www.pexels.com/photo/picture-of-eiffel-tower-338515/

➔ Ivan Barma and Postnik Jakovlev, Saint Basil's Cathedral, Moscow, Russia, 1555–1561. Дмитрий Трепольский / Pexels / Public Domain

SPATIALITY AND SITUATIONALITY OF MEMORY

Our recollections are situational and spatialized memories, they are memories attached to places and events. It is hard to recall, for instance, a familiar or iconic photograph as a two-dimensional image on photographic paper; we tend to remember the depicted object, person, or event in its full spatial reality. It is obvious that our existential space is never a two-dimensional pictorial space, it is a lived and multi-sensory space saturated and structured by memories and intentions. We keep projecting meanings and signification onto everything we encounter, I have rarely disagreed with the views of Joseph Brodsky, one of my house gods, but when he argues that after having seen touristic buildings, such as Westminster Abbey, the Eiffel Tower, Saint Basil's cathedral, the Taj Mahal or the Acropolis, "We retain not their three-dimensional image but their printed version," and concludes that "Strictly speaking, we remember not a place but our postcard of it,"[11] I have to disagree with the poet. We do not remember the postcard but the real place pictured in it. A recalled image is always more than the once-seen image itself. In my view, Brodsky presents a rushed argument here, perhaps misguided by Susan Sontag's ideas of the power of the photographed image in her seminal book, *On Photography*.[12]

Pictures, objects, fragments, insignificant things, all serve as condensation centers for our memories. Jarkko Laine, the Finnish poet, writes about the role of objects in his memory: "I like looking at these things. I don't seek esthetic pleasure in them . . . nor do I recall their origins: that is not important. But even so, they all arouse memories, real and imagined. A poem is a thing that arouses memories of real and imagined things . . . The things in the window act like a poem. They are images that do not reflect anything . . . I sing of the things in the window."[13]

The significance of objects in our processes of remembering is the main reason why we like to collect and have familiar or peculiar objects around us; they expand and reinforce the realm of memories, and eventually, of our very sense of self. Few of the objects we possess are really needed strictly for utilitarian purposes; their function is social and mental. "I am what is around me," argues Wallace Stevens,[14] whereas Noël Arnaud, another poet, claims: "I am the space, where I am."[15] These condensed formulations by two poets emphasize the intertwining of the world and the self as well as the externalized ground of remembrance and identity.

A room can also be individualized and taken into one's possession by turning it into a place of dreaming; the acts of memorizing and dreaming are interrelated. As Bachelard puts it: "The house shelters daydreaming, the house protects the dreamer, the house allows one to dream in peace."[16] A fundamental quality of a landscape, a house, and a room is its capacity to evoke and contain a feeling of

11 Brodsky, A place as good as any, op. cit., p. 37.

12 Sontag, Susan (1978). *On Photography*. London: Penguin Books.

13 Laine, Jarkko (1982). (Starting a Conversation). *Parnasso* 6: 323–324.

14 Stevens, Wallace (1990). Theory. In: *The Collected Poems* (ed. Wallace Stevens), 86. New York, NY: Vintage Books.

15 Noël Arnaud, as quoted in Bachelard, *The Poetics of Space*, op. cit., p. 137.

16 Bachelard, *The Poetics of Space*, op. cit., p. 6.

← Ustad Ahmad Lahauri, the Taj Mahal, Agra, India, 1632.
Roney John / Pexels / Public Domain

safety, familiarity, and at-homeness and to stimulate fantasies. We are not capable of deep imagination outdoors in wild nature; profound imagination calls for the focusing intimacy of a room. For me, the real measure of the quality of a town is whether I can imagine myself falling in love there.

THE LIVED WORLD

We do not live in an objective world of matter and facts, as commonplace naïve realism tends to assume. The characteristically human mode of existence takes place in the worlds of possibilities, molded by the human capacity of remembrance, fantasy, and imagination. We live in mental worlds, in which the material and the spiritual, as well as the experienced, remembered, and imagined, constantly fuse into each other. As a consequence, the lived reality does not follow the rules of space and time as defined and measured by the science of physics. I wish to argue that the lived world is fundamentally "unscientific," when measured by the criteria of western empirical science. In fact, the lived world is closer to the reality of a dream than any scientific description. In order to distinguish the lived space from physical and geometrical space, we can call it existential space. Lived existential space is structured on the basis of meanings, intentions, and values reflected upon it by an individual, either consciously or unconsciously; existential space is a unique quality interpreted through the memory and experience of the individual. Every lived experience takes place at the interface of recollection and intention, perception and fantasy, memory and desire. T.S. Eliot brings forth the important pairing of opposites in the end of his fourth quartet, "Little Gidding": "What we call the beginning is often the end. And to make an end is to make a beginning . . . We shall not cease from exploration. And the end of all our exploring will be to arrive where we started. And know the place for the first time."[17]

17

Eliot, T. S. (1971). *Four Quartets*, 58–59. London: Harcourt Brace Jovanovich.

On the other hand, collective groups or even nations, share certain experiences of existential space that constitute their collective identities and sense of togetherness. We are, perhaps, held together by our shared memories more than by an innate sense of solidarity. I wish to recall here the famous sociological study by Lawrence Halbwachs that revealed that the ease of mutual communication between old Parisians living within a distinct quarter was grounded in their rich and shared collective memories.

The lived space is also the object and context of both the making and experiencing of art as well as architecture. Art projects a lived reality, not mere symbolic representations of life. The task of architecture, also, is "to make visible how the world touches us," as Merleau-Ponty wrote of the paintings of Paul Cézanne.[18] We live in the "flesh of the world," to use a notion of the philosopher, and landscapes and architecture structure and articulate this existential flesh, giving it specific horizons and meanings.

18 Merleau-Ponty, Maurice (1964)). Cezanne's doubt. In: *Sense and Non-Sense* (ed. Maurice Merleau-Ponty), 19. Evanston, IL: Nortwestern University Press.

EXPERIENCE AS EXCHANGE

The experience of a place or space is always a curious exchange; as I settle in a space, the space settles in me. I live in a city and the city dwells in me. We are in a constant exchange with our settings; simultaneously we internalize the setting and project our own bodies, or aspects of our body schemes, on the setting. Memory and actuality, perception and dream merge. This secret physical and mental intertwining and identification also take place in all artistic experience.

Erik Gunnar Asplund and Sigurd Lewerentz, The Woodland Crematorium, Stockholm, Sweden, 1940.
Holger.Ellgaard / Wikimedia Commons / CC BY-SA 3.0
https://www.flickr.com/photos/bjargot/43231753935

Juhani Pallasmaa, Korundi Art Center Concert Hall, Rovaniemi, Finland, 2010.
Courtesy of Juhani Pallasmaa

19 Brodsky, "An immodest proposal." In: Brodsky, *On Grief and Reason*, op. cit., p. 206.

20 Hrabal, Bohumil (1990). *Too Loud a Solitude*, 1. London: Harcourt, Inc.

In Joseph Brodsky's view, every poem tells the reader "Be like me."[19] Here lies the ethical power of all authentic works of art; we internalize them and integrate them with our very sense of self. A fine piece of music, poetry, or architecture becomes a part of my physical and moral self. The Czech writer Bohumil Hrabal gives a vivid description of this bodily association in the act of reading: "When I read, I don't really read; I pop a beautiful sentence in my mouth and suck it like a fruit drop or I sip it like a liqueur until the thought dissolves in me like alcohol, infusing my brain and heart and coursing on through the veins to the root of each blood vessel."[20]

Remembering is not only a mental event; it is also an act of embodiment and projection. Memories are not only hidden in the secret electrochemical processes of the brain; they are also stored in

Michelangelo Buonarroti, the Laurentian Library, Florence, Italy, 1519–1571.
Yuri Turkov / Alamy Stock Photo
https://www.alamy.com/visiting-laurentian-library-biblioteca-medicea-laurenziana-in-florence-italy-image546315506.html?imageid=28F31F2C-22D2-4F04-9FF4-2DF0BCE49F9B&p=195033&pn=2&searchId=17752a4ef7b990a031e8f301b4fac7c8&searchtype=0

our skeletons, muscles, and skin. All our senses and organs think and remember.

THE EMBODIED MEMORY

I can recall the hundreds of hotel rooms around the world, which I have temporarily inhabited during my five decades of traveling, with their furniture, color schemes and lighting, because I have invested and left parts of my body and my mind in these anonymous and insignificant rooms. The protagonist of Marcel Proust's *In Search of Lost Time* reconstructs similarly his very identity and location through his embodied memory: "My body, still too heavy with sleep to move, would endeavor to construe from the pattern of its tiredness the position of its various limbs, in order to deduce therefrom the direction of the wall, the location of the furniture, to piece together and give a name to the house in which it lay. Its memory, the composite memory of its ribs, its knees, its shoulder blades, offered it a whole series of rooms in which it had at one time or another slept, while the unseen walls, shifting and adapting themselves to the shape of each successive room that it remembered, whirled it in the dark . . . my body, would recall from each room in succession the style of the bed, the position of the doors, the angle at which the sunlight came in at the windows, whether there was a passage outside, what I had had in mind when I went to sleep and found there when I awoke."[21] We are again encountering an experience that brings to mind a fragmented Cubist composition. We are taught to think of memory as a cerebral capacity, but the act of memory engages our entire body.

21 Proust, Marcel (1992). *In Search of Lost Time*. Vol. I. *Swann's Way*, 4–5. London: Random House.

"Body memory is . . . the natural center of any sensitive account of remembering," philosopher Edward S. Casey argues in his seminal book, *Memorizing: A Phenomenological Study*, and concludes: "There is no memory without body memory."[22] In my view, we could say even more; body is not only the locus of remembrance, it is also the site and medium of all creative work, including the work of the architect.

22 Casey, Edward S. (2000). *Memorizing: A Phenomenological Study*, 148–172. Bloomington, IN: Indiana University Press.

MEMORY AND EMOTION

In addition to being memory devices, landscapes and buildings are also amplifiers of emotions; they reinforce sensations of belonging or alienation, invitation or rejection, tranquility or despair. A landscape or work of architecture cannot, however, create feelings. Through their authority and aura, they evoke and strengthen our own emotions and project them back to us as if these feelings of ours had an external source. In the Laurentian Library in Florence, I confront my own sense of metaphysical melancholy awakened and projected back by Michelangelo's architecture. The optimism that I experience when approaching the Paimio Sanatorium is my own sense of hope evoked and strengthened by Alvar Aalto's optimistic architecture. The hill of the meditation grove at the Woodland Cemetery in Stockholm, for instance, evokes a state of longing and hope through an image that is an invitation and a promise. This architectural image of landscape evokes simultaneously remembrance and imagination like the composite painted image of Arnold Böcklin's *Isle of the Dead*. All poetic images are condensations and microcosms.

"House, even more than the landscape, is a psychic state," Bachelard suggests.[23] Indeed, writers, film directors, poets, and painters do not just depict landscapes or houses as unavoidable geographic and

23 Bachelard, *The Poetics of Space*, op. cit., p. 72.

physical settings of the events of their stories; they seek to express, evoke, and amplify human emotions, mental states, and memories through purposeful depictions of settings, both natural and man-made. "Let us assume a wall: what takes place behind it?," asks the poet Jean Tardieu,[24] but we architects rarely bother to imagine what happens behind the walls we have erected. The walls conceived by architects are usually mere estheticized constructions, and we see our craft in terms of designing esthetic structures rather than evoking perceptions, feelings, and fantasies.

Artists seem to grasp the intertwining of place and human mind, memory, and desire, much better than we architects do, and that is why these other art forms can provide such stimulating inspiration for our work as well as for architectural education. There are no better lessons of the extraordinary capacity of artistic condensations in evoking microcosmic images of the world than, say, the short stories of Anton Chekhov, and Jorge Luis Borges, or Giorgio Morandi's minute still lifes, consisting of a few bottles and cups on a table top.

SLOWNESS AND REMEMBERING – SPEED AND FORGETTING

"There is a secret bond between slowness and memory, between speed and forgetting . . . the degree of slowness is directly proportional to the intensity of memory: the degree of speed is directly proportional to the intensity of forgetting," suggests Milan Kundera.[25] With the dizzying acceleration of the velocity of time today and the constant speeding up of our experiential reality, we are seriously threatened by a general cultural amnesia. In today's accelerated life, we can finally only perceive, not remember. In the society of the spectacle, we can only marvel, not remember. Speed and transparency weaken remembrance, but they have been fundamental fascinations of Modernity since the proclamation of F.T. Marinetti in the Futurist Manifesto almost a full century ago: "The world's magnificence has been enriched by a new beauty: the beauty of speed,"[26] and Karl Marx's prophecy: "Everything that is solid . . . melts into the air."[27] Today, even architecture seeks the sensation of speed, instant seduction and gratification, and turns autistic, as a consequence. The architectural confession of Coop Himmelb(l)au illustrates this aspiration for dramatized architectural action and speed: "The aesthetics of the architecture of death in white sheets. Death in tiled hospital rooms. The architecture of sudden death on the pavement. Death from a rib-cage pierced by a steering shaft. The path of the bullet through a dealer's head on 42nd Street. The aesthetics of the

24

As quoted in Perec, Georges (1992). *Tiloja ja avaruuksia* (Species of Spaces), 72. Helsinki: Loki-Kirjat.

25

Kundera, Milan (1966). *Slowness*, 39. New York, NY: HarperCollins.

26

Marinetti, Filippo Tommaso, The Futurist Manifesto (1909). Available at: https://www.arthistoryproject.com/artists/filippo-tommaso-marinetti/the-futurist-manifesto/ (accessed July 2025).

27

Marx, Karl and Engels, Frederick (1888). *The Communist Manifesto*. London: William Reeves. "All fixed, fast-frozen relations, with their train of ancient and venerable prejudices and opinions, are swept away, all newformed ones become antiquated before they can ossify. All that is solid melts into air, all that is holy is profaned, and men at last are forced to face . . . the real conditions of their lives and their relations with their fellow men." Available at: https://www.marxists.org/archive/marx/works/download/pdf/Manifesto.pdf (accessed July 2025).

peep-show sex in washable plastic boxes. Of the broken tongues and the dried-up eyes."[28]

28 Coop Himmelb(l)au, "Die Fascination der Stadt," as quoted in Vidler, Anthony (1999). *The Architectural Uncanny*, 76. Cambridge, MA: The MIT Press.

In my view, however, architecture is inherently a slow and quiet, emotionally a low-energy art form in comparison with the dramatic arts of sudden affective impact. Its role is not to create strong foreground figures or feelings, but to establish frames of perception and horizons of understanding. The task of architecture is not to make us weep or laugh, but to sensitize us to be able to enter all emotional states. Architecture is needed to provide the ground and projection screen of remembrance and emotion.

I believe in an architecture that slows down and focuses human experience instead of speeding up or diffusing it. In my view, architecture has to safeguard memories and protect the authenticity and independence of human experience. Architecture is fundamentally the art form of emancipation, and it makes us understand and remember who we are.

ARCHITECTURAL AMNESIA

There are different kinds of architecture in relation to memory: one that cannot recall or touch upon the past, and another that evokes a sense of depth and continuity. There is also an architecture that seeks to remember literally, like the architectural works of Postmodernism, and another that creates a sense of deep time, and epic continuity without any direct formal reference, as the works of Alvar Aalto, Dimitris Pikionis, and Carlo Scarpa. These are products of a "poetic chemistry," to use an evocative notion of Bachelard.[29] Every significant and true work sets itself in a respectful dialogue with the past, both distant and immediate. At the same time that the work defends itself as a unique and complete microcosm, it revives and revitalizes the past. Every true work of art occupies a thick and layered time instead of mere contemporaneity.

29 Bachelard, Gaston (1983). *Water and Dreams: An Essay on the Imagination of Matter*, 46. Dallas, TX: The Pegasus Foundation.

There is yet another dimension in architectural memory. Architectural images, or experiences have a historicity and ontology of their own. Architecture begins with the establishment of a horizontal plane; consequently, the floor is the "oldest" and most potent element of architecture. The wall is more archaic than the door or the window, and projects a deeper meaning as a consequence. Modernity has suffered from another kind of amnesia as architectural elements and images have become abstracted and detached from their origins and ontological essences. The floor, for instance, has forgotten its origin as leveled earth, and turned into mere constructed horizontal planes. In fact, as Bachelard suggests, human constructions of the technological age have forgotten verticality altogether, and turned into mere horizontality. Today's skyscrapers consist of stacked horizontality and have lost the sense of verticality, the fundamental ontological difference between below and above, Hell and Heaven. Also, the floor and the ceiling have become identical horizontal planes. The window and the door are often mere holes in the wall. I do not have the space here to elaborate on this theme of the historicity of architectural images and the current architectural amnesia resulting from the loss of the historicity of experiences; I merely point at the mental significance of this dimension.

THE TENSES OF ART

I venture to suggest that in its very essence artistic work is oriented toward the past rather than the future. Brodsky seems to support this view as he argues: "There is something clearly atavistic in the process of recollection, if only because such a process never is linear. Also the more one remembers, the closer perhaps one is to dying."[30]

30
Brodsky, Joseph (1986). Less than one. In: *Less Than One* (ed. Joseph Brodsky), 30. New York, NY: Farrar, Straus & Giroux.

In any significant experience, temporal layers interact; what is perceived interacts with what is remembered, the novel short-circuits with the archaic. An artistic experience always awakens the forgotten child hidden inside one's adult persona.

There are fabricated images in today's architecture and art that are flat and without an emotional echo, but there are also novel images that resonate with remembrance. The latter are mysterious and familiar, obscure and clear, at the same time. They move us through the remembrances and associations, emotions, and empathy that they awaken in us. Artistic novelty can move us only provided it touches something that we already possess in our very being. Every profound artistic work surely grows from memory, not from rootless intellectual invention. Artistic works aspire to bring us back to an undivided and undifferentiated oceanic world. This is the *Omega* that Teilhard de Chardin writes about, "the point from which the world appears complete and correct."[31]

31
As quoted in Valjakka, Timo (ed.) (1995). *Juhana Blomstedt: muodon arvo* (Juhana Blomstedt: the value of form). Helsinki: Painatuskeskus.

We are usually conditioned to think that artists and architects ought to be addressing the future readers, viewers, and users of their products. Joseph Brodsky is very determined, indeed, about the poet's temporal perspective: "When one writes, one's most immediate audience is not one's own contemporaries, let alone posterity, but one's predecessors."[32] "No real writer ever wanted to be contemporary," Jorge Luis Borges argues in the same vein.[33] This view opens up another essential perspective on the significance and role of remembrance; all creative work is collaboration with the past and with the wisdom of tradition. "Every true novelist listens for that suprapersonal wisdom [the wisdom of the novel], which explains why great novels are always a little more intelligent than their authors. Novelists who are more intelligent than their books should go into another line of work," Milan Kundera argues.[34] The same observation is equally true of architecture; great buildings are fruits of the wisdom of architecture, they are products of a collaboration, often unconscious, with our great predecessors as much as they are works of their individual creators. Only works that are in vital and respectful dialogue with their past possess the mental capacity to survive time and stimulate viewers, listeners, readers, and occupants in the future.

32 Brodsky, Joseph, Letter to Horace. In: *On Grief and Reason*, op. cit., 439.

33 di Giovanni, Norman Thomas, Halpern, Daniel, and MacShane, Frank (ed.) (1994). *Borges on Writing*, 53. Hopewell, NJ: The Ecco Press.

34 Kundera, Milan (2000). *The Art of the Novel*, 158. New York, NY: HarperCollins.

NEWNESS, TRADITION, AND IDENTITY 5

Existential Content and Meaning in Architecture

An interest in the significance of tradition is today usually seen as nostalgia and conservatism; in our age, obsessed with progress, our eyes are exclusively fixated on the present and future. During the past few decades, uniqueness and newness have become the prevailing criteria of quality in architecture, design, and art. The coherence and harmony of landscapes and cityscapes, and their rich historical layering are no longer seen as essential objectives of architecture. Artistic uniqueness and formal invention have, in fact, replaced the quest for existential meaning and emotive impact, to say nothing of the desire for a spiritual dimension or beauty.

In his acceptance speech of the 2012 Pritzker Architecture Prize in Beijing, the Chinese Laureate Wang Shu confessed that he had begun his career with works in the then prevailing Postmodern and Deconstructionist idioms, but he had eventually realized that his country was losing its connection with the Chinese tradition and cultural identity. After this realization he endeavored to tie his architecture to the long and deep cultural traditions of China.[1] This was an unexpectedly outspoken message in the presence of top Chinese officials.

1
A memorized reference to Wang Shu's speech at the Pritzker Architectue Prize Ceremony in the Great Hall of the People in Beijing on May 25, 2012.

In his more recent work, Wang Shu has, indeed, succeeded in creating buildings, such as the Xiangshan Campus and the Historical Museum at Ningbo, which seem to reconnect with the invisible undercurrents of timeless Chinese images and traditions. These buildings do not echo any distinct formal attributes of the country's rich architectural past, but they evoke atmospheres and moods that make one feel a depth of time and being grounded in history. This sense of rootedness does not lie on a formal language or allusions but the architectural logic itself, its cultural deep structure, as it were. This architecture also projects comforting and enriching

Eight Meditations on Architecture, First Edition. Juhani Pallasmaa. Edited by Matteo Zambelli.

experiences of participation in a meaningful historical continuum. The architect's repeated use of re-cycled materials, such as old bricks and roof tiles, speaks of inherited crafts, timeless and selfless labor, and a sense of collective and shared identity passed on to the coming generations.

Visiting Wang Shu's buildings made me recall Louis Kahn's powerful Parliament Buildings in Dacca, which project an authoritative condensation of traditions, ageless and contemporary, geometric and mystical, European and Oriental. Kahn's architecture in Bangladesh succeeds in giving a proud and optimistic cultural identity to a new Islamic state with ancient traditions. These examples show that a respectful attitude to traditions does not imply regressive traditionalism, but its acknowledgment as a source of meaning, inspiration, and emotional rooting.

THE ECSTASY OF NEWNESS

The loss of the sense of historicity and evolutionary identity is clearly becoming a major concern in numerous countries developing at the accelerated rate of today's aggressive investment strategies, expedient methods of construction, and universal architectural fashions. But, is newness a relevant aspiration and criterion of quality in art and architecture? Is a future without its constitutive past even conceivable?

Our ultra-materialistic and hedonistic consumer culture seems to be losing its capacity to identify essences of life and experience as well as to be deeply affected by them. Quality, nuance, and expressive subtlety are replaced by such quantifiable aspects as size, loudness, shock value, and strangeness. The interest in uniqueness and newness shifts the artistic encounter from a genuine and autonomous experience to a comparative and quasi-rational judgment. Intellectual speculation replaces emotive sincerity, and experiential quality is unnoticeably replaced by quantitative assessment.

Newness is expected to evoke interest and excitement, whereas any reference to the traditions of the artform in question, to say nothing of intentionally attempting to strengthen the continuum of tradition, are seen as reactionism and a source of boredom. Already in the 1980s, Germano Celant, one of the postmodern critics, used such notions as "contemporaryism," "hyper-contemporary," "terror of the contemporary," and "the vertigo of nowness" and referred to "a pathological and conformist anxiety . . . that turns the present into an absolute frame of reference, an undisputable truth."[2] Today we can undoubtedly speak of "a vertigo of newness" when thinking of the scene of art and architecture during the first decade of the third millennium. New artistic images keep emerging like an "unending rainfall of images," to use an expression of Italo Calvino.[3]

2
Celant, Germano (1988). *Unexpressionism – Art beyond the Contemporary*, 5, 6, and 10. New York, NY: Rizzoli International Publications.

3
Calvino, Italo (1988). *Six Memos for the Next Millennium*, 57. New York, NY: Vintage Books.

The constant and obsessive search for newness has already turned into a distinct repetitiousness and monotony; unexpectedly the quest for uniqueness seems to result in sameness, repetition, and boredom. Newness is a formal surface quality without a deeper mental echo that would energize the work and its repeated experiencing. The Norwegian philosopher Lars Fr. H. Svendsen points out this paradoxical phenomenon in his book, *A Philosophy of Boredom*: "In this objective something new is always sought to avoid boredom with the old. But as new is sought only because of its newness, everything turns identical, because it lacks all other properties but newness."[4] "Boredom with the old" becomes replaced by boredom with the new.

4
Svendsen, Lars (2012). *A Philosophy of Boredom*. London: Reaktion Books. Pallasmaa translated the sentence from the Finish version of the book (Svendsen, Lars Fr. H. [2005]. *Ikävystymisen Filosofia*, 75. Helsinki: Kustannusosakeyhtiö Tammi) into English.

Artistic newness is generally associated with radicalism – the new is expected to surpass previous ideas in quality and effect and to cast prevailing tradition down from the throne. But is there really any identifiable progress in art and architecture, or are we only witnessing changing approaches to fundamental existential motives? What is the quality that makes us experience a 25,000-year-old cave painting with the same affect and impact as any work of our own day? Hasn't art always been engaged in expressing the human existential condition? Shouldn't art be oriented toward the timeless questions of existence rather than the appeal of the momentary and fashionable? Shouldn't art and architecture seek deep and permanent essences of human existence instead of obsessively trying to generate a passing experience of newness? I do not believe that any profound artist is directly interested in newness or self-expression, as art is too deeply engaged in deep existential issues to be concerned with such passing aspirations. "No real writer ever tried to be contemporary," Jorge Luis Borges bluntly asserts.[5]

5
di Giovanni, Norman Thomas, Halpern, Daniel, and MacShane, Frank (ed.) (1994). *Borges on Writing*, 53. Hopewell, NJ: The Ecco Press.

Newness is usually relate to extreme individuality and self-expression, but self-expression is another questionable objective in art. Indeed, since the emergence of the modern era, art and architecture have been increasingly seen as areas of self-expression. However, Balthus (Count Balthasar Klossowski de Rola), one of the finest figurative painters of the twentieth century, expresses a contrary view: "If a work only expresses the person who created it, it wasn't worth doing . . . Expressing the world, understanding it, that is what seems interesting to me."[6] Later, the painter reformulated his argument: "Great painting has to have universal meaning. This is really no longer so today and this is why I want to give painting back its lost universality and anonymity, because the more anonymous painting is, the more real it is."[7] Echoing the painter's view, we can say that we also need to give architecture back its lost universality and anonymity, because the less subjective architecture is, the more real it is, and the more it has the capacity to support our individual identities. The more subjective a work is, the more it focuses on the subjectivity of the author, whereas works that are open to the world provide a ground of identification for others. Just think of the assuring sense of the real evoked by the vernacular building traditions around the world.

6 Roy, Claude (1996). *Balthus*, 18. New York, NY: Little, Brown and Company.

7 Balthus (2001). *Balthus in His Own Words: A Conversation with Cristina Carrillo de Albornoz*, 6. New York, NY: Assouline.

Balthus also scorns self-expression as an objective of art: "Modernity, which began in the true sense with the Renaissance, determined the tragedy of art. The artist emerged as an individual and the traditional way of painting disappeared. From then on the artist sought to express his inner world, which is a limited universe: He tried to place his personality in power and used paintings as a means of self-expression."[8] The painter's concern clearly applies to architecture, also, although architects rarely write about the mental dimensions in their work.

8 Ibid., p. 6.

TRADITION AND RADICALITY

In his Harvard lectures of 1939, Igor Stravinsky, the arch-modernist and arch-radical of music, presents an unexpectedly forceful criticism of artistic radicalism and the rejection of tradition: "Insubordination boasts of just the opposite and does away with constraint in the ever-disappointed hope of finding in freedom the principle of strength. Instead, it finds in freedom only the arbitrariness of whim and the disorders of fancy."[9] In the composer's view, the rejection of tradition eliminates the communicative ground of art: "Individual caprice and intellectual anarchy, which tend to control the world in which we live, isolate the artist from his fellow-artists and condemn him to appear as a monster in the eyes of the public; a monster of originality, inventor of his own language, of his own vocabulary, and of the apparatus of his art. The use of already employed materials and of established forms is usually forbidden him. So he comes to the point of speaking an idiom without relation to the world that listens to him. His art becomes truly unique, in the sense that it is incommunicable and shut off on every side."[10] The fact that Stravinsky's *The Rite of Spring* was considered so radical at its time that its

9 As quoted by Stravinky, Igor (1947). *Poetics of Music: In the Form of Six Lessons*, 76–77. Cambridge, MA: Harvard University Press.

10 Ibid., pp. 73–74.

premiere in Paris in 1913 turned into a cultural riot, gives an added significance to the composer's view of the dialectics of tradition and artistic radicalism.

I wish to reiterate that newness and uniqueness alone are hardly relevant aspirations for art. Meaningful artistic works are embodied existential expressions that articulate experiences and emotions of our shared human situation. Works of art, from poetry to music, painting to architecture, are metaphoric representation of the human existential encounter with the world, and their quality arises from the existential content of the work, i.e. its capacity to re-present and experientially actualize and energize this very encounter. Great works of architecture and art restructure, sensitize and enrich our experiences of our encounters with the world. As Maurice Merleau-Ponty significantly points out: "We come to see not the work of art, but the world according to the work."[11] A fresh and sensitized articulation of the fundamental artistic issues gives the work its special emotive power and life force. Constantin Brancusi formulates the artistic aim forcefully: "The work must give immediately, at once, the shock of life, the sensation of breathing."[12] This master sculptor's requirement also applies to architecture; an architecture that does not evoke sensations of life remains a mere formalist exercise. Formal, cultural, and sociological criteria and preconceptions, such as uniqueness, have only a subservient value in relation to the mental task of art. When art is seen in its existential dimension, uniqueness as a formal quality loses its significance.

11

As quoted in McGilchrist, Iain (2010). *The Master and His Emissary*, 409. New Haven, CT: Yale University Press.

12

As quoted in Shanes, Eric (1989). *Brancusi*, 67. New York, NY: Abbeville Press.

Another arch-radical, Ezra Pound, the Imagist poet, also confesses his respect for tradition and the historical continuum of various artforms as he points out the importance of the ontological origins of each artform: "Music begins to atrophy when it departs too far from dance . . . poetry begins to atrophy when it gets too far from music."[13] Similarly, in my view, architecture turns into mere formalist visual esthetics when it departs from its originary motives of domesticating space and time for human occupation through distinct primal encounters, such as the four elements, gravity, verticality and horizontality, as well as the metaphoric representation of the act of construction. Architecture withers into a meaningless formal game when it loses its echo of the timeless myths and traditions of building. Instead of portraying newness, true architecture makes us aware of the entire history of building and it restructures our reading of the continuum of time. The view that is often disregarded today is that architecture structures our understanding of the past just as much as

13

Pound, Ezra (1987). *ABC of Reading*, 14. New York, NY: New Directions.

➔

Wang Shu (Amateur Architecture Studio), Ningbo History Museum, Ningbo, China, 2008.
Arcaid Images / Alamy Stock Photo
https://www.alamy.com/exterior-view-of-the-ningbo-historic-museum-zhejiang-china-image396817997.html

Louis Kahn, Bangladesh National Parliament House, Bangladesh, 1961–1982. Jubair / Adobe Stock https://www.flickr.com/photos/mashfiq13/5936038912

it suggests images of future. Every masterpiece re-illuminates the history of the artform and makes us look at earlier works in new light. "When one writes verse, one's most immediate audience is not one's own contemporaries, let alone posterity, but one's predecessors," Brodsky asserts.[14]

14 Brodsky, Joseph (1997). Letter to Horace. In: *On Grief and Reason* (ed. Joseph Brodsky), 439. New York, NY: Farrar, Straus & Giroux.

CULTURAL IDENTITY

Cultural identity, a sense of rootedness and belonging are an irreplaceable ground of our very humanity. Our identities are not only in dialogue with our physical and architectural settings as we grow to be members of countless contexts and cultural, social, linguistic, geographic, as well as esthetic identities. Our identities are not attached to isolated things, but the continuum of culture and life; our true identities are not momentary as they have their historicity and continuity. Instead of being mere occasional background aspects, all these dimensions, and surely dozens of other features, are constituents of our very personality. Identity is not a given fact or a closed entity. It is an exchange; as I settle in a place, the place settles in me. Spaces and places are not mere stages for our lives, as they are "chiasmatically" intertwined, to use a notion of Maurice Merleau-Ponty. As this philosopher argues: "The world is wholly inside, and I am wholly outside myself."[15] Or, as Ludwig Wittgenstein concludes: "I am my world."[16]

15 Merleau-Ponty, Maurice (1962). *The Phenomenology of Perception*, 407. London: Routledge & Kegan Paul.

16 Wittgenstein, Ludwig (1922). *Tractatus Logico-Philosophicus*, 84e. London: Kegan Paul, Trench, Trubner & Co.

The significance I am giving to tradition, not only as a general sense of cultural history, but also as the need to understand the specificity and locality of culture, raises critical concerns about today's careless practice of designing in alien cultures merely for commercial interests. As anthropologists, such as Edward T. Hall, have convincingly shown, the codes of cultures are so deeply ingrained in the human unconscious and pre-reflective behavior, that essences of culture take a lifetime to learn. Do we really have the right to execute our designs in cultures that are very different from our own, merely for our own economic interests? Isn't this yet another form of colonialization?

ARCHITECTURE AND IDENTITY AS EVOLUTIONARY PROCESSES

Let me be clear, I do not support nostalgic traditionalism or conservatism, I merely wish to argue that the continuum of culture is an essential – although mostly unconscious – ingredient of our lives as well as of our individual creative work. Creative work is always collaboration: it is collaboration with countless other thinkers, architects, and artists, but it is collaboration also in the sense of humbly and proudly acknowledging one's role in the continuum of tradition. Every innovation in thought – both in the sciences and the arts – is bound to arise from this ground and be projected back into this most honorable context. Anyone working in the mental sphere, who believes he/she has arrived at his/her achievement alone is simply self-centered and naïve.

Architectural and artistic works arise in the continuum of culture, and they seek their role and position in this continuum. Jean Genet expresses this idea of presenting the work to the tradition touchingly, indeed: "In its desire to require real significance, each work of art must descend the steps of millennia with patience and extreme caution and meet, if possible, the immemorial night of the dead, so that the dead recognize themselves in the work."[17] When a work of apparently extraordinary uniqueness is not accepted in this ever-expanding gallery of artistic tradition, it will be quickly forgotten as a mere momentary curiosity. On the other hand, even the most original and revolutionary work that touches upon essential existential qualities, in addition to its initial novelty and shock value, ends up reinforcing the continuum of artistic tradition and becomes part of it. This is the basic paradox of artistic creation: the most radical of works end up clarifying and strengthening tradition. The Catalan philosopher Eugenio d'Ors gives a memorable formulation to this paradox: "Everything which is not tradition is plagiarism."[18] The philosopher's cryptic sentence implies that works of art that are not supported and continuously revitalized by the constant blood circulation of tradition are doomed to remain mere plagiarism in the realm of arrogant and pretentious newness. These works do not have an artistic life force, and they are doomed to turn into mere curiosities of the past.

17

Genet, Jean (1987). *Giacomettin ateljeessa* (In Giacometti's Atelier), 15. Helsinki: Kustannusosakeyhtiö Taide. Translation Juhani Pallasmaa.

18

Stravinsky, op. cit., p. 57. Igor Stravinsky includes this sentence in his book, *The Poetics of Music* (1962), however, without any reference to the source, Eugenio d'Ors. Curiously also, Luis Buñuel, the arch-radical of cinema, refers to the same thought in his autobiography *My Last Sigh* (1982), however, correctly crediting the Catalan philosopher.

The most eloquent and convincing defense of tradition is surely T.S. Eliot's essay "Tradition and Individual Talent" (1929), but its wisdom has been sadly forgotten today. He states that tradition is not a static "thing" to be inherited, preserved, or possessed, as true tradition has to be reinvented and recreated by each new generation. Instead of valuing mere factual history, the poet argues for the significance of "a historical sense," an internationalized mental dimension. It is this historical sense that ties the artist and the architect to the continuum of culture and provides the backbone of his/her language and its comprehensibility. The fundamental issues of identity in terms of the questions "who are we?" and "what is our relationship to the world?" are constitutive. This historical sense also brings about collective cultural meanings as well as a societal purposefulness. It is this historical sense that gives profound works their combined humility, patience, and calm authority, whereas works that desperately aspire for novelty and uniqueness always appear arrogant, strained, and impatient. Although T.S. Eliot's essay has been frequently referred to, I wish to quote its most essential message which is more pertinent today in the age of globalization than ever before:

"Tradition is a matter of much wider significance. It cannot be inherited, and if you want it, you must obtain it by great labour. It involves, in the first place, the historical sense . . . and the historical sense involves a perception, not only of the pastness of the past, but of its presence; the historical sense compels a man to write [and to design] not merely with his own generation in his bones, but with a feeling that the whole of the literature [architecture] . . . has a simultaneous existence and composes a simultaneous order. This historical sense, which is a sense of the timeless as well as of the temporal and of the timeless and the temporal together, is what makes a writer [an architect] traditional and it is at the same time what makes a writer [an architect] most acutely conscious of his place in time, of his own contemporaneity. No poet, no artist of any art, has his complete meaning alone. His significance, his appreciation is the appreciation of his relation to the dead poets and artists. You cannot value him alone; you must set him, for contrast and comparison, among the dead."[19]

19

Eliot, T. S. (1932). Tradition and Individual Talent. In: *Selected Essays 1917–1932*, 4. New York, NY: Harcourt, Brace & Company.

The poet's arguments make it clear that creative work is always bound to be a collaboration, a collective effort of the artist with his/her contemporaries as well as predecessors. The views of the artistic thinkers I am quoting in this chapter also demystify the myth of the solitary and isolated genius. Great works of art and architecture cannot arise from cultural ignorance; they emerge in the midst of the evolving story of the history of the art form. The masterpieces emerge equipped with a capacity for eternal comparison and dialogue.

TRADITION AND INNOVATION

I want to repeat that I do not wish to praise tradition because of a nostalgia for the past. Neither am I writing about traditionalism as an alternative to individual invention, but about an embodiment of the essence of tradition as a necessary precondition for meaningful creativity. I write about the value of tradition because of its fundamental significance for the course of culture and human identity, as well as for the arts or any other creative endeavor. Tradition maintains and safeguards the collective and accumulated existential wisdom of countless generations. It also gives a reliable direction to the new and maintains the comprehensibility and meaning of the new.

It is clear that artistic meanings cannot be invented, as they are mostly unconscious and pre-reflective existential re-encounters of primal human experiences, emotions, and myths. As Alvaro Siza has written, "Architects don't invent anything, they transform reality."[20] In the case of Siza himself, this attitude of humility has produced more lasting qualities in architecture than the self-assurance of many of his celebrated colleagues, who have deliberately adopted the role of a radical formal innovator. The continuum of tradition provides the ground from which all human meaning arises. Architectural meaning is always contextual, relational, and temporal. Great works achieve their density and depth from the echo of the past, whereas the voice of the products of superficial novelty remain feeble, incomprehensible, and meaningless.

20

As quoted in Frampton, Kenneth (2002). Introduction. In: *Labour, Work and Architecture: Collective Essays on Architecture and Design* (ed. Kenneth Frampton), 18. London: Phaidon Press.

THE GROUND OF CULTURE

Tradition is mostly a unconscious system that organizes and maintains a sense of historicity, context, coherence, hierarchy, and meaning in the constant forward flow of culture. A coherence of tradition is created by the firm foundation of culture, not by any singular and isolated characteristics or ideas.

The quick collapse of this collective mental foundation during the past decades is already a serious obstacle for education in the creative fields. It is difficult, indeed, or often totally impossible, to teach architecture when there is no inherited tradition of knowledge in relation to which new knowledge can be understood and structured. The fragmentation of knowledge into isolated facts and bits of information, due to the dominance of new digital search media, reinforces the lack of an integrating background of culture, and gives rise to a rapid fragmentation of the world-view. A wide knowledge of classical literature and arts has been a crucial ingredient of an understanding of culture as a background and context for novel thought and artistic creativity. How do you teach architecture and art when the mention of almost any historically important name or phenomenon is met with an ignorant stare? Our personal identities are not objects, they are not things; our identities are dynamic processes that build upon the core of an inherited cultural tradition. The sense of self can only arise from the context of culture and its historicity.

In today's widely publicized and applauded avant-garde architecture, formal uniqueness is sought *ad absurdum* at the cost of functional, structural, and technical logic, as well as of human perceptual and sensory realities. Architectural entities are conceived as a-historical, separate, and disembodied objects detached from their context, societal motivation, and dialog with the past.

It is likely that societies and nations do not possess a capacity to learn; only individuals do. It is sad to observe that city after city, country after country, seem to go through the same fundamental mistakes that others, slightly further in cultural and economic development, have already committed earlier. Particularly the ecstasy of wealth seems to blind societies, make them undervalue or neglect their own histories, traditions, and identities. In the case of newly wealthy contemporary societies, it is as if, at the moment of sudden wealth, we become ashamed of our past, regardless of its human integrity and qualities of its settings. It is as if we suddenly want to forget who we are and from where we have come.

What is at stake in the loss of the lived sense of tradition is our very identity and sense of historicity. We are fundamentally historical beings, both biologically and culturally. It is totally reasonable to think that we are all millions of years old; our body remembers our entire evolutionary past by means of the biological relics in our bodies, such as the tailbone from our arboreal life, the *plica semilunaris* of our eyes from our Saurian life, and the remains of gills in our lungs from our primordial fish life.

In his book on slowness, Milan Kundera argues that forgetting is in direct relation to speed, whereas remembering calls for slowness.[21] The obsessively accelerated change of fashion and life style makes an accumulation of tradition and memory mentally difficult. As Paul Virilio has suggested, the main product of contemporary societies seems to be speed. Indeed, two of the disturbing characteristics of the Postmodern era, according to philosophers like David Harvey and Fredric Jameson, are shallowness and the lack of an overall view of things.[22]

21

Kundera, Milan (1996). *Slowness*. New York, NY: HarperCollins.

22

See Harvey, David (1990). *The Condition of Postmodernity*. Oxford: Blackwell, and Jameson, Fredric (1991). *Postmodernism, or the Cultural Logic of Late Capitalism*. Durham, NC: Duke University Press.

THE TASK OF ARCHITECTURE

The primary task of architecture continues to be to defend and strengthen the wholeness and dignity of human life, and to provide us with an existential foothold in the world. The first responsibility of the architect is always to the inherited landscape or urban setting; a profound building has to enhance its wider context and give it new meanings and esthetic qualities. Responsible architecture improves the landscape of its location and gives its lesser architectural neighbors new qualities instead of degrading them. It always enters a dialogue with the existent conditions; profound buildings are not self-centered monologues. Buildings mediate deep narratives of culture, place, and time, and architecture is in essence always an epic art form. The content and meaning of art – even of the most condensed poem, minimal painting, or simplest house – are epic in the sense of being a metaphor for human existence in the world.

The fascination with newness is characteristic of modernism at large, but this obsession has never been as unquestioned as in our age of mass consumption and surreal materialism. Designed aging of products, as well as the adoration of youth, are deliberate psychological mechanisms at the service of ever-accelerated consumption. However, these characteristics are also the ingredients of today's collective mental pathology. Also architecture is increasingly promoting distinct life styles, images, and personalities instead of strengthening the individual's sense of the real and of him/herself.

The task of architecture is not to create dream worlds, but to reinforce essential causalities, processes of rooting, and the sense of the real. The fascination with novelty is deeply connected to the self-destructive ideology of consumption and perpetual growth. Instead of contributing to meaningful and coordinated landscapes and cityscapes, the structures of today's businesses (and almost everything is considered business in the world of fluid capital) turn into self-centered and self-indulgent commercial advertisements. Whereas responsible buildings are deeply rooted in the historicity of their place and they contribute to a sense of time and cultural continuum, today's monuments of selfishness and novelty flatten the sense of history and time. This experience of flattened reality leaves us as outsiders in our own domicile; in the middle of today's abundance we have become consumers of our own lives and increasingly homeless. Yet, as Aldo van Eyck insisted: "Architecture should facilitate Man's homecoming."[23]

23 Hertzberger, Herman, van Roijen-Wortmann, Addie, and Strauven, Francis (1982). *Aldo van Eyck*, 65. Amsterdam: Stichting Wonen.

Great works possess a timeless freshness and they present their embodied enigma always anew as if we were looking at the work for the first time: the greater a work is, the stronger is its resistance to time. As Paul Valéry suggests: "An artist is worth a thousand centuries."[24] Newness has a mediating role in revealing the existential dimension through fresh and unexpected metaphors. Only in the sense of the perpetually recharged and re-energized image, is timeless newness a quality in artistic and architectural works. This is where also anonymity turns into a specific value. Such works constitute the realm of tradition and they are reinforced by the authority and aura of this continuum. I personally like to repeatedly revisit certain masterworks of painting and architecture, and re-read my favorite books to find myself equally fascinated and moved each time. I have had the fortune of visiting the Villa Mairea by Alvar Aalto in the industrial community of Noormarkku (1937–1939) numerous times during half a century, but at each new visit this architectural miracle welcomes me with the same freshness and a stimulating sense of expectation and wonder. This is the power of a true artistic tradition that halts time and reintroduces the already known with a seductive new freshness and intimacy. This is also the kind of architecture that empowers both the dweller and the occasional visitor, and strengthens his/her sense of being and identity.

24 Valéry, Paul (1956). *Dialogues*, XIII. New York, NY: Pantheon Books.

Alvar Aalto, Villa Mairea, Noormarkku, Finland, 1937–1939.

■ ■ ■

In our age . . . there is coming into existence a new kind of provincialism, not of space, but of time; one for which history is merely the chronicle of human devices which served their turn and have been scrapped, one for which the world is the property solely of the living, a property in which the dead hold no shares.

—T.S. Eliot[25]

25

Eliot, T. S. (1944). *What Is a Classic?* 30. London: Faber and Faber Limited. Available at: http://bracchiumforte.com/PDFs/tseliot.pdf (accessed December 2025).

6 WISDOM AND MODESTY

Where is the wisdom we have lost in knowledge?
Where is the knowledge we have lost in information?

—T.S. Eliot[1]

1 Eliot, T. S. (1934). *The Rock*, 7. New York, NY: Harcourt, Brace & Co.

2 Gardner, Howard (1999). *Intelligence Reframed: Multiple Intelligences for the 21st Century*, Chapters 3 and 4. New York, NY: Basic Books. Gardner first lists seven categories of intelligence: linguistic, logical, mathematical, musical, bodily-kinesthetic, spatial, and interpersonal and intrapersonal, but later adds three further categories: naturalistic, spiritual, and existential intelligences.

3 In my writings, I have added three categories: emotional, esthetic, and ethical intelligences.

4 Brodsky, Joseph (1997). An immodest proposal. In: *On Grief and Reason* (ed. Joseph Brodsky), 208. New York, NY: Farrar, Straus & Giroux.

In our current culture, which reveres information, knowledge and expertise, wisdom is usually seen as an especially acute intelligence. However, wisdom is not related to these capacities or mental qualities. Besides, the current understanding of intelligence itself is regrettably narrow, as it is usually defined as the distinct cerebral ability measured by the normative IQ Intelligence Test. The psychologist Howard Gardner has suggested 10 additional criteria for the standard intelligence test.[2] In my lectures and essays I have added three further dimensions of intelligence to the psychologist's already long list of criteria for intelligence. The most important of these added capacities, in my view, is the existential intelligence, which arises from a rich and deep sense of life.[3] Wisdom is most closely related to the comprehensive and accumulated field of life experience in existential intelligence, which is especially pertinent in the practice of architecture; life itself projects the dynamic ground of architecture.

Wisdom appears as a quiet, modest, observing, and listening attitude, never ambitious, loud, arrogant, or aggressive. It is a hidden, synthetic, and ethical mode of simultaneously lived experience and creative overview and vision. This stance arises from a distinct externality and distance, combined with an empathic identification with the situation. Wisdom has a verb form rather than being a substantive; wisdom is silent ethical energy. It is a form of intuitive and internalized, natural, existential, and lived understanding. True wisdom also fuses ethical and esthetic judgments. Joseph Brodsky, the Nobel Laureate poet, points out the interaction of these two mental qualities: "Man is an aesthetic creature before he is an ethical one."[4] The primacy of the ethical judgment suggested by the poet is

Eight Meditations on Architecture, First Edition. Juhani Pallasmaa. Edited by Matteo Zambelli.

thought-provoking. The social psychiatrist Erich Fromm also combined the qualities of beauty and truth: "Beauty is not the opposite of the *ugly*, but of the *false*."[5]

5

Fromm, Eric (1968). *The Revolution of Hope: Toward a Humanized Technology*, 75. New York, NY: Harper & Row. Italics in original. Available at: https://archive.org/details/revolutionofhope00from/page/n5/mode/2up?q=false (accessed October 2025).

Instead of a factual and intellectual assessment of distinct things, wisdom implies a lived, internalized, and emotively felt judgment, withdrawal, and a distinct simultaneous identification with the issues at a distance. Wise observation and judgment fuse, or push back, details and secondary characteristics of the situation. This instinctual fusion of details and entities, similarities and differences, resembles our atmospheric perception, which also fuses countless sensory experiences into a singular unconsciously fused and felt experience. Wise observation fuses generality, knowledge, ethical evaluation, and empathy into one judgment, as well as the envisioned consequences of alternative choices. Wisdom connects intuition and vision, generality and specificity, ethical judgment and empathic association, nearness and distance, forward view and responsibility; it is in essence an outsider's existentially internalized judgment. Instead of an intellectualized evaluation of things, it is a lived and existentially evaluated judgment. Somewhat unexpectedly, as Brodsky suggests, wisdom is also close to the experience of beauty, which is a similarly integrated judgment, that fuses intellect and emotion with sensory and esthetic judgments. Beauty also engaged consciousness of time: "The language of beauty is the language of timeless reality," as the philosopher Karsten Harries suggests.[6]

6

Harries, Karsten (1982). Building and the terror of time. *Perspecta: The Yale Architectural Journal* 19: 63.

While knowledge is grounded in certainty, wisdom arises from the acceptance of doubt and uncertainty, as well as the imminent possibility of failure; wisdom is fragile and modest. It is not necessarily a result of specific education, trained skill or societal position; a traditional fisherman, hunter, farmer, and craftsman may possess a remarkable silent and embodied wisdom in his/her work, sense of life, and human relations. A natural sense of beauty is also mediated by traditions; traditional societies have built harmonious buildings and made beautiful objects without any esthetic education or specific intentions. Traditions, in general, are carriers of silent, unformalized wisdoms, which are mediated by lived, sensory, and practical experiences, and the accumulated, hidden, and wordless intelligence of life itself, grounded in the silent understanding of the entities and interactions of things and their imminent destinies. Knowledge and skills are distinct focused facts, whereas wisdom arises from a general relatedness and a natural life-supporting and positive perspective. There is also an esthetic dimension in wisdom, as deep wisdom is miraculous, admirable, deeply touching, and beautiful. Besides, wisdom is always based on truth.

In our post-industrial cultures, broken into countless isolated specializations, we are especially in need of the unifying and guiding visions of existential wisdom. Human cultures are specific sets of beliefs and collective wisdom, developed and accumulated through time. Wisdom is generally expected of philosophers, writers, poets, and religious and political leaders, who are all expected to have an inclusive view of society and culture and their destinies. Through the constant increase of information, the huge sphere of political thinking, decision-making and action, is especially in a deep need of wisdom. Political decisions are expected to be based on a synthesizing judgment and mediation between opposing and conflicting views and aspirations. Yet, this is the quality that is usually missing in today's discourse and decision-making. Undoubtedly, wisdom should be regarded as a required qualification for political decision-makers. In addition to technical, esthetic, and empathic sensibilities, the architect also needs human wisdom. Architecture operates as much in the sphere of human experiences, values, and emotions as in the physical acts of construction, and architectural design implies continuous evaluation, choice, and decision-making.

Our current culture is rushing thoughtlessly toward an unknown future, such as total computerization and the quickly widening use of artificial intelligence, disregarding the currently established scientific fact, that it takes roughly 50,000 years for an acquired human capability to become part of the human genome; from the biological perspective, we are hopelessly slow in our natural evolution. Through the speed of technological development, we are suppressing our biologically derived capacities and rhythms. It is evident that the gap between our biological essence and our self-made technoculture, goals, and values, is dramatically widening. In the current quasi-rational culture of persuasion, insistence, and manipulation, wisdom is a disappearing quality. We live in a culture of constantly focusing attention and the simultaneous acceleration of speed; as a consequence, we are losing wide and deep general views, that could support wisdom. Human attention and knowledge are becoming increasingly focused, but we need wide views, understanding, and wisdom to survive as a species.

A wise person keeps him/herself outside of the center of action, as true understanding arises from the internalization and grasping of large entities through simultaneous and irreconcilable observations, the merging of peripheral and focused attention, as well as simultaneous views in time, backwards and forwards. In our intoxication with the near future, we are losing the layered wisdoms of time and past life.

The technological societies are split into countless unrelated domains of expertise, individuals, and groups, who are assumed to know and master ever-narrowing areas of specific knowledge or activity. The wise person seeks an unfocused, general view of things, as sharp and focused vision would turn him/her into an expert and specialist with a narrow view. Expertise is a focused and limited capacity, whereas wisdom arises from a diffuse and comprehensive understanding of the situational essence of the issue in question. Expertise is valid only within its limited and constrained area, whereas wisdom is the capacity to grasp wide and complex entities and causalities, usually even consisting of conflicting dimensions and details. Put simply, structuring a situation of logically irreconcilable characteristics calls for a different attitude and capacity than expertise. Many of the seminal governmental and societal tasks, such as political decisions, management, planning, and architecture, characteristically consist of conflicting realities, intentions, and interests. The real situations of cultural and societal life usually merge numerous dimensions of reality and, consequently, they cannot be resolved purely through focused expertise, intellect, reason, or logic.

In his inaugural lecture as Member of the Academy of Finland in 1955, Alvar Aalto pointed out the irreconcilable inner structure of architectural tasks: "In every case one must achieve the simultaneous solution of opposites. Nearly every design task involves tens, often hundreds, sometimes thousands of different contradictory elements, which are forced into a functional harmony only by man's will. This harmony cannot be achieved by any other means than those of art."[7] Aalto saw art as the skill of mediation and artistic synthesis, but his statement above could well terminate in the words ". . . those of wisdom."

Architecture is undoubtedly a field that calls more for wisdom than expertise, as it usually concerns countless human lives, activities, experiences, and values, which do not arise from logic. Architecture is always based on a vision of future life. In today's world, architecture is frequently seen as mere problem-solving, and architectural projects are, accordingly, commonly called "solutions" by architects

7

Aalto, Alvar (1985). "Art and technology," lecture at the Academy of Finland, October 3, 1955. In: *Sketches: Alvar Aalto* (ed. Göran Schildt). Cambridge, MA: The MIT Press.

themselves. The use of this notion turns architecture into an act of rational solving of equations, revealing a fundamental misunderstanding of architecture. The art of architecture creates experiential and relational meanings and values, which do not arise from logic; they arise from visions and personal convictions. An architectural work is more a personal confession than problem-solving. Architecture does not primarily solve anything, as it mediates our relationships (movements, actions, physical and sensory conditions, as well as our relationships and mental experiences and values) with the world, both natural and man-made; architecture opens up, connects, mediates, and facilitates, instead of solving problems. Architecture is an unavoidable and irreplaceable embodied and mental mediation between us and the world, not a given or closed problem to be solved by intelligence, skill, or expertise. The art of architecture creates human values, and they cannot be intellectually projected. Indeed, Maurice Merleau-Ponty argues significantly: "We come to see not the work of art, but the world according to the work."[8] This argument reveals the relational, mediating, and dialogical essence of all artistic works, especially of architecture. Artistic works are always about something else than their material selves, and architecture is about the world, and human life and values in that very world. However, true architecture is about a situation that does not exist, yet architecture mediates an understanding of historicity and time, and it is simultaneously deeply engaged in the potential life in the future.

8

Merleau-Ponty, Maurice (1996). *The Phenomenology of Perception*. New Delhi: Motilal Banarsidass Publishers, as quoted in McGilchrist, Iain (2009). *The Master and His Emissary*, 100. New Haven, CT: Yale University Press.

Joseph Brodsky, the Nobel Laureate poet, is critical of our culture of expertise: "In the business of writing what one accumulates is not expertise but uncertainties."[9] In the poet's view, even master craftsmen are engaged in uncertainties rather than the certainties of the expert. Wisdom acknowledges the evolution and change of phenomena through time and contains a temporal understanding fusing the time perspective in its judgment. For the wise person, time loses its linear chronology and becomes flexible. In the reality of ideas and artistic expressions, time gives up its absolute nature; an artistic work, which may be 25,000 years old, such as the cave paintings of Lascaux, is mentally just as vivid, powerful, and moving as any works of art of today. On the other hand, masterpieces of our time often valorize works that may well be hundreds of years old. The world of art is a field of endless present tense and interaction, and the history of art is an irreplaceable source of estheticized wisdom and grace. No wonder, Paul Valéry writes: "An artist is worth a thousand centuries."[10] Whereas Karsten Harries, the philosopher, writes that architecture is not only about domesticating space, "It has provided

9

Brodsky, Joseph (1998). Less than one. In: *Less Than One* (ed. Joseph Brodsky), 17. New York, NY: Farrar, Straus & Giroux.

10

Valéry, Paul (1956). *Dialogues*, vol. XIII. New York, NY: Pantheon Books.

defences against the terror of time . . . The language of beauty is the language of timeless reality."[11]

11
Harries, op. cit., pp. 57, 63.

Knowledge and skills can be studied, taught, and learned, but wisdom grows and matures by itself through lived life, intense work, and experience. In its very essence, wisdom is always contextual; the wise person sees and feels the phenomenon in its total context, interactions, dynamics, and potentials. In traditional societies, wisdom relied on culturally inherited mythical and symbolic knowledge or magic, while, in our self-claimed age of reason, it is an exceptional and rare human gift altogether. Wisdom is not a conceptualized and structured mental construction; it is a natural ability to sense the essences, hierarchies, and interactions of things. Wisdom is our sixth sense.

The legendary speech of the Indian Chief Seattle of 1854 to a distinct audience, that included the first Governor of Washington Territory, is a humbling example of wisdom arising from authentic life experience. It is a historical document of the opposition of intelligence and wisdom; the white man wanted to buy the land on which the Indians historically had lived, but the red man could not even understand this desire. "How can you buy or sell the sky, the warmth of the land? The idea is strange to us. If we do not own the freshness of the air and the sparkle of the water, how can you buy them? Every part of this earth is sacred to my people. Every shining pine needle, every clearing and humming insect is holy in the memory and experience of my people. The sap which comes through the trees carries the memories of the red man."[12] Wisdom arises from lived emotional assurance, an acute sense of identity and solidarity, not from an intellectual control of facts, legal positions, or ownership.

12
Indian Chief Seattle, speech in 1864. There are several memorized versions of this famous speech on Google.

Wisdom is usually related to age and life experience, as only deeply layered and internalized experiences of life can prepare a person for the required diffuse attention, impartiality, and unfocused judgment. Wisdom calls for forgetting, just as much as remembering. By its very nature, it is a quality of an individual, hardly a collective virtue. The common view today suggests that responsible decisions in demanding situations call for intelligence, but emotive, empathic, and existential capacities are more essential. The choices of wisdom are usually based on emotive and visionary, rather than rational certainties. Philosopher Mark Johnson claims: "Emotions are not second-rate cognitions; rather they are affective patterns of our encounter with our world, by which we take the meaning of things at a primordial level . . . Emotions are a fundamental part of human meaning."[13] Wisdom fuses knowledge and emotion, intelligence and memory, reason and vision, certainty and doubt, as well as the embodied and the mental. It also calls for imagination, and in fact, wisdom is fundamentally an imaginative skill and gift. Imagination is an integral part of wisdom, as the wise person is capable of imagining and imaginatively living potential situations without words and concepts. But, most importantly, wisdom has an essential ethical and esthetical component, as there is no wisdom without ethical judgment and moral responsibility. Wisdom is primarily an existential gift – it arises from existential poetic and ethical intuition – and it is undoubtedly the highest and rarest of human qualities.

13

Johnson, Mark (2007). *The Meaning of the Body: Aesthetics of Human Understanding*, 18, 66. Chicago, IL: University of Chicago Press.

SPIRITUALITY IN ARCHITECTURE 7

Architecture, Art, and Existential Sacredness

I am not conscious of the miracle of faith, but I often live that of ineffable space, the consummation of plastic emotion.

—Le Corbusier[1]

Architecture has no presence. A work is an offering to the Sanctuary.

—Louis I. Kahn[2]

I want to claim that the sacred needs architecture if it is not to wither, and that similarly architecture needs the sacred.

—Karsten Harries[3]

1

As cited in Curtis, William J. (1986). *Le Corbusier: Ideas and Forms*, 179. London: Phaidon.

2

Kahn, Louis (1991). Silence, reprinted in: *Louis I. Kahn: Writings, Lectures, Interviews* (ed. Alessandra Latour), 232. New York, NY: Rizzoli International Publications, Inc.

3

Harries, Karsten (2010). Untimely meditations on the need for sacred architecture. In: *Constructing the Ineffable* (ed. Karla Cavarra Britton), 49. New Haven, CT: Yale University Press.

THE MENTAL TASK OF ARCHITECTURE

The ontological task of architecture is usually seen in providing physical shelter from external threats and the elements. Yet, we can argue that the most fundamental task of architecture is to create the experience of placeness, to define our location and domicile in relation to the homogeneous, placeless, and meaningless "natural" space that extends to infinity. Architectural constructions place and focus us in the world and they provide a framing or horizon for perceiving and understanding our existential situation. The experience of place implies the perception of the spatial configuration as a distinct gestalt, image, or atmosphere that can be identified or named, and on which a specific human meaning can be projected. The experiential places of our life-world structure our awareness as well as the understanding of ourselves; we cannot mentally exist in a non-place. "I am the space where I am," as the French poet Noël Arnaud says.[4]

4

Noël Arnaud, as cited in Bachelard, Gaston (1969). *The Poetics of Space*, 137. Boston, MA: Beacon Press.

Architecture is usually regarded as the art of articulating space, but it structures and domesticates both space and time to be lived and inhabited. As Karsten Harries, the philosopher, writes that architecture is not only about domesticating space, "It has provided defences against the terror of time . . . The language of beauty is the language of timeless reality."[5] Cities, buildings, and places also structure our experiences of time through giving the measureless and endless natural time a human scale, and making the continuum of time conceivable to the human mind. The historicity and duration of the material world with its processes of aging, wear, and patina turn into instruments of measuring time. Thus the temporal layering of man-made structures has a significant mental task. With its layered historicity the human habitat materializes and concretizes the passage of time and life.

5

Harries, Karsten (1982). Building and the terror of time. *Perspecta: The Yale Architecture Journal* 19: 57–63.

Buildings are simultaneously instrumental devices and artistic expressions, objects of utility and metaphysical contemplation. Since time immemorial, architectural structures have also concretized hierarchies and marked the worlds of divinities and mortals. Rudolf Wittkower describes the metaphysical intention of Renaissance architecture as follows: "The belief in the correspondence of macrocosm and microcosm, in the harmonic structure of the universe, in the comprehension of God through the mathematical symbols of centre, circle and sphere – all these closely related ideas which had their roots in antiquity, and belonged to the undisputed tenets of medieval philosophy and theology, acquired new life in the Renaissance."[6] Yet, as in all other art forms, the essence of architectural expression lies in the human existential condition, the very enigma of life and origins.

6

Wittkower, Rudolf (1988). *Architectural Principles in the Age of Humanism*, 39. New York, NY: St. Martin's Press.

In addition to its practical purposes, architecture marks the domains of the ineffable and the numinous. The experience of architectural sacredness is generated equally by the image of a Greek temple in the Mediterranean landscape as a worldly metaphor of cosmic order, the dramatic sense of material and gravity, light and shadow of a vaulted Romanesque space, the rising of the gaze into the heights of a Gothic cathedral, the illusory space and movement evoked by the structures, sculptures, and paintings in a Baroque church, or the opening of the interior of an ascetic modern chapel to the landscape, that makes us experience our connectedness with nature and cosmos. These are all architectural experiences that guide our attention and thoughts beyond the material and utilitarian essences of construction.

These are all familiar images of sacred architecture, but a sacred experience may also be evoked by worldly settings without any specific and deliberate intention for sacredness.

SACREDNESS IN ARTISTIC AND RELIGIOUS EXPERIENCE

The experience of spirituality evoked by a work of art or architecture is essentially a different category than the experience of religious sacredness. The latter is associated with specific places, events, phenomena, or objects (e.g. the Holy Land, the Holy Sepulchre, the Last Supper, the Holy Spirit, the Blessed Trinity, the Holy Sacraments, etc.), which have been denominated as sacred in the Holy Word, or which have otherwise been sanctified by a religious order. Thus, religious sacredness implies the encounter of an object or space which has been specifically named or designated as sacred. On the contrary, the spirituality invoked by a secular artistic or architectural work is a personal and individual existential experience, which obtains its impact and aura – to use Walter Benjamin's notion – without specific religious symbolism or connotation, through the inherent nature of human experience. Such an experience may arise, for example, from an exceptional sense of place or space, purity of form, intense materiality or color, or a transcendent illumination.

The narrative or symbolic representation of mythical and sacred events has historically been one of the central themes of artistic works, but even in these representations of explicit religious events, the actual experience of sacredness arises from artistic qualities, suggestions, and associations irrespective of any deliberate, religious symbolism. An artistic and architectural experience of spirituality, detached from deliberate devotional purposes, seems to arise from a nameless and unintentional experiential origin, which is initiated by a sensitized encounter of the self and the world. This experience arises from the holiness of life itself and deep existential experiences of being.

THE GROUND OF ARTISTIC SACREDNESS

Beauty invokes images of a utopian and spiritualized reality. The pure shapes of Constantin Brancusi's sculptures do not possess an explicit religious content, but irrespective of their actual subject matter – a human figure, fish, bird, or a primordial egg shape, for instance – their radiant beauty makes them appear harbingers of otherness, a more perfect and timeless world. Similarly, the contemporary pollen, honey and milk works of Wolfgang Laib exude an air of fragility and holiness through their experiential purity and association with the origins of life; they also appear as images of original human innocence.

➔
Wolfgang Laib, Pollen from Hazelnut, MoMA, New York City, New York, USA, 2013. Jessica Sheridan / Flickr https://www.flickr.com/photos/kaitlinmarie/8608517994

Louis Kahn, Salk Institute, La Jolla, San Diego, California, 1959–1965. Jason Taellious / Flickr / CC BY-SA 2.0 https://www.flickr.com/photos/dreamsjung/3021667238

In the art form of architecture, even buildings constructed for earthly purposes can project experiences of sacredness in the same way that an extraordinarily beautiful painting, devoid of deliberate religious subject matter, can evoke the air of sacredness through the touching purity of its intention. The marble courtyard of Louis Kahn's Salk Institute in La Jolla, California, seen against the horizon line of the Pacific Ocean, turns the entire sky into the celestial ceiling of this ascetic outdoor space, and the authoritative space silences the visitor to cosmic reflection. Luis Barragán's minute structures in Mexico for domestic and other mundane purposes, such as horse stables and drinking troughs, similarly create dreamlike microcosms, images of metaphysical transcendence and paradise. Although architecture operates in the world of realities, such as climate, gravity, materials, technical means and skills, it always aspires to ideals. Without this inner idealizing tendency architecture turns into mere banal construction. In Alvar Aalto's view, profound architecture always aspires to the image of paradise: "Architecture . . . has an ulterior motive . . ., the idea of creating paradise. That is the only purpose of our buildings . . . We wish to build a paradise on earth for man."[7]

7 Alvar Aalto, lecture at the Jubilee Meeting of the Southern Sweden Master Builders' Society in Malmö, 1957. Cited in Schildt, Göran (ed.) (1997). *Alvar Aalto in His Own Words*, 215. Helsinki: Otava Publishing Company.

The sense of spirituality and sacredness can also be encountered in esthetically unself-conscious and unassuming vernacular settings and objects, as in Walker Evans' touching photograph "The Burrough's Family Kitchen" (Hale County, Alabama, 1936). Esthetic purity and utilitarian rationality, sensuality. and restraint can be fused into a virtuous beauty, resulting in a sense of sacredness as in the Shaker architecture and objects. A sense of holiness is equally evoked by the pitch-black interior of the primordial Finnish peasant's chimneyless smoke hut, which projects images of the serenity and sacredness of a simple and severe life; the shining blackness of soot on the walls turns into a symbol of a home, of cleanness, and purity. The protective, calming, and focusing essence of a home here attains metaphysical qualities; the home turns into a space of devotion and an expression of existential gratitude.

THE SUBLIME EXPERIENCE

The experience of architectural sacredness arises from the specificity and singularity of the space, which surpasses the sphere of everyday normality. This sacredness is not necessarily explicitly intended or symbolized; it arises from existential meanings, which we ourselves project onto the space. An exceptional landscape, a solemn urban space, or the mere site of a former house erased by fire, which has already been taken over by vegetation, evoke impressions and significations beyond the commonplace. These encounters ignite the fire of our imagination and we feel empathy for the simple life lived in these settings. As a place or a space transcends its mere utilitarian purpose, it evokes our empathy and directs our awareness beyond everyday reality. An extraordinary quality of the human mind is the capacity of our imagination to reflect particular meanings on our experiences. This is how even a non-representational image acquires its meaning and experienced qualities; we "become" the object that we are intensely observing. Current research in mirror neurons suggests that we are neurologically equipped to subconsciously simulate and imitate aspects of our world through our body, senses, and imagination. Joseph Brodsky acknowledges this mimetic power of artistic imagery in his suggestion that any great poem purposefully commands the reader: "Be like me."[8] We internalize the dignity and beauty of the piece of art that impresses the reader. These unconscious associations and meanings even guide and direct perceptions. Contrary to common understanding, perception is not an autonomous and mechanical function of the senses; it is defined and determined by the meanings we unconsciously project onto the perceived phenomenon, and the percept merges with imagination and evocations of memory.

8
Brodsky, Joseph (1997). An immodest proposal. In: *On Grief and Reason* (ed. Joseph Brodsky), 206. New York, NY: Farrar, Straus & Giroux.

Natural beauty, particular scenery, or even specific conditions of weather often awaken feelings of serenity and sacredness. It is meaningful that atmospheres of nature are sometimes associated with religious spaces, as in the expressions "the Church of Nature," or "the Sanctuary of the Forest." Such conditions of nature appear perfect and meaningful, and they evoke the reading of intentionality and, consequently, the existence of the Creator with his divine purposes.

Since the Romantic landscape paintings of the nineteenth century, the notion of sublime beauty has implied a view of the world which surpasses human scale and possesses powerful and even terrifying qualities. The enigmatic landscapes of Caspar David Friedrich, as well as of the great nineteenth-century American landscape painters, exemplify this sublime dimension in the art of painting. The experience of solemn serenity is similarly expressed in art works of our time, such as Barnett Newman's and Mark Rothko's immense canvases. In architectural experience, the category of the sublime is associated with a scale beyond the human measure, or with severe simplicity and geometry. The Egyptian pyramids, or the Peristyle of the Karnak Temple create a sublime and absolute silence through their immense stone structures of super-human scale. These are structures and spaces, which seem to have emerged before the creation of time. The relentless geometry of Louis Kahn's buildings as well as the uncompromising esthetic perfection of Mies van de Rohe's structures evoke equally sublime beauty, suggesting an air of the sacred. In their very esthetic absoluteness, these buildings seem to reveal the metaphysical and hidden order of reality.

Also Le Corbusier refers to the qualities of architecture which cannot be expressed in words: "When a work reaches a maximum of intensity, when it has the best proportions and has been made with the best quality of execution, when it has reached perfection, a phenomenon takes place that we may call 'ineffable space'. When this happens, these places start to radiate . . . It belongs to the domain of the ineffable, of that which cannot be said."[9]

EMBODIED UNDERSTANDING

The artistic meanings of works of art and architecture are not given iconographic or intellectual significations; they are ineffable and beyond verbal mediation, "that which cannot be said," as Le Corbusier confesses above. They are generated by the viewer's own intentions and experiences. Our very being-in-the-world is fused with an embodied and sensory understanding, through which we "understand" the "meaning" of our life situation as well as of the works of art that we encounter. "Essences and facts are incommensurable, and the one who begins with facts, will never end up with essences . . . understanding is not a quality entering our human reality from outside; it is the natural content of being," Jean-Paul Sartre writes.[10] Sartre's poignant statement implies that understanding and meaning are intertwined in our existential experience itself. According to the poetic notion of Maurice Merleau-Ponty, "We live in the flesh of the world."[11] This implies that we are not outsiders and spectators of our world, but inseparable ingredients of this very universe; the world is constituted through us and we are actualized in the world. Indeed, as Ludwig Wittgenstein exclaims, "I am my world."[12]

Openness to interpretation and a layered richness of association are ingredients of all significant artistic works. They are not intellectual arguments or conventionalized symbols; they are existential objects, which place themselves directly in our awareness and experience of being. As Merleau-Ponty states: "We come to see not the work of art, but the world according to the art of work."[13] A profound work is always about something else than its apparent subject matter or physical essence. "When a painter presents us an image of a field

9 Le Corbusier, in an interview recorded at La Tourette, 1961. Cited in Wogenscky, André (2006). *Le Corbusier's Hands*, 81. Cambridge, MA: The MIT Press.

10 Sartre, Jean-Paul (1993). *The Emotions: An Outline of a Theory*, 9. New York, NY: Carol Publishing Co.

11 Maurice Merleau-Ponty uses the expression "the flesh of the world" in several contexts, when writing about the intertwining of the world and the human mind.

12 Wittgenstein, Ludwig (1972). *Tractatus Logico-Philosophicus and Notebooks 1914–1916*, 68. Helsinki: Werner Söderström.

13 Maurice Merleau-Ponty, as quoted in McGilchrist, Iain (2009). *The Master and His Emissary: The Divided Brain and the Making of the Western World*, 409. New Haven, CT: Yale University Press.

Barnett Newman, Voice of Fire, 1967.
Youngjim / Wikimedia Commons / CC BY-SA 4.0
https://www.flickr.com/photos/neesam/51396901376

← Pyramids of Giza, Giza, Giza Governorate, Egypt, 2600–2500 BCE. Matheus De Moraes Gugelmim / Pexels / Public Domain https://www.pexels.com/photo/pyramids-in-giza-in-egypt-20290834/

→ The Great Hypostyle Hall of the Temple of Karnak, Luxor, Egypt, 1290–1224 BCE. AXP Photography / Pexels / Public Domain https://www.pexels.com/photo/hieroglyph-covered-sandstone-columns-in-the-karnak-great-hypostyle-hall-18991548/

or a vase with flowers, his paintings are windows open to an entire world," Jean-Paul Sartre writes.[14] In other words, instead of mediating symbolism, profound works of art have their impact directly on our existential sense through embodied simulation and empathy. "Tintoretto did not choose the yellow rift in the sky above Golgatha to signify or evoke anguish. Not an anguish of the sky or the sky of grief; it is a materialized anguish and grief, which has turned into that yellow rift in the sky," Sartre writes of Jacopo Tintoretto's *Crucifixion* (1565), pointing out the magical "thingness" of artistic effects.[15]

14

Sartre, Jean-Paul (1978). *What Is Literature?* 272. Gloucester, MA: Peter Smith.

15

Ibid., p. 3.

We experience the world and ourselves momentarily as if redirected and rearticulated by the artistic object. The experience is not the encounter of an object outside ourselves, but an intertwining of the object and our consciousness. The experiencing is a kind of exchange; we project our emotions and intentions onto the object, whereas the object lends us its authority, its "aura," that entices unique associations and feelings in us. A powerful artistic experience is, above all, an intense encounter with oneself. Indeed, when we sense a deep melancholy in Michelangelo's stairway hall of the Laurentian Library in Florence, we are really confronted with our own but hidden melancholy. Our individual existential experience is momentarily reinforced and amplified through the consciousness of a great artist. This is the merciful generosity and equality of art. It enables us to sense and identify reactions and emotions concealed from our everyday consciousness by cultural code or personal unconscious sensoring.

Works of art open up channels of feeling, understanding, and sharing for us, that would not be available to us without the artistic work. Works of art also present us with phenomena of beauty, the spiritual realm, and transcendence that possibly would not otherwise be available or present for us. Artistic experience is an act of compassion that opens to the world.

As Jean-Paul Sartre explains: "It is the joint effort of author and reader which brings upon the scene that concrete and imaginary object which is the work of the mind. There is no art except for and by others[16] . . . Thus, reading is a pact of generosity between author and reader."[17] So is architecture.

16

Sartre, Jean-Paul (2001). *Basic Writings* (ed. Stephen Priest), 264. London: Routledge.

17

Ibid., p. 271.

Jannis Kounellis, untitled, 1980.
Jean-Pierre Dalbéra / Flickr / CC BY 2.0
https://www.flickr.com/photos/dalbera/48164053541/in/photostream/

IMAGES OF FORM, MATTER, AND IMMATERIALITY

In his book, *Water and Dreams*,[18] Gaston Bachelard makes a distinction between images of form and images of matter, and suggests that the latter are capable of evoking deeper emotional responses than the former. Early modernity focused on form, whereas materiality has become more central in the artistic expressions of the past few decades. In the works of Jannis Kounellis, for instance, everyday materials such as plates of steel, rocks, sacks of hemp, heaps of coal, and carcasses of animals, attain touching poetic expressions. These works exude a sense of enigma and destiny, and they suggest sacred rites and rituals. The monochromatic and gilded surfaces of Yves Klein's paintings create an air of holiness in the same way as the golden auras of saints in icon paintings. Klein's paintings are, in fact, icons devoid of pictorial contents, or connections with any specific religious themes. Also James Turrell's ethereal light works possess an iconic presence, as they guide the viewer to the very limit of his/her perceptual capacities and experience of being. Does the mysterious light of the work exist physically and objectively, or is one looking at an illusory projection of one's own nervous system? Am I looking at a miracle? What does truly and objectively exist, and what is true in one's experiential and existential perspective? The dark light of Mark Rothko's and Ad Reinhardt's paintings leads the viewer to another borderline, which lies beyond intellectual and verbal definitions. As Arthur Zajonc argues in his book, *Catching the Light: The Entwined History of Light and Mind*, we could not see light without our mental inner light.[19] It is a mental limit, beyond which new conditions of being and awareness seem to prevail. What is the ground of existential understanding? Have I reached the borderline of my very existence? "I see black light," were the last words of Victor Hugo.[20]

The materiality of architecture and the material uniformity evoke experiences of serenity. The Klippan Church of Sigurd Lewerentz near Malmö is constructed solely of dark burnt bricks. This church is an enclosed world, an architectural microcosm that directs the visitor's awareness and thoughts to the ultimate shore of life. Its monolithic materiality, more than light, gives the space a mysterious and therapeutic darkness and shadow. The dark crack in the brick floor brings Mother Earth, death, and the afterlife into one's consciousness; the visitor is granted a glimpse into the final abyss of time. The experience of nostalgia and sorrow humbles the visitor and integrates him/her with a healing sense of time.

18

Bachelard, Gaston (1982). *Water and Dreams: An Essay on the Imagination of Matter*, 107. Dallas, TX: The Pegasus Foundation.

19

Zajonc, Arthur (1993). *Catching the Light: The Entwined History of Light and Mind*, 5. Oxford: Oxford University Press.

20

The writer articulated the majesty of darkness in his poem:
"O darkness, the sky is a gloomy precinct
Whose door you close, and whose key the soul owns;
And night divides itself in half, being diabolical and holy,
Between Ilis, the black angel, and Christ, the starry Human Being."
Victor Hugo, Dernière Gerbe, 26 November 1976. Available at: https://www.azquotes.com/quote/908653 (accessed December 2025).

➔

James Turrell, Sky Space, Salzburg, Austria, 2006. Anton kurt / Wikimedia Commons / CC BY-SA 3.0 https://commons.wikimedia.org/wiki/File:Sky_Space_Salzburg_05.jpg

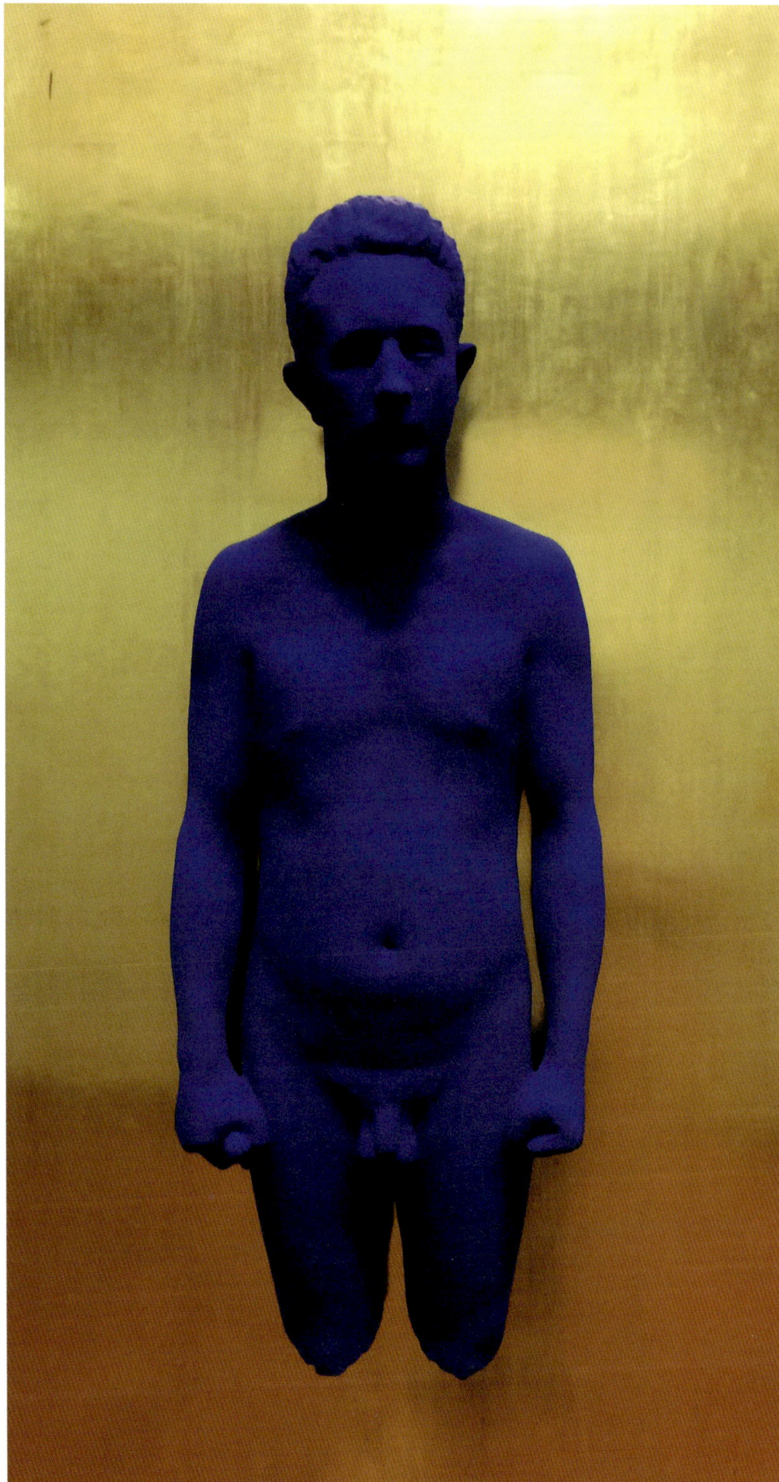

➔ Yves Klein, Portrait Relief of Claude Pascal, 1962. Lorenzofaoro / Wikimedia Commons / CC BY-SA 4.0 https://commons.wikimedia.org/wiki/File:Yves_Klein,_the_new_blue.jpg

➔ Pekka Pitkänen, The Chapel of the Holy Cross, Turku, Finland, 1963–1967. © Mikko Laaksonen

➔ Tadao Ando, Church of Water, Shimukappu-mura, Japan, 1988. 準建築人手札網站 Forgemind ArchiMedia / Flickr / CC BY 2.0 https://www.flickr.com/photos/eager/5298044021/in/photostream/

The ascetic religious spaces of Aarno Ruusuvuori and Pekka Pitkänen in Finland and of Tadao Ando in Japan, cast in concrete, create similar feelings of the spiritual, focusing through their material uniformity, and emptiness, and the ultimate restraint and dialectics of matter, space, and light. Silence has an authoritative voice in these ascetic spaces.

VOICES OF OBJECTS

Even objects are capable of mediating metaphysical and sacred meanings without reference to conventional symbolization. In Walker Evans' famous interior of a poor southern sharecropper's shack, a tin washing bowl and a white linen towel radiate the nobility and sacredness of humble life. Poverty and suffering project a strangely dignified radiance. Human dignity seems to emerge in scarcity and need, and disappear in prosperity and abundance. In the surreal materialism and obsessive consumption of today, the dignity of the human soul is lost.

"The higher material level the society has, the more effort it needs to devote toward a spiritual development," the deeply religious film director Andrei Tarkovsky argues.[21] "I have a feeling that mankind has stopped having faith in itself . . . For me, man is above all a spiritual being, and life's purpose is in the development of this. If man is unable to do this, the society degenerates," the film director continues.[22]

21

Olofsson, Anders (1986). Nostalghia. In: *Tanken på en hemkomst* (The thought of returning home) (ed. Magnus Bergh and Birgitta Munkhammar), 150. Stockholm: Alfa Beta Bokförlag.

22

Ibid., p. 158.

The everyday utilitarian Shaker objects, as well as the refined objects of traditional Japanese and Finnish peasant cultures evoke equally moving images of the dignity and holiness of severe life. True beauty arises from limits and reduction rather than from unconstrained and wilful choice. The bottles, vessels, and cups on a table top in Giorgio Morandi's minute still lifes are, indeed, impressive witnesses of the power of artistic reduction and compression; mere household objects, embedded in their soft silence, suffice to represent the entire universe of human experience. In the words of the Russian film director Andrei Tarkovsky, "The [artistic] image is not a specific *meaning* . . . but the entire world is reflected in it as in a drop of water."[23] These images do not depict mere common objects; they represent the metaphysical enigma of human existence. They pose the mysterious question of the nature of being. To be, to exist, is the ultimate verb, and these insignificant objects share this mysterious and monumental act with us.

23

Tarkovsky, Andrei (1986). *Sculpting in Time*, 100. London: Bodley Head Ltd.

BEAUTY AND GOODNESS

The experience of the spiritual in a natural phenomenon or a work of art and architecture is a reflection of a longing for sacredness and beauty. This experience materializes the human desire for a reality that surpasses the limits of our mortal existence, "the timeless reality," as suggested by Harries. Beauty provides a promise of a mode of existence beyond temporality, mortality, and moral doubts. In the artistic experience the categories of beauty, goodness, and truth are fused, as the experience of beauty evokes and maintains the possibility of a better world. "The purpose of evolution, believe it or not, is beauty, which survives it all and generates truth simply by being a fusion of the mental and the sensual,"[24] as the poet Joseph Brodsky writes. "Aesthetics is the mother of ethics,"[25] he concludes.

24
Brodsky, op. cit., p. 207.

25
Ibid., p. 208.

The experience of beauty calls for the capacities of empathy and compassion; the work becomes momentarily a part of one's personal experience of existence and self. The ugliness or beauty expressed by the artistic image turns into experiences of one's own body and mind. A culture, which loses its longing for and appreciation of beauty, is surely on its way to losing its capacity of empathy and compassion as well as its very life force. Living in this quasi-rational time of ours, we are in a desperate need of the mental emancipation that the spiritual and artistic dimensions can provide to human thought, emotion, and imagination. The concept of esthetics has become empty of its ethical, ritualistic, and spiritual echoes and flattened into pure retinal pleasure. As Frank Stella famously asserted, "What you see is what you see."[26]

26
Exhibition entitled: "What You See Is What You See", Frank Stella and the Anderson Collection at SFMOMA (San Francisco Museum of Modern Art), June 11–September 6, 2004.

Profound beauty is always a promise, a glimpse into a perfect and timeless world. "The experience of the beauty of the environment promises a genuine homecoming," Harries writes optimistically.[27]

27
Karsten Harries, "Transcending Aesthetics: Architecture and the Sacred," lecture in the "Transcending Architecture: Aesthetics and Ethics of the Numinous" symposium at the Catholic University of America, October 7–8, 2011, lecture manuscript, pp. 1–2. The book of the conference is available at: https://students.aiu.edu/submissions/profiles/resources/onlineBook/i5r5b6_Transcending_Architecture_Sacred_Space.pdf (accessed October 2025).

SACREDNESS AND LIGHT

The air of spirituality and holiness in a religious space derives from various experiential properties, such as scale, form, materiality, and color. Acoustic qualities as well as evocations of touch and scents can also be part of the impression of sacredness that detaches us from the commonplace reality and directs our consciousness toward spiritual feelings and emotions.

Yet, the most subtle and expressive medium in the language of architecture is light. Ultimate human emotions, such as grief and

➔ Juha Leiviskä, Myyrmäki Church, Vantaa, Finland, 1984.
David Karlin / Alamy Stock Photo https://www.alamy.com/stock-photo-the-white-interior-with-strong-vertical-lines-of-myyrmki-church-vantaa-124307784.html?imageid=D5F10B51-8F0B-4D96-8797-3A6E10E02CF8&p=354891&pn=1&searchId=54866751c39ffd28e62db0b293622c04&searchtype=0

joy, melancholy and ecstasy, sorrow and bliss, may all be expressed through light, but hardly through any of the material ingredients of architecture. A building is constructed of matter, but the essence of its space is always determined by illumination. Also the impression of sacredness in a religious space usually arises from the specific character of its illumination. Religious light reveals and heals, mediates and unifies. The contained and articulated light inside the religious building differs from the worldly "natural" light outside in the same way as existential space differs from physical space.

"Light alone does not make light. There must be darkness for light to become light – resplendent with dignity and power. Darkness, which kindles the brilliance of light and reveals light's power, is innately a part of light . . . Today, when all is cast in homogeneous light, I am committed to pursuing the interrelationship of light and darkness," Tadao Ando explains his intentions in the design of his church of light.[28]

28 Ando, Tadao (1995). Church of Light. In: *Tadao Ando: Complete Works* (ed. Francesco Dal Co), 471. London: Phaidon.

The Church of the Three Crosses by Alvar Aalto in Imatra (1957) as well as Juha Leiviskä's more recent Myyrmäki Church in Vantaa (1984) and the Männistö Church in Kuopio (1992) are impressive examples of contemporary religious spaces, in which light creates an atmosphere of dignity, integrity, and hope. Light is simultaneously the messenger of life and of the transcendent dimension beyond. The spaces of these churches also invoke the calming and comforting light of the Nordic landscape and the forest; these spaces guide us back to the Nature of all origins.

EXPERIENCING ARCHITECTURE

A powerful work of art creates a kind of a short circuit of consciousness by means of weakening our rational capacities of deduction, and inviting primordial emotional reactions. "Literature is made at the frontier between the self and the world, and in the act of creation that frontier softens, becomes permeable, allows the world to flow into the artist and the artist to flow into the world," as Salman Rushdie writes.[29] This fusion of the world and the self, described here by a writer, applies to all artistic experience. A similar fusion takes place in encounters with architecture, although the mental impact of architecture usually appears as a less dramatic form of unconscious pre-understanding, that directs and conditions the act of experience itself. We do not encounter the world or the object of our attention from outside as a separate entity, but we share our very existence with it.

29 Salman Rushdie, "Is Nothing Sacred?" Available at: https://granta.com/is-nothing-sacred/ (accessed October 2025).

Architecture frames and focuses human perceptions and existential experiences, and provides them with a distinct horizon of understanding and meaning. When viewed through a window, the landscape is already pre-selected and pre-viewed by the building itself. A natural scene or a condition of weather is experienced differently when framed and interpreted through an architectural device than when confronted unmediated in its natural state. Gaston Bachelard actually criticizes Martin Heidegger's view of the inherent human anxiety of being thrown into the world: "[The house] is the human being's first world. Before he is 'cast into the world', as claimed by certain hasty metaphysics, man is laid in the cradle of the house."[30] From the very beginning of our existence, our relationship with the world is unavoidably articulated by architectural structures.

30 Bachelard, *The Poetics of Space*, op. cit., p. 7.

The specific task of ecclesiastic architecture is to create mental conditions for the confrontation of the basic essences of life and faith. The impact of a religious space – or of any architectural space, for that matter, which touches our emotions deeply – is born from the bodily, sensory, and mental language of architecture itself. Sir Colin St John Wilson explains the secret and pre-reflective power of architecture as follows: "It is as if I am being manipulated by some subliminal code, not to be translated into words, which acts directly on the nervous system and imagination, at the same time stirring intimations of meaning with vivid spatial experience as though they were one thing. It is my belief that the code acts so directly and vividly upon us because it is strangely familiar; it is in fact the first language we ever learned, long before words, and which is now recalled to us through art, which alone holds the key to revive it."[31]

31 Wilson, Sir Colin St John (1979). Architecture – public good and private necessity. *RIBA Journal*.

Religious symbols serve to connect the ecclesiastic space with specific theological contexts and ideas, but the true emotional impact arises from architecture's own spatial, material, and sensory language. This is an existentially grounded and embodied language, the meanings of which precede words and concepts, as St John Wilson suggests. Architectural meanings are ineffable because they express and articulate pre-cognitive existential experiences and significations arising from our being-in-the-world. Architecture implies autonomous metaphysical thinking through images and impressions specific to this art form of construction and its tectonic language, which directly address the body and the mind.

THE HOLINESS OF SETTINGS

Since we are capable of identifying and being deeply affected by sacred spaces of alien cultures, the experience of architectural

sacredness must transcend the boundaries of religious ideologies. When the encounter of architectural sacredness is detached from the connotations and symbolism of specific religions, it turns into a meta-religious and existential experience. The most moving encounter with the sacred dimension, for me personally, was a visit, 35 years ago, to the Bandiagara Canyon in Mali, south of the Saharan Desert, to study the architecture and artifacts of the Dogon culture. I had a feeling that every stone, tree, object, and human act had its divine purpose and origin. I learned only later that the Dogons, in fact, actually repeat phases of their complex cosmogony in each of their daily acts and, thus, continue the creation of the world every single day. Their world is constantly being created; it is always *in statu nascendi*, in a divine present tense of becoming. Even the smallest aspects of nature and life obtain specific meanings from this collectively understood and incontestable mythical ground.

I have also encountered silencing sacredness in the raked sand garden of the Ryōan-ji Zen Temple in Kyoto, with its 15 moss-covered stones, set on a rectangular sand court, as its sole motif. This minimal still life turns into a hypnotic image of the cosmos and the untouchable authority of the sacred. The imagery shifts from the foaming waves of a primordial ocean to mountain peaks puncturing the sublime landscape of billowing clouds.

ONE-DIMENSIONAL REALITY

The feeling of sacredness in architecture as well as the arts is a category of experience arising from our encounter of a timeless, archetypal, or mythical existence. Our worldly, materialistic, and obsessively rationalistic culture has, however, turned into a depressive and unsatisfactory life style by imprisoning life in a one-dimensional reality. In his seminal book, *One-Dimensional Man*, Herbert Marcuse argues that the citizens of the industrial societies themselves become one-dimensional as "the second reality" of human experience disappears, and along with this reduction, the tension between the everyday world and the world of ideals is lost.[32] He uses the provocative expression "the radical Empiricist onslaught." In Marcuse's view, our materialist and hedonistic culture aspires to fuse the dimension of ideals into everyday life and, thus, to create a paradise on earth. Marcuse writes: "Today's novel feature is the flattening out of the antagonism between culture and social reality through the obliteration of the oppositional, alien, and transcendent elements in the higher culture by virtue of which it constituted *another dimension* of reality. This liquidation of *two-dimensional* culture takes place

32

Marcuse, Herbert (1964). *One-Dimensional Man: Studies on the Ideology of Advanced Industrial Society*. Boston, MA: Beacon Press.

Bandiagara Escarpment, Mopti Region, Mali. Wikimedia Commons: Ferdinand Reus / Wikimedia Commons / CC BY-SA 2.0 https://commons.wikimedia.org/wiki/File:Bandiagara_escarpment_1.jpg

not through the denial and rejection of the 'cultural values', but through their wholesale incorporation into the established order, through their reproduction and display on a massive scale."[33]

This sad development described by the famous social psychiatrist even annuls the task of myths and art as mediators between the two mental and experiential realities. In our materialist and consumer culture, architecture has been totally instrumentalized and buildings fail to sustain the spiritual and ideal dimension of our mental lives. In addition to providing shelter for our bodies and activities, architecture should also house our dreams and memories, and provide ground for imagination and hope.

It is evident that the ethical and humane task of architecture and all art is to defend the authenticity and autonomy of human experience, as well as the existence of the transcendental realm, the experience of the sacred.

■ ■ ■

Modern man's most urgent need is to discover the reality and value of the inner subjective world, to discover the symbolic life . . . The symbolic life in some form is a prerequisite for psychic health.

—Edward F. Edinger[34]

Architecture has no presence. Only a work of architecture has presence, and that at its best is an offering of architecture itself . . . Architecture is the reaching out for the truth . . . All Bach cared about was the truth. Undefinable, unmeasurable truth. And, so it is with architecture. It's a search for the truth.

—Louis I. Kahn[35]

Zen Ryōan-ji, Ukyō-ku, Kyoto, Kyoto Prefecture, Japan, 1450 (completed). Jean-Pierre Dalbéra / Wikimedia Commons / CC BY 2.0 https://commons.wikimedia.org/wiki/File:Le_jardin_zen_du_temple_Ry%C3%B4an-ji_%28Kyoto,_Japon%29_%2832162405237%29.jpg

33 Ibid., p. 57. Italics in original.

34 Edinger, Edward F. (1992). *Ego and Archetype.* Boston, MA: Shambhala.

35 Louis Kahn, lecture at Drexler University Architectural Society, Philadelphia, November 5, 1968. Cited in Wurman, Richard Saul (1986). *What Will Be Has Always Been: The Words of Louis I. Kahn*, 27 and 208. New York, NY: Rizzoli International Publications, Inc.

THE COMPLEXITY OF SIMPLICITY 8

The Inner Structure of the Artistic Image

The means with which one paints can never be simple enough. I have always forced myself to become simpler. But the maximum simplicity coincides with the maximum fullness. The simplest means frees the eye for vision to the maximum of clarity. And in the long run only the simplest means is convincing. But courage has always been required in order to be simple. I think there's nothing harder in the world. Those who work with simple means should never be afraid of becoming apparently trite.

—Henri Matisse[1]

Making the simple complicated is commonplace, making the complicated simple, awesomely simple, that's creativity.

—Charles Mingus, jazz musician[2]

1 Henri Matisse, in a conversation with Gotthard Jedlich, 1952. The text was displayed in the exhibition "Henri Matisse: Arabesque, Scuderia del Quirinale," Rome, 2015.

2 The quote originates in a letter by Michael Matiisen to the author, dated January 2013.

We tend to think of simplicity and complexity as polar and exclusive opposites. When speaking of phenomena in logic, this view may well be acceptable, but our mental lives and artistic imagery do not follow rules of rationality and logic. While the logical processes focus, the emotive artistic exploration opens up and widens; a logical entity is exclusive, whereas an artistic imagery aspires for inclusivity. The objective of art is always to evoke something about the entity of human existential experience. And our minds are in constant flux of images, thoughts, associations, recollections, emotions, and dreams. This existential and mental fusion of irreconcilable categories is the essential realm of art.

In his book, *The Philosophy of No: A Philosophy of the New Scientific Mind*, Gaston Bachelard, the French philosopher of science and poetic imagery (whose book *The Poetics of Space* has been one of the most influential texts in architectural theory since its publication in 1958),

Eight Meditations on Architecture, First Edition. Juhani Pallasmaa. Edited by Matteo Zambelli.

argues that all scientific thought develops along a predestined path: from animism through realism, positivism, rationalism and complex rationalism to dialectic rationalism.[3] "The philosophical evolution of a special piece of scientific knowledge is a movement through all these doctrines in the order indicated," he argues.[4] In my view, artistic thinking aspires to advance in the opposite direction; the arts work their way from the realist, rational, intellectual, and analytic understanding of the world back toward a unifying mythical and animistic experience, and art seeks to re-mythicize, re-enchant, and re-eroticize our relationship with the world.

3

Bachelard, Gaston (1968). *The Philosophy of No: A Philosophy of the New Scientific Mind*, 15. New York: The Orion Press.

4

Ibid., p. 16.

Paradoxically, the notion of simplicity is commonly used both in a pejoritative sense and in acknowledgment of a distinct quality. Also the notion of complexity has a dual essence, it implies both something chaotic or unresolved, and a synthetic unity of a multifaceted field of phenomena. To further confuse the interplay of the two notions in the arts, the fundamental meaning of artistic and architectural works is always beyond the material work itself, as it evokes and mediates relationships and horizons of perception, feeling, and understanding. As Maurice Merleau-Ponty points out: "We come to see not the work of art, but the world according to the work."[5] This philosopher's observation also applies to architecture; a profound building frames and guides our perceptions, actions, thoughts, and feelings, instead of being the objective itself. It projects an epic narrative of human life and culture. As a consequence, the entire complexity of life becomes part of even the simplest of artistic or architectural works. As Jean-Paul Sartre suggests: "If the painter presents us with a field or a vase of flowers, his paintings are windows which are open on the whole world."[6] This openness to the world of feeling and interpretation is an inherent quality of all profound artistic images.

5

Maurice Merleau-Ponty, as quoted in McGilchrist, Iain (2010). *The Master and His Emissary: The Divided Brain and the Making of the Western World*, 409. New Haven, CT: Yale University Press.

6

Sartre, Jean-Paul (1978). *What Is Literature?* 272. Gloucester, MA: Peter Smith.

Instead of analyzing and separating things, art is fundamentally engaged in merging and fusing opposites. Alvar Aalto, the Finnish master architect, for one, argued that only by means of uniting opposites, can an artistic work achieve meaningfulness. "Whatever our task . . . In every case [of creative work] opposites must be reconciled . . . Almost every formal assignment involves dozens, often hundreds, sometimes thousands of conflicting elements that can be forced into functional harmony only by an act of will. This harmony cannot be achieved by any other means than art."[7]

7

Aalto, Alvar. "Taide ja tekniikka" (Art and technology), lecture, Academy of Finland, October 3, 1955, cited in (1997). *Alvar Aalto in His Own Words* (ed. Göran Schildt), 174. Helsinki: Otava Publishing Company, Ltd.

The art form of architecture is logically an "impure," or "messy" category, as it contains and fuses ingredients from conflicting and even irreconcileable categories, such as materiality and feeling, construction and esthetics, physical facts and beliefs, knowledge and dreams, past and future, means and ends. In fact, it is hard to imagine a more complex and internally more conflicting human endeavor than architecture.

Such an array of unrelated and conflicting factors, aspects, requirements, and concerns can only be brought to a synthesis – or harmony, to use Aalto's notion – through a creative process based on deep mental identification, embodied metaphors and the fusion of doubt and certainty, emotion and judgment, intuition and feeling, belief and desire. The mediating and reconciliatory task of architecture is twofold; it fuses a multitude of dimensions into an experiential and structured entity, and it serves as an essential fusion of the world and the self. In this fusion we are encountering the miracle of the poetic image and imagination. Architectural projects and propositions are lived spatial metaphors which have their impacts largely on a pre-reflective and unconscious level. Sir Colin St John Wilson, the architect of the British Library, whose former house at Cambridge currently houses the Wittgenstein archive, describes this impact convincingly: "It is as if I am manipulated by some subliminal code, not to be translated into words, which acts directly on the nervous system and imagination, at the same time stirring intimations of meaning with vivid spatial experience as though they were one thing. It is my belief that the code acts so directly and vividly upon us because it is strangely familiar; it is in fact the first language we ever learned, long before words . . . now recalled to us through art, which alone holds the key to revive it."[8]

The utterly reductive spatial works of the American artist Fred Sandback exemplify the perceptual interplay of an extremely simple image and an unexpectedly complex and sensorially subtle experience. In their material essence his works are as minimal as artworks can possibly be, only a few thin lines stretched in space. They could be regarded as "minimalism," but the artist himself did not like the label and preferred to call his pieces "sculptures" or "constructions."[9] The notion of minimalism is altogether problematic, as usually the characterization is based on a purely formal understanding of the work, or a process of deliberate formal simplification as a stylistic preconception. Sandback defines his works as "simple facts" without any representational intentions.[10] Yet, the artist's statement of his conscious intention cannot void the perceptual and cognitive processes that his works set in motion in the observer's mind. Regardless of the artist's expressed view, his works automatically complete their *gestalt* in the viewer's mind, and seek their meanings. Frank Stella

8

Wilson, Colin St John (1979). Architecture – public good and private necessity. *RIBA Journal* (March).

9

Sandback, Fred (2005). Untitled. In: *Fred Sandback* (ed. Friedeman Malsch and Christiane Meyer-Stoll). Ostfildern-Ruit: Hatje Cantz Verlag.

10

"A sculpture made with just a few lines may seem very purist or geometric at first. My work isn't either of these things. My lines aren't distillations or refinements of anything. They are simple facts, issues of my activity that don't represent anything beyond themselves. My pieces are offered as concrete, literal situations and not as indications of any other sort of order," in ibid., p. 106.

famously described his intention: "What You See Is What You See,"[11] but in the phenomenon of art, what you experience is never what you actually see. A profound work opens up a wide field of images, meanings, associations, recollections, and intuitions. Every great work of art is an open excavation. In the light of current neurological studies, the process of "seeing" is far more complex than has been assumed; the process of perception always fuses observation, memory, and imagination and it is essentially a creative act.

11
Exhibition entitled: "What You See Is What You See," Frank Stella and the Anderson Collection at SFMOMA (San Francisco Museum of Modern Art), June 11–September 6, 2004.

The hidden complexity of Sandback's spatial configurations arises from our perceptual mechanism, the *gestalt* power of geometry, and the convention of reading spatiality in a drawing, as well as from the essential and unavoidable ambivalences and tensions between the material and imaginative realities in art. Besides, we constantly seek meaning, because the act of giving meaning is built into our system of perception itself. Sandback's nearly immaterial lines of acrylic yarn, tensioned in space, are essentially philosophical questions: why and how does a spatial image arise, and what is the reality of this mental unreality? Why does a thing exist rather than not?

Sandback's works are essentially spatial drawings; his lines make us see a specifically shaped figure of space, an imaginary volume set on the floor, leaning against a wall, or suspended in the air. The connected lines, arranged as planar configurations in a corner of a gallery, or suspended between the walls, ceiling, and/or floor, lose their linear nature as a drawing, as they become immaterial spaces with ideated materiality. The air inside the imaginative figure seems denser and of a slightly different consistency than the air outside the figure. The nonexistent plane even acquires an experiential color and weight. This artistic alchemy is particularly effective in the constructions of four lines that make us conceive a rectangular plane leaning against a wall or away from it. The imagined rectangle transforms into a sheet of glass-like transparent, but non-existent matter, and the construction seems paradoxically both to invoke an imaginary volume and to annul weight and gravity. The outward leaning "plane" seems to be in danger of falling over, whereas the "plane" leaning against the wall appears to bend due to its own weight. These experiences or perceptions are likely to be a result of our empathetic capacity brought about by our mirror neurons and systems; we feel the imaginary plane through our unconscious bodily mimesis, or embodied simulation, and our combined sense of balance and gravity. Similarly, we experience the weight and ideated movement of Richard Serra's pieces of steel through our

Fred Sandback, "Fred Sandback at the University of Helsinki," Helsinki, Finland, 2023. © Saara Mansikkamäki / Helsingin Sanomat

Fred Sandback, "Fred Sandback at the University of Helsinki", Helsinki, Finland, 2023.

muscles and bones, skin, and sense of balance. We re-enact what we see through the empathetic capacity of our body. Without being consciouss of it, we become the artistic work that we are looking at, listening to, or reading. "Be like me" is the demand of every poem to its reader, according to Joseph Brodsky,[12] and this unconscious identification applies to all art, including architecture.

12
Brodsky, Joseph (1997). An immodest proposal. In: *On Grief and Reason* (ed. Joseph Brodsky), 206. New York, NY: Farrar, Straus & Giroux.

Yet, visual tricks and illusions are mere perceptual demonstrations of the psychologist or the magic of an illusionist, whereas an artistic impact calls for a metaphoric and existential content. Profound artistic works are always about the world and the perceiver's own life situation and consciousness. A work of art makes us encounter a specific world, which is not symbolic, but real in its own right. What are the hidden metaphors of Sandback's constructions? Don't his works question the assumptions of naive realism, and don't they reveal to us the relativity and dialectical nature of our experience

Fred Sandback, "Fred Sandback at the University of Helsinki", Helsinki, Finland, 2023.
© Andrés Villaveces

of reality? We do not live in a given and objective world, but one of our own making, and this world and our self constitute an entity and continuum. "In a word, the [artistic] image is not a certain *meaning* . . . but an entire world reflected in a drop of water," as the great Russian film director Andrei Tarkovsky[13] suggests.

A work of art has a double existence: it takes place in its own reality of matter and execution, on the one hand, and in an imaginative world of perception, association, thought, and emotion, on the other. We do not usually see the silhoutte of a figure as an independent line because we perceive the physical object that it encloses, and we name that very object. The focusing on one aspect of our perceptual field tends to make us lose sight of the other aspects. We do not primarily experience the physical matter of sculpture either, as we perceive the volume and shape of the piece in its suggestive and imaginative reality. Similarly, in a building we do not experience the

13

Tarkovsky, Andrei (1986). *Sculpting in Time: Reflections on the Cinema*, 110. London: The Bodley Head.

Richard Serra, Dirk's Pod, Novartis-Campus, Basel, Switzerland, 2005. Michal Sikorski / Alamy Foto Stock https://www.alamy.it/la-scultura-gigante-dirks-pod-di-richard-serra-ha-dedicato-questa-scultura-al-fotografo-dirk-reinartz-novartis-campus-basilea-svizzera-dirks-pod-sc-image596683974.html?imageid=212E1C1B-B311-4610-A0D3-5FD667D5BCE8&p=266810&pn=1&searchId=05cff594265f2b61edd95f00ae0c759c&searchtype=0

meaningless physical space as we are affected by the architecturally articulated space possessing specific intentionalities and meanings. Art makes visible the invisible and gives meaning to the meaningless. A tension between these two realities is fundamental to the magic of art.

The ultimate ideal of all art (and an impossibility, we must admit) is to fuse the complexity of human experiences into a singular image, or "the oceanic feeling" of unity and oneness of the child in the mother's womb, as psychoanalytic thinking suggests. Rainer Maria Rilke writes touchingly about the ingredients of this poetic condensation: "[V]erses are not, as people imagine, simply feelings . . . they are experiences. For the sake of a single verse, one must see many cities, men and things, one must know the animals, one must feel how the birds fly and know the gesture with which the little flowers open in the morning."[14] The poet continues his list of experiences required for the writing of a single verse for the length of a full page. He lists roads leading to unknown regions, unexpected encounters and separations, childhood illnesses and withdrawals into the solitude of rooms, nights of love, screams of women in labor, and tending the dying. But even all of this together is not sufficient to create a line of verse. In the poet's view, one has to forget all of this and have patience to wait for the distilled return of these experiences. Only after all our life experiences have turned to our own blood within us, "not till then can it happen that in a most rare hour the first word of a verse arises in their midst and goes forth from them."[15] The poet's powerful description makes clear that a poem is not a formal invention; it is a poetically constructed world.

14 Rilke, Rainer Maria (1992). *The Notebooks of Malte Laurids Brigge*, 26. New York, NY: W.W. Norton & Company.

15 Ibid., p. 27.

In the mental and artistic realms, a special form of complexity in simplicity is the archetype. The concept originates in Sigmund Freud's idea of "archaic remnants" of the mind. Later, Carl Jung defined the archetype as a tendency of an image to evoke distinct associations, feelings, and meanings in our collective memory. Again, the openness and layered structure of the mental phenomenon are essential – a wealth of associations mediated by a collectively identifiable image, instead of a specific and closed meaning. In their desire to fuse the primordial mythical past and the lived actuality, works of art tend to approach the concept of the archetype, or these works touch upon a hidden imagery of premordial power.

Barnett Newman, the American Abstract Expressionist painter, entitled some of his paintings, consisting of a single linear element against the background of a single color, *Onements*. The painter condenses a multitude of existential experiences into an ultimately simple image. Kazimir Malevich's painting of a black square on white ground and Yves Klein's mono-chromatic paintings, as well as James Turrell's skyspaces, are similar *onements*, which fuse the multiplicity of experiences into a singular indivisible whole. There are no "elements" in these works, only their singularity. Do they represent simplicity or complexity?

These works derive their richness from their enigmatic nature; they are inexhaustible generators of questions and feelings. The experience of encountering a work of art is not simply a matter of looking at or hearing the work. The process is a complex interaction and exchange between the work and the embodied mind of the person experiencing it. Ingredients of one's individual memory as well as archetypal meanings and feelings enter the process; the encounter unveils layers of the work at the same time that the work unveils layers of the perceiving mind. In Lucio Fontana's famous slashed canvases, for instance, the violent act of gashing is certainly present as an unconscious mimetic experience; when looking at his works, I feel the threatening sharpness of the blade, and the "pain" of the canvas being slashed. Viewing an artwork is not unlike an archeological excavation in which both the depth of the work and the perceiving mind are being simultaneously excavated.

The difficulty of determining something as simple or complex in an artwork arises from the fact that any artistic image – a painting, a poem, a piece of music, or architectural space – exists simultaneously in two realms, first, as a material phenomenon in the physical world, and second, as a mental image in the unique individual experience. In the first sense, the *Black Square* of Malevich is just a simple geometric figure in black against a white background, executed by the painter's brush. However, the painted surface, crackled by time, gives the painting a sense of uniqueness and authenticity, reality, and age, beyond its geometric essence, as well as its iconic authority and aura. Old icon paintings possess a similar authority and radience. The work is in a dialogue with artistic works before its creation as well as with ones that have come after it. Its mental image is numerous things at the same time, which connect it to existential, philosophical, metaphysical, religious, and symbolic fields. The viewer's imagination and autonomous search for meaning set a never-ending process of association and interpretation in motion. It is the provocative indefinability and openness of the poetic suggestion that

give it its evocative richness, sense of life, and mental complexity. Simplicity turns into labyrinthian complexity. A profound artistic or architectural work is always a never-ending mental rhizom. Devoid of the enigmatic suggestiveness of the poetic image, a square remains a mere lifeless geometric figure without deeper meanings and the capacity to evoke emotions. Profound architectural simplicity condenses imagery and meaning similarly. The geometry of architectural constructions and spaces turns into spatial mandalas, devices that mediate between the cosmos, the world, and the self. Also in architecture, formal simplicity, devoid of poetic intention and richness of feeling, results in mere construction.

Barnett Newman, Voice of Fire, 1967. Youngjim / Wikimedia Commons / CC BY-SA 4.0 https://commons.wikimedia.org/wiki/File:Voice_Of_Fire,_National_Art_Gallery,_2015.jpg

The Wittgenstein House, which Ludwig Wittgenstein designed and built in Vienna in 1928, is an illuminating case regarding the necessary interaction of formal simplicity and complexity of context and content. Conceived by a major philosopher of the twentieth century, it is undoubtedly a product of serious and precise thinking, which has reduced all architectural elements into their minimum essence. The fact that Wittgenstein had the intermediate floor plate chiseled away and recast 3 centimeters higher convinces us of the author's uncompromising architectural ambition. However, the building

Ludwig Wittgenstein, Wittgenstein House, Vienna, Austria, 1926–1928. Aldo Ernstbrunner / Wikimedia Commons / CC BY-SA 3.0 AT https://upload.wikimedia.org/wikipedia/commons/7/7c/Wittgensteinhaus.jpg

➔ James Turrell, The Light Inside, MFAH, Houston, Texas, 1999.

remains curiously mute and lifeless. What seems to be missing in this ultra-rational piece of architecture is the mental complexity and contextual dialogue, sense of embodiment and poetic sensuality. "I am not interested in erecting a building, but in . . . presenting to myself the foundation of all possible buildings," Wittgenstein himself confessed.[16] It seems that exactly this rationalized generality makes the Wittgenstein House appear mute; it feels like a logical formula for a house rather than a specific and authentic building in the "flesh of the world," to use the suggestive notion of Maurice Merleau-Ponty.[17] The work hardly evokes associations, or feelings, it merely exists as itself and reflects its uncompromising system of proportions and structure.

Today's Minimalist architecture usually implies the application of a formal stylistic preconception, whereas meaningful artistic simplicity and abstraction are a result of a laborious and gradual process. The word "abstraction" suggests misleadingly a subtraction or reduction of contents and meaning, but a pregnant artistic abstraction, that has the capacity to touch our emotions and charge our imaginations, can only arise from the opposite process of distillation or compression. Constantin Brancusi, the master sculptor, gives us a significant piece of advice: "Simplicity is not an end in art, but one arrives at simplicity in spite of oneself, in approaching the real essence of things . . . simplicity is at bottom complexity and one must be nourished on its essence to understand its significance."[18] What does the artist mean by "in spite of himself"?; does he suggest that simplicity has its own gravity that pulls the artist to go for it regardless of his true nature?

A true abstraction condenses countless ingredients of the creative exploration into an artistic singularity. At the same time, the work takes a determined distance from the subjectivity of the author toward universality and anonymity. Balthus (Balthasar Klossowski de Rola), one of the greatest figurative painters of last century, makes a surprising and thought-provoking comment on artistic expression. "If a work only expresses the person who created it, it wasn't worth doing . . . Expressing the world, understanding it, that is what seems interesting to me."[19] Later, Balthus re-formulated his argument: "Great painting has to have a universal meaning. This is really no longer so today and this is why I want to give painting back its lost anonymity, because the more anonymous painting is, the more real it is."[20] This is a thought-provoking argument, but the same argument could surely be made of architecture. In its obsessive search for uniqueness, the architecture of our time has often become meaningless.

16
Ludwig Wittgenstein, Wikipedia. See en.wikipedia.org/wiki/Haus_Wittgenstein

17
Merleau-Ponty, Maurice (1969). The Intertwining-The Chiasm. In: *The Visible and the Invisible* (ed. Claude Lefort). Evanston, IL: Northwestern University Press. The writer describes the notion of the flesh in the following way: "My body is made of the same flesh as the world . . . and moreover . . . this flesh of my body is shared by the world" (ibid., p. 248), and "The flesh (of the world or my own) is . . . a texture that returns to itself and conforms to itself" (ibid., p. 146).

18
Constantin Brancusi in "1926 Brancusi Exhibition Catalog – Brummer Gallery, New York," republished in Shanes, Eric (1989). *Brancusi*. New York, NY: Abbeville Press.

19
Balthus, cited in Roy, Claude (1996). *Balthus*, 18. New York, NY: Little, Brown and Company.

20
Balthus (2001). *Balthus in His Own Words: A Conversation with Christina Carrillo de Albornos*, 6. New York, NY: Assouline.

All meaningful works of art are microcosms, miniaturized and condensed representations of a metaphoric and idealized world. This is an internal universe of the work itself, the *Weltinnenraum*, to use a beautiful notion of Rilke.[21] The poetic image keeps guiding our minds to constantly new contexts; clarity contains inviting obscurity, and formal simplicity turns into an experiential complexity. "What is there more mysterious than clarity?," Paul Valéry, the poet, asks.[22] William James, the visionary American psychologist, describes the essential fluidity and open-endedness of mental imagery: "Every definite image in the mind is steeped and dyed in the free water that flows around it. With it goes the sense of its relations, near and remote, the dying echo of whence it came to us, the dawning sense of whither it is to lead. The significance, the value of the image, is all in the halo or penumbra that surrounds and escorts it."[23] Clarity has value in art only when it projects a potent field of criss-crossing associations and impression. The simplest of poetic images, that arises from an authentic process of artistic distillation, keeps suggesting images and echoes, and endlessly seeking new meanings.

The associative imagery of art is existential rather than esthetic and it addresses our entire sense of being. Instead of offering mere visual pleasure, architecture, also, stirs up deep layers of the mind and sense of self, or more precisely, true architectural images evoke multi-sensory and embodied memories, making the architectural entity part of our bodily constitution and sense of existence. Through our body, we re-enact and mimic unconsciously whatever we encounter in the world; this is called "embodied simulation." As neurological studies have recently confirmed, every meaningful work of art and architecture actually changes our brain, behavior, and self-understanding.[24]

In addition to the sphere of the arts, the interaction of simplicity and complexity is especially impressive and inspiring in the natural and biological world. Here the constant interaction of simple principles and causalities creates a never-ending flow of subtle variations and complexities. The complexity of the biological world is normally underestimated as we tend to overvalue our own understanding and achievements. Edward O. Wilson, the world's leading myrmecologist and the spokesman of Biophilia, the science and ethics of life, makes the staggering argument, that the "superorganism" of a leafcutter ant community is "one of the evolution's master clockworks, tireless, repetitive and precise, and more complicated than any human invention and unimaginably old."[25] No wonder complicated traffic systems

21 Enwald, Liisa (1997). Lukijalle (To the Reader). In: *Hiljainen taiteen sisin: kirjeitä vuosilta 1900–1926* (The Silent Innermost Core of Art: Letters 1900–1926) (ed. Rainer Maria Rilke), 8. Helsinki: TAI-teos.

22 Valéry, Paul (1956). Eupalinos or the Architect. In: *Dialogues*, 107. New York, NY: Pantheon Books.

23 James, William (1983). *Principles of Psychology*. Cambridge, MA: Harvard University Press.

24 Fred Gage, as cited in Eberhard, John Paul (2015). Architecture and neuroscience: A double helix. In: *Mind in Architecture* (ed. Sarah Robinson and Juhani Pallasmaa), 135. Cambridge, MA: The MIT Press.

25 Wilson, Edward O. (1984). *Biophilia: The Human Bond with Other Species*, 37. Cambridge, MA: Harvard University Press.

are designed today using models of ant behavior, and new types of super-fast computers are being developed using our own neural network as the model. At the same time, Semir Zeki, a neurobiologist and professor of neuroaesthetics, who has applied the recent knowledge of the neurosciences to artistic phenomena, suggests "a theory of aesthetics that is biologically grounded."[26] What else could beauty be than nature's ultimate principle of bringing complexity into the stunning coherence of seemingly self-evidently simple beauty? Joseph Brodsky declares this view with the assurance of a great poet: "The purpose of evolution, believe it or not, is beauty."[27]

26 Zeki, Semir (1999). *Inner Vision: An Exploration of Art and the Brain*, 1. Oxford: Oxford University Press.

27 Brodsky, op. cit., p. 208.

I wish to end my chapter on the interplay of simplicity and complexity in the arts with Constantin Brancusi's powerful and poetic statement on the fundamental requirement of a true artistic work: "Art must give suddenly, all at once, the shock of life, the sensation of breathing."[28]

28 Brancusi, as cited in Shanes, op. cit., p. 67.

BIBLIOGRAPHY

Bachelard, Gaston (1968). *The Philosophy of No: Essay on a Philosophy of the New Scientific Spirit.* New York, NY: The Orion Press.

Bachelard, Gaston (1969). *The Poetics of Space.* Boston, MA: Beacon Press.

Bachelard, Gaston (1982). *Water and Dreams: An Essay on the Imagination of Matter.* Dallas, TX: The Pegasus Foundation.

Bachelard, Gaston (1984). *The Flame of a Candle.* Dallas, TX: The Dallas Institute Publications.

Balthus (2001). *Balthus in His Own Words: A Conversation with Christina Carrillo de Albornos.* New York, NY: Assouline.

Böhme, Gernot (2017). *Critique of Aesthetic Capitalism.* Milan: Mimesis International.

Borges, Jorge Luis (2000). *This Craft of Verse.* Cambridge, MA: Harvard University Press.

Brodsky, Joseph (1997a). *Watermark.* London: Penguin Books.

Brodsky, Joseph (1997b). *On Grief and Reason.* New York, NY: Farrar, Straus & Giroux.

Brodsky, Joseph (1998). *Less than One.* New York, NY: Farrar, Straus & Giroux.

Buñuel, Luis (1984). *My Last Sigh.* New York, NY: Random House Inc.

Calvino, Italo (1981). *If on a Winter's Night a Traveler.* New York, NY: Harcourt Brace & Company.

Calvino, Italo (1988). *Six Memos for the Next Millennium.* New York, NY: Vintage Books.

Carriére, Jean-Claude (2000). Answering the sphinx. In: *Conversations about the End of Time* (ed. Catherine David, Frédéric Lenoir, and Jean-Philippe de Tonnac). London: Penguin Books.

Casey, Edward S. (ed.) (2000). *Remembering: A Phenomenological Study.* Bloomington, IN, Indiana University Press.

Cavarra, Britton Karla (2010). *Constructing the Ineffable.* New Haven, CT: Yale University Press.

Celant, Germano (1988). *Unexpressionism–Art beyond the Contemporary.* New York, NY: Rizzoli International Publications.

Curtis, William J. (1986). *Le Corbusier: Ideas and Forms.* London: Phaidon.

Dal Co, Francesco (1995). *Tadao Ando: Complete Works.* London: Phaidon.

Darwin, Charles (1859). *On the Origin of Species: A Facsimile of the First Edition.* Cambridge, MA: Harvard University Press.

Eight Meditations on Architecture, First Edition. Juhani Pallasmaa. Edited by Matteo Zambelli.

Darwin, Charles and Ghiselin, Michael T. (1874). *The Descent of Man and Selection in Relation to Sex.* New York, NY: Prometheus Books.

David, Catherine, Lenoir, Frédéric, and de Tonnac, Jean-Philippe (ed.) (2000). *Conversations about the End of Time.* London: Penguin Books.

de Anda Alanis, Enrique X. (1989). *Luis Barragán: Classic of Silence.* Bogota: Collection Somosur.

de Waal, Frans (2010). *The Age of Empathy: Nature's Lessons for a Kinder Society.* New York, NY: Broadway Books.

Dewey, John (1980). *Art as Experience.* New York, NY: The Berkley Publishing Company.

di Giovanni, Norman Thomas, Halpern, Daniel, and MacShane, Frank (ed.) (1994). *Borges on Writing.* Hopewell, NJ: The Ecco Press.

Dirac, Paul (1963). The Evolution of the Physicist's Picture of Nature. *Scientific American* 208.

Dirac, Paul (2019). *La bellezza come metodo. Saggi e riflessioni su fisica e matematica* (Beauty as method. Essays and reflections on physics and mathematics). Milan: Raffaello Cortina Editore.

Eberhard, John Paul (2015). *Mind in Architecture* (ed. Sarah Robinson and Juhani Pallasmaa). Cambridge, MA: The MIT Press.

Edinger, Edward F. (1992). *Ego and Archetype.* Boston, MA: Shambhala.

Ehrenzweig, Anton (1975). *The Psycho-Analysis of Artistic Vision and Hearing: An Introduction to a Theory of Unconscious Perception.* London: Sheldon Press.

Eliot, T. S. (1932). Tradition and Individual Talent. In: *Selected Essays 1917–1932.* New York, NY: Harcourt, Brace & Company.

Eliot, T. S. (1934). Choruses from The Rock. In: *The Rock.* New York, NY: Harcourt, Brace & Co.

Eliot, T. S. (1944). *What Is a Classic?* London: Faber and Faber. Available at: http://bracchiumforte.com/PDFs/tseliot.pdf

Eliot, T. S. (1964). *Selected Essays.* New York, NY: Harcourt, Brace & World.

Eliot, T. S. (1988). *Four Quartets.* London: Harcourt Brace Jovanovich, Publishers.

Frampton, Kenneth (2002). *Labour, Work and Architecture: Collective Essays on Architecture and Design.* London: Phaidon Press.

Fromm, Erich (1968). *The Revolution of Hope: Toward a Humanized Technology.* New York, NY: Harper & Row.

Gardner, Howard (1999). *Intelligence Reframed: Multiple Intelligences for the 21st Century.* New York, NY: Basic Books.

Genet, Jean (1987). *Giacomettin ateljeessa* (In Giacometti's Atelier). Helsinki: Kustannusosakeyhtiö Taide.

Giedion, Sigfried (1952). *Space, Time and Architecture: The Growth of a New Tradition.* Cambridge, MA: Harvard University Press.

Harries, Karsten (1982). Building and the terror of time. *Perspecta: The Yale Architectural Journal* 19: 59–69.

Harries, Karsten (1998). *The Ethical Function of Architecture.* Cambridge, MA: MIT Press.

Harvey, David (1992). *The Condition of Postmodernity.* Oxford: Blackwell.

Hawking, Stephen (2013). *My Brief History*. New York, NY: Penguin Random House.

Hertzberger, Herman, van Roijen-Wortmann, Addie, and Strauven, Francis (ed.) (1982). *Aldo van Eyck*. Amsterdam: Stichting Wonen.

Hrabal, Bohumil (1990). *Too Loud a Solitude*. London: Harcourt, Inc.

Huyghe, René (1955). *Dialogue with the Visible: Understanding Painting*. Paris: Flammarion.

Iliescu, Sanda, Eight Aesthetic Propositions, unpublished manuscript, 2006.

James, William (1983). *Principles of Psychology*. Cambridge, MA: Harvard University Press.

Jameson, Fredric (1991). *Postmodernism, or the Cultural Logic of Late Capitalism*. Durham, NC: Duke University Press.

Johnson, Mark (2007). *The Meaning of the Body: Aesthetics of Human Understanding*. Chicago: University of Chicago Press.

Juni'chirō, Tanizaki (1977). *In Praise of Shadows*. New Haven, CT: Leete's Island Books.

Kahn, Louis (1991). *Louis I.Kahn Writings, Lectures, Interviews* (ed. Alessandra Latour). New York, NY: Rizzoli International Publications.

Kundera, Milan (1966). *Slowness*. New York, NY: HarperCollins.

Kundera, Milan (2005). *The Art of the Novel*. London: Faber and Faber.

Laine, Jarkko (1982). *"Tikusta Asiaa"* (Starting a Conversation). Helsinki: Parnasso.

Levin, David Michael (1993). *Modernity and the Hegemony of Vision*. Berkeley, CA: University of California Press.

Lightman, Alan (1993). *Einstein's Dreams*. New York, NY: Pantheon Books.

Malsch, Friedeman and Meyer-Stoll, Christiane (ed.) (2005). *Fred Sandback*. Ostfildern-Ruit: Hatje Cantz Verlag.

Marcuse, Herbert (1964). *One-Dimensional Man: Studies on the Ideology of Advanced Industrial Society*. Boston, MA: Beacon Press.

Marx, Karl and Engels, Frederick (1888). *The Communist Manifesto*. London: William Reeves. Available at: https://www.marxists.org/archive/marx/works/download/pdf/Manifesto.pdf

Mason, Lawrence, Scott, Poole, Sarpaneva, Pia, and Carpenter, James (ed.) (2005). *James Carpenter*. Blacksburg, VA: Architecture Edition.

Mayne, Thomas and Pran, Peter (ed.) (2006). *Ligang Qiu*. Beijing, China: DUT Press.

McCarter, Robert (1991). *Frank Lloyd Wright: A Primer on Architectural Principles*. New York, NY: Princeton Architectural Press.

McGilchrist, Iain (2009). *The Master and His Emissary: The Divided Brain and the Making of the Western World*. New Haven, CT: Yale University Press.

Merleau-Ponty, Maurice (1962). *Phenomenology of Perception*. London: Routledge and Kegan Paul.

Merleau-Ponty, Maurice (1964). *Signs*. Evanston, IL: Northwestern University Press.

Merleau-Ponty, Maurice (1969). *The Visible and the Invisible* (ed. Claude Lefort). Evanston, IL: Northwestern University Press.

Merleau-Ponty, Maurice (1992). *Sense and Non-Sense.* Evanston, IL: Northwestern University Press.

Nussbaum, Martha (1995). *Poetic Justice: The Literary Imagination and Public Life.* Boston, MA: Beacon Press.

Olofsson, Anders (1986). Nostalghia. In: *Tanken på en hemkomst* (ed. Magnus Bergh and Birgitta Munkhammar). Stockholm: Alfa Beta Bokförlag.

Ortega y Gasset, José (1968). *The Dehumanization of Art and Other Essays on Art, Culture, and Literature.* Princeton, NJ: Princeton University Press.

Overbye, Dennis, "Remembrance of Things Future: The Mystery of Time." *New York Times,* June 28, 2005.

Pallasmaa, Juhani (ed.) (1995). *Animal Architecture.* Helsinki: Museum of Finnish Architecture.

Perec, Georges (2008). *Species of Spaces and Other Pieces.* London: Penguin Classics.

Picard, Max (1988). *The World of Silence.* Washington, DC: Gateway Editions.

Pirzig, Robert M., "An Author and Father Looks Ahead at the Past", *The New York Times Book Review,* March 4, 1984.

Plummer, Henry (1987). *Poetics of Light.* Tokyo: A+U, Extra Edition.

Pound, Ezra (1987). *ABC of Reading.* New York, NY: New Directions Publishing Corporation.

Proust, Marcel (1992). *In Search of Lost Time: Swann's Way.* Trans. C.K. Scott Moncrieff and Terence Kilmartin. London: Random House.

Prum, Richard O. (2018). *The Evolution of Beauty: How Darwin's Forgotten Theory of Mate Choise Shapes the Animal World – and Us.* New York, NY: Anchor Books.

Rasmussen, Steen Eiler (1993). *Experiencing Architecture.* Cambridge, MA: MIT Press.

Rentschler, Ingo, Herzberger, Barbara, and Epstein, David (1988). *Beauty and the Brain: Biological Aspects of Aesthetics.* Berlin: Birkhäuser Verlag.

Rilke, Rainer Maria (1992). *The Notebooks of Malte Laurids Brigge.* Trans. M.O. Herter Norton. New York, NY: W.W. Norton & Co.

Rilke, Rainer Maria (1997). *Hiljainen Taiteen Sisin: kirjeitä Vuosilta 1900–1926* (The Silent and Intimate Core of Art: Letters 1900–1926) (ed. Liisa Envald). Helsinki: Tai-teos.

Rispa, Paul (ed.) (1995). *Barragán: The Complete Works.* London: Thames and Hudson.

Roy, Claude (1996). *Balthus.* New York, NY: Little Brown and Company.

Rushdie, Salman, "Is Nothing Sacred?" (1990). Available at: https://granta.com/is-nothing-sacred (accessed May 2024).

Ruskin, John (1980). *The Lamp of Beauty: Writings on Art.* Ithaca, NY: Cornell University Press.

Saint, Augustine (2012). *The Confessions* (ed. David Vincent Meconi). San Francisco: Ignatius Press. Available at: https://ia600202.us.archive.org/28/items/confessionsofsta00augu/confessionsofsta00augu.pdf

de Saint Exupéry, Antoine (1991). *Wind, Sand and Stars.* London: Penguin Books.

de Saint Exupéry, Antoine (2019). *The Little Prince.* Glasgow: Farshore.

Sartre, Jean-Paul (1978). *What Is Literature?* Gloucester, MA: Peter Smith.

Sartre, Jean-Paul (1993). *The Emotions: An Outline of a Theory.* New York, NY: Carol Publishing Co.

Sartre, Jean-Paul (2001). What Is Literature? In: *Basic Writings* (ed. Stephen Priest). London: Routledge.
Scarry, Elaine (1999). *On Beauty and Being Just.* Princeton, NJ: Princeton University Press.
Schildt, Göran (ed.) (1985). *Sketches: Alvar Aalto.* Cambridge, MA: The MIT Press.
Schildt, Göran (ed.) (1997). *Alvar Aalto in His Own Words.* Helsinki: Otava Publishing Company.
Seamon, David (ed.) (1993). *Dwelling, Seeing and Designing: Toward a Phenomenological Ecology.* Albany, NY: State University of New York Press.
Shanes, Eric (1989). *Constantin Brancusi.* New York, NY: Abbeville Press.
Sontag, Susan (1986). *On Photography: Reality and Image in our Society.* Harmondsworth: Penguin Books.
Stevens, Wallace (1990). *The Collected Poems.* New York, NY: Vintage Books.
St John Wilson, Sir Colin (1979). Architecture – public good and private necessity. *RIBA Journal* (March).
Stokes, Adrian (1978). *The Critical Writings of Adrian Stokes.* London: Thames & Hudson.
Stravinsky, Igor (1947). *Poetics of Music: In the Form of Six Lessons.* Cambridge, MA: Harvard University Press.
Svendsen, Lars (2012). *A Philosophy of Boredom.* London: Reaktion Books.
Tarkovsky, Andrei (1986). *Sculpting in Time.* Austin, TX: University of Texas Press.
Turrell, James (2000). *The Thingness of Light* (ed. Scott Poole). Blacksburg, VA: Architecture Edition.
Valéry, Paul (1956). *Dialogues.* New York, NY: Pantheon Books.
Valéry, Paul (1932). *Eupalinos or the Architect.* Oxford: Oxford University Press.
Valjakka, Timo (ed.) (1995). *Juhana Blomstedt: muodon arvo* (Juhana Blomstedt: the value of form). Helsinki: Painatuskeskus.
Vidler, Anthony (1999). *The Architectural Uncanny.* Cambridge, MA: MIT Press.
Virilio, Paul (1994). *Katoamisen Estetiikka* (The Esthetics of Disappearance). Tampere: Gaudeamus.
Wilson, Edward O. (1984). *Biophilia: The Human Bond with Other Species.* Cambridge, MA: Harvard University Press.
Wittgenstein, Ludwig (1922). *Tractatus Logico-Philosophicus.* London: Kegan Paul, Trench, Trubner & Co.
Wittkower, Rudolf (1988). *Architectural Principles in the Age of Humanism.* London: St. Martin's Press.
Wogenscky, André (2006). *Le Corbusier's Hands.* Cambridge, MA: MIT Press.
Wohlleben, Peter (2016). *The Hidden Life of Trees: What They Feel, How They Communicate – Discoveries from A Secret World.* Vancouver: Greystone Books.
Wright, Frank Lloyd (1954). *The Natural House.* New York, NY: Horizon Press.
Wright, Frank Lloyd (1960). *Frank Lloyd Wright: Writings and Buildings* (ed. Edgar Kaufman and Ben Raeburn). New York, NY: Horizon Press.

Wurman, Richard Saul (1986). *What Will Be Has Always Been: The Words of Louis I. Kahn.* New York, NY: Rizzoli International Publications, Inc.

Zajonc, Arthur (1993). *Catching the Light: The Entwined History of Light and Mind.* Oxford: Oxford University Press.

Zeki, Semir (1999). *Inner Vision: An Exploration of Art and the Brain.* Oxford: Oxford University Press.

Zumthor, Peter (2006). *Atmosphere: Architectural Environments Surrounding Objects.* Basel: Birkhäuser.

INDEX

A

Aalto, Alvar, 18, 30, 58, 70, 72, 95, 104, 122, 130, 131
aesthetic capitalism, 1
The Age of Empathy (de Waal), 11
Aldo van Eyck, 9, 89
Ando, Tadao, 18, 118, 122
archaic remnants, 138
archetype, 138
architectural amnesia, 72–73
architectural light, 16, 18
architecture
  art of, 96
  biological time in, 52
  of desolation, 38
  ethical dimension, 1
  as evolutionary process, 84–86
  experiencing, 122–123
  holiness of settings, 123, 125
  intelligence and, 7–8
  and memory, 56–57
  mental task of, 99–100
  need and, 3
  newness, tradition, and, 75–90
  one-dimensional reality, 125, 128
  qualities of, 106
  sacredness and, 101, 104
  simplicity, 129–144
  space of time, 35–52
  spirituality in, 99–128
  sublime experience, 104–106
  task of, 89–90
  time perspective in, 55–56
  tradition and radicality, 78–79, 84
  voices of objects, 118
Arnaud, Noël, 59, 99
art
  as cultural deviation, 3
  ethical dimension, 1
  history of, 9
  and novelty, 50–51
  objective of, 8
  as self-expression, 8
  as symbol, 49
  tenses of, 73–74
Art as Experience (Dewey), 7
artistic image, inner structure of, 129–144
artistic newness, 77
artistic quality, 1
artistic sacredness, 101, 104
Atmosphere: Architectural Environments Surrounding Objects (Zumthor), 6

B

Bachelard, Gaston, 16, 45, 47, 50, 56, 59, 72, 113, 129
Basic Writings (Sartre), 111
beauty
  art and, 8
  and atmosphere, 6
  biological perspective, 9–10
  empathy, and integrity, 10–11
  and ethics, 1–3
  ethics of limits, 3–4
  and goodness, 119
  holistic essence of, 5–7
  intelligence and experience, 7–8
  obsession with newness, 2
  quality in mathematics, 4
  quality in sciences, 4

Eight Meditations on Architecture, First Edition. Juhani Pallasmaa. Edited by Matteo Zambelli.

beauty (*continued*)
role of, 2
in science, 4–5
and timelessness, 2
and truth, 4
Bell, Daniel, 37
Biophilia: The Human Bond with Other Species (Wilson), 10, 145
Böhme, Gernot, 1
Borges, Jorge Luis, 2, 44, 71, 74
Brancusi, Constantin, 79, 101, 144, 146
Brodsky, Joseph, 4, 6, 10, 47, 57, 73, 92, 96, 105, 134

C
Calvino, Italo, 38, 77
capitalism, 1
Casey, Edward S., 70
Catching the Light: The Entwined History of Light and Mind (Zajonc), 113
Celant, Germano, 76
Coop Himmelb(l)au, 38, 71
The Craft of Verse (Borges), 2
Critique of Aesthetic Capitalism (Böhme), 1
cultural identity, 75, 76, 84
culture, 87–88

D
Darwin, Charles, 10
de Saint-Exupéry, Antoine, 7, 57
de Waal, Frans, 11
The Dehumanization of Art and Other Essays on Art, Culture and Literature (Ortega), 2
The Descent of Man, and Selection in Relation to Sex (Darwin), 10
Dewey, John, 7
Dirac, Paul A.M., 4

E
Ehrenzweig, Anton, 44
Einsteins Dreams (Lightman), 35
Eliot, T. S., 66, 85–86
emotions, 6, 10, 50, 70, 97
The Emotions: An Outline of a Theory (Sartre), 106
Enwald, Liisa, 145
esthetics
ethics and, 3
meaning of, 4
role of, 9
of speed, 38
The Ethical Function of Architecture (Harries), 1, 3
ethics
and beauty, 1–3
of limits, 3–4
Eugenio d'Ors, 85
The Evolution of Beauty (Prum), 10
Experiencing Architecture (Rasmussen), 13

F
The Flame of a Candle (Bachelard), 16
Fromm, Eric, 4, 93

G
Gardner, Howard, 7, 92
Genet, Jean, 51, 85
Giedion, Sigfried, 36

H
Harries, Karsten, 1, 2, 44, 56, 93, 100
Hawking, Stephen, 36

I
identity, 84–86
If on a Winter's Night a Traveler (Calvino), 39
Iliescu, Sanda, 41
In Praise of Shadows (Tanizaki), 30–32
Indian Chief Seattle, 97
Inner Vision: An Exploration of Art and the Brain (Zeki), 10
innovation, 86–87
Intelligence Reframed (Gardner), 7

J
James, William, 145
Johnson, Mark, 6, 97
Jung, Carl, 138

K
Kahn, Louis, 18, 76, 104
Keats, John, 7
Kundera, Milan, 71, 88

L
Laine, Jarkko, 59
Le Corbusier, 16, 106

Leonardo da Vinci, 3
light
  alienating, 27
  architectural, 16, 18
  black, 23, 26–27
  and color, 23
  experiencing space, 13–14
  liquified, 18
  multi-sensory touch, 14
  and place, 14–15
  sacredness and, 119, 122
  and shadow, 15–16
  thingness of, 32–33
Lightman, Alan, 35
The Little Prince (de Saint-Exupéry), 7

M
Marcuse, Herbert, 125
Marx, Karl, 71
The Master and His Emissary: The Divided Brain and the Making of the Western World (McGilchrist), 5
McGilchrist, Iain, 5
Memorizing: A Phenomenological Study (Casey), 70
memory
  and architecture, 56–57
  embodied, 69–70
  and emotion, 70–71
  slowness and, 71–72
  spatiality and situationality of, 58–59, 66
Merleau-Ponty, Maurice, 6, 8, 14, 96, 106, 130, 144
minimalism, 131
Minkowski, Hermann, 36
modern space-time, 36–37

N
Newman, Barnett, 138
newness, ecstasy of, 76–78
The Notebooks of Malte Laurids Brigge (Rilke), 57
Nussbaum, Martha, 4

O
On Beauty and Being Just (Scarry), 4
On Photography (Sontag), 59
On the Origin of Species (Darwin), 10
On Writing (Borges), 51, 74
One-Dimensional Man (Marcuse), 125
Ortega y Gasset, José, 2

P
A Philosophy of Boredom (Svendsen), 2, 77
The Philosophy of No: A Philosophy of the New Scientific Mind (Bachelard), 50, 129
Picard, Max, 56
Poetic Justice (Nussbaum), 4
The Poetics of Space (Bachelard), 13, 56, 59, 70
Pound, Ezra, 79
Pritzker Architecture Prize, 75
Proust, Marcel, 37–41, 69
Prum, Richard O., 10
The Psychoanalysis of Artistic Vision and Hearing: An Introduction to a Theory of Unconscious Perception (Ehrenzweig), 44

R
Rasmussen, Steen Eiler, 13
Reed, Carol, 13
Rilke, Rainer Maria, 57–58, 138
Rushdie, Salman, 122
Ruskin, John, 45

S
Sandback, Fred, 131, 132, 134
Sartre, Jean-Paul, 106, 111, 130
Scarry, Elaine, 4
Sculpting in Time (Tarkovsky), 1, 8, 118, 135
In Search of Lost Time (Proust), 37, 38, 69
Shu, Wang, 75–76
Six Memos for the Next Millennium (Calvino), 77
Slowness (Kundera), 88
solutions, 95
Sontag, Susan, 59
Space, Time and Architecture (Giedion), 36
Stella, Frank, 119, 131
Stevens, Wallace, 18, 59
Stokes, Adrian, 47, 49
Svendsen, Lars, 2, 40, 77

T
Tanizaki, Junichirô, 30
Tardieu, Jean, 71
Tarkovsky, Andrei, 7–8, 26, 47, 118, 135

time
collapse of, 37–40
museums of, 40–41
perfection and imperfection, 44–45
reversed, 51–52
in science and fiction, 35–36
space and, 36–37
symbol and reality, 49–50
time-free perception, 44
water and, 47, 49
tradition, 75–90
Turrell, James, 6, 23, 32, 113, 139

U

The Universe in a Nutshell (Hawking), 36

V

Valéry, Paul, 15, 41, 43, 90, 96, 145

W

Water and Dreams (Bachelard), 45, 72, 99, 113, 123
Watermark (Brodsky), 4
Weyl, Hermann, 4
What Is Literature? (Sartre), 111, 130
Wilson, Colin St John, 123, 131
Wilson, Edward O., 10, 145
wisdom and modesty, 92–98
Wittgenstein, Ludwig, 84, 106, 141, 144
Wittkower, Rudolf, 100
The World of Silence (Picard), 40, 56
Wright, Frank Lloyd, 11, 30, 49

Z

Zajonc, Arthur, 113
Zeki, Semir, 10, 146
Zumthor, Peter, 6, 18

eight meditations on architecture

eight meditations on architecture

ALBERTO CAMPO BAEZA

Edited by MATTEO ZAMBELLI

Alberto Campo Baeza Essays, translated from Spanish by Penelope Eades

WILEY

CONTENTS

1 **BEAUTY** / Relentlessly Seeking Beauty 157

2 **LIGHT** / Architectura Sine Luce Nulla Architectura Est 179

3 **TIME** / The Suspension of Time 200

4 **MEMORY** / Aula Ingenti Memoriae 211

5 **UNIVERSALITY** / On Surrender and Universality 226

6 **WISDOM** / On the Wisdom of the Architect 234

7 **ON DIVINE PROPORTION** 245

8 **ESSENTIALITY** / More with Less 250

Bibliography **257**

Afterword / Western Light
Paolo Zermani **261**

Index **269**

BEAUTY 1

Relentlessly Seeking Beauty

Quid est ergo pulchrum? Et quid est pulchritudo?

—Saint Augustine[1]

Do we perchance love anything but the beautiful? What then is the beautiful? And what is beauty? What is it that allures and unites us to the things we love; for unless there were a grace and beauty in them, they could not possibly attract us to them?

—Saint Augustine[2]

1 Augustine, Saint (2012). *The Confessions* (ed. David Vincent Meconi). Book 4, Chapter XIII, 4. San Francisco, CA: Ignatius Press. Available at: https://ia600202.us.archive.org/28/items/confessionsofsta00augu/confessionsofsta00augu.pdf (accessed September 2025)

2 Ibid.

PURPOSE

After many years working as an architect, teaching as a university professor and putting my ideas on paper, the reason why I pursue my work, I must confess, what I truly seek with all my heart and with all my soul, relentlessly, is beauty.

Can an architect confess this so overtly? Can any creator state outright that what he is seeking is beauty? That is what poets and musicians and painters and sculptors, all artists, do.

But I am convinced that by achieving beauty in architecture with this "art with necessary reason," as the classics used to say, we succeed in making a happier place for mankind.

Beauty, *Venustas*, together with *Utilitas* and *Firmitas*, are the three principles whose fulfillment Vitruvius demanded from Architecture. Achieving *Venustas*, having previously fulfilled the requirements of *Utilitas* and *Firmitas*, is the best way of making people happier, which is the aim not only of Architecture but also of all creative work. Sáenz de Oíza explained it better than I can in "The Dream of Paradise" when he said: "I declare that the works of Architecture are

Eight Meditations on Architecture, First Edition. Alberto Campo Baeza. Edited by Matteo Zambelli.

instruments for transforming reality into a splendid and regained Paradise from which through our own fault we were expelled and which we have again been readmitted to thanks to the powers of transformation of Architecture."[3] *Venustas*, beauty, as a means to regaining Paradise lost, happiness.

Similarly, Carvajal spoke of "orderly beauty" and his "desire to create efficiency and beauty at the same time such as only true architects seek to do." "The beauty that we contemplate, being ours, we can use to engender beauty, operatively, in our works. Thus beauty becomes a driving force and not just a consequence."[4]

Over the past number of years I have written about many of the masters of Spanish contemporary architecture and, in attempting to summarize all that seemed to me most substantial in them, I developed a collection of texts under the heading of beauty. Bald beauty for Sota, volcanic beauty for Oíza, chiseled beauty for Carvajal, rebellious beauty for Fisac, and beauty itself for Barragán. It was my understanding then that beauty was the cause and the aim of the creative work of the masters. And now, with the passage of time, I see it with ever greater clarity. Beauty!

REASON: CERVANTES, GOYA, GOETHE

Beauty in architecture goes hand in hand with reason. I have defended and still defend reason as the architect's primary and principal instrument to attain beauty. Although this may be true for all the arts, it is imperative for architecture.

Cervantes

Those who have read *Don Quixote* do not usually pause at those exceptional pages in which Cervantes prefaces his universal work. And Cervantes himself confesses that he wrote the prologue later. He also confesses that it is the piece of writing to which he devoted most time. Thus he wrote: "Loving reader: thou wilt believe me, I trust, without an oath, when I tell thee it was my earnest desire that *this offspring of my brain*[5] should be as beautiful, ingenious, and sprightly as it is possible to imagine."[6] So, having made it clear that reason was his principal work tool, he declares his unshakeable desire to capture beauty with it.

When I wrote that architecture is a built idea,[7] I was merely making the claim that architecture, and any creative work, must

3
Francisco Javier Sáenz de Oíza refers to the Robie House, Fallingwater, Taliesin West, the Johnson Wax Headquarters, the Guggenheim in New York, and Frank Lloyd Wright's Mile High Skyscraper in Illinois. Francisco Javier Sáenz de Oíza, "El sueño del Paraíso," *A&V*, 31 August 1995. Available at: https://arquitecturaviva.com/articulos/el-sueno-del-paraiso (accessed March 2025).

4
Unidentified bibliographic reference [Editor's note].

5
Italics by Alberto Campo Baeza [Editor's note].

6
de Cervantes, Miguel (n.d.). *Adventures of Don Quixote de la Mancha*, 3. New York, NY: Thomas Y. Crowll & Co., no. 13 Astor Palace. Available at: https://upload.wikimedia.org/wikipedia/commons/2/2b/Adventures_of_Don_Quixote_de_la_Mancha_%28IA_cu31924027657075%29.pdf (accessed September 2025).

7
Alberto Campo Baeza refers to his collection of essays entitled (2015). *The Built Idea*. Beijing, China: Oscar Riera Ojeda Publishers.

be the product of thought, of reason, and of understanding, as we read in Cervantes.

And when that reason is missing, then bizarre architectures appear which, being so often "against nature," produce the amazement and the adoration of this ignorant society of ours that bows before these works as if they were the temples of a new religion.

Goya

"The sleep of Reason Produces Monsters," Goya tells us in the marvelous aquatint that presides over the office of the President of the Royal Academy of Fine Arts of San Fernando. It is number 43 of the 80 etchings that make up the series of Los Caprichos, published by Goya in 1799. Goya also wrote a lesser-known text, in the form of a list of comments, the original of which is conserved in the Archive of the Prado Museum. In that text, commenting on etching 43, Goya writes: "Fantasy abandoned by reason produces impossible monsters," but goes on to say that "united with her, she is the mother of the arts and the origin of their marvels." In other words, reason needs imagination to open the doors to beauty. How could we not agree with Goya!

God forbid that I should wish to compare myself with Cervantes or Goya, but it is with this spirit that I have wished and still wish to build all my works: trying to conquer beauty with all my soul, with the weapons of reason and of imagination. With "Le dur désir de durer" (the dour desire to endure) as the primary impulse of creation, as Paul Éluard[8] tells us. With the intention of remaining in the memory of humankind. Or as Federico García Lorca said with such simple and lovely words: "I write to be loved."

Goethe

And it would seem that Goethe agreed with Cervantes and Goya in defending reason as the best pathway to beauty when, referring to the painters of his time, he said that "they must dip their brushes into the bottle of reason." Of course, he then adds: "and architects into Winckelmann."[9] Tired of the unreasonable digressions being produced around him, Goethe, with these emphatic words, strongly advocated the recovery of reason.

8

There are two books that have the phrase "Le dur désir de durer" in their titles: Éluard, Paul and Chagall, Marc (1950). *Le dur désir de durer*. Paris: Bordas, and Paul Éluard and Man Ray (1960). *Le dur désir de durer. Le temps déborde*. Paris: Seghers.

9

Unidentified bibliographic reference [Editor's note].

REASON: PLATO AND SAINT AUGUSTINE

Reason as man's primary tool in achieving beauty. But what is beauty?

In *The Banquet,* Plato proposed beauty as *splendor veri,* the splendor of truth.[10] Over the centuries, further nuances were added to this proposal by other thinkers who, carrying on from Plato, fine-tuned his words with the most interesting of accents. Jacques Maritain sums it up very well: "*Splendor veri,* said the Platonists; *splendor ordinis,* said Saint Augustine, adding that 'unity is the form of all beauty'; *splendor formae,* said Saint Thomas."[11] However, coursing through the veins of all these formulas is an irrepressible ambition to discover deeper explanations. If truth must be at the heart of all architectural creation that aspires to beauty, how could we consider order and form to be less important? Truth and order and form. "Form, as we well know, is not something superimposed; it is generated by the very material that reveals itself in it,"[12] as José Angel Valente so wisely wrote when honoring Chillida. How could we as architects not subscribe to form as the "material that reveals itself in it" in achieving beauty?

And I cannot resist mentioning here Saint Augustine's considerations in identifying beauty with the Supreme Maker: "Too late did I love Thee, O Fairness, so ancient, and yet so new! Too late did I love Thee! For behold, Thou wert within, and I without, and there did I seek Thee; I, unlovely, rushed heedlessly among the thing of beauty Thou madest. Thou wert with me, but I was not with Thee. Those things kept me far from Thee, which, unless they were in Thee, were not. Thous calledst, and criedst aloud, and forcedst open my deafness. Thou didst gleam and shine, and chase away my blindness. Thou didst exhale odours, and I drew in breath and do pant after Thee. I tasted, and do hunger and thirst. Thou didst touch me, and I burned for The peace."[13]

INVESTIGATION, PRECISION, AND TRANSCENDENCE

Let us not, however, go off on intricate philosophical or theological tangents but return to the route that leads to beauty via architecture.

And, indeed, the motto on the shield of the AA Architectural Association in London says: "Design with Beauty, Build in Truth," which is an accurate summary of what we are discussing right now.

←
Francisco Goya, El sueño de la razón produce monstruos (The Sleep of Reason Produces Monsters), 1799. incamerastock / Alamy Stock Photo https://www.alamy.com/francisco-goya-the-sleep-of-reason-produces-monsters-etching-1799-image247856198.html?imageid=F8DDF09D-1581-47C0-B640-A5FEF09559B6&p=16392&pn=1&searchId=a803592b5e58b900562e8d5024220ab7&searchtype=0

10
Plato never wrote the sentence "Beauty is the *splendor veri* (splendor of truth)". As Jacques Maritan said, it is generally attributed to platonist [Editor's note].

11
Maritain, Jacques (1974). *Art and Scholasticism with Other Essays*, 20. London: Sheed and Ward. Available at: https://archive.org/details/bmshri.artscholasticism0000jacq_r3h6/page/20/mode/2up?q=splendor+veri (accessed September 2025).

12
Valente, José Angel (1999). Chillida o la transparencia. In: *Chillida 1957–1997*, Exhibition Catalogue, 1. Editorial Fibulas, Galería Antonio Machón, November–December.

13
Saint Augustine, *The Confessions*, cit., p. 16.

On the occasion of his Doctorate Honoris Causa conferral by the University of Oporto, I was asked to write a text on Álvaro Siza in which I enlarged on what I consider to be his three principal qualities as an architect – as a factor of beauty more than anything else – being the three characteristics that I consider as inherent in all architecture that participates in that longed-for beauty: an investigative nature, poetic precision, and the capacity to transcend.

Investigative Nature

One reaches beauty in architecture in the wake of rigorous, profound work that can and must be considered a true work of research. Beauty is something profound, precise, and concrete that rocks the very foundations of human civilization, which makes time stand still, and ensures that the created work remains durable in time and in the memory of man. For beauty in architecture is not something superficial, vague, or diffuse, but the work of real research.

Not one of my projects has ever been just "another one." In each and every one of them, I have given my all. Each new project has been and is for me an opportunity to seek and find beauty. Each and every one of them has been conceived and designed and built with maximum intensity. With the intense conviction that architecture is the most beautiful work in the world.

I have said "no" many times to many projects in which I wasn't given enough freedom or which I considered were not interesting enough to devote my time to them. Some may call this pedantic. But I believe this is the only way that one can create, that one can live creating, living with the intensity that makes this life worthwhile. All creators understand this very well: poets and writers, musicians, and painters and sculptors worth their salt.

When Xavier Zubiri was awarded the National Research Prize in 1982, in his acceptance speech he thanked the Spanish people for being capable of understanding that philosophy is a true labor of research. On many occasions I have recommended to my students that they replace the word philosophy with the term architecture in that illuminating text and they will discover that the result is surprisingly close. Because architecture is a true labor of research. And as Zubiri himself advised in his address, quoting Saint Augustine: "Seek as those seek who still have not found, and find as those find who are still seeking."[14]

14 Saint Augustine. *On the Trinity*, Book IX, Chapter 1, In what way we must inquire concerning the Trinity. Available at: https://www.monergism.com/thethreshold/sdg/augustine/On%20The%20Trinity%20-%20Augustine.pdf (accessed July 2025).

Poetic Precision

And the beauty we are talking about comes to architecture hand in hand with precision – that same precision with which poetry is chiseled. When I defend the poetic nature that all architecture in search of beauty must have, I am not defending something vague and diffuse. I am looking for the precision required in poetry to achieve beauty, which is the same precision that I look for in architecture.

María Zambrano defined poetry as "the word in harmony with the number."[15] What better way to define the precision inherent in poetry? A word, which in one position says nothing special, when placed in the right place is capable of moving us and making time stand still right there. The same is true, with the same precision, in architecture. Because if poetry is words conjugated with precision, capable of moving the hearts of men, so too is architecture with its materials.

15 Unidentified bibliographic reference [Editor's note].

Capacity to Transcend

Beauty in architecture appears when it is capable of transcending us. Architecture that achieves beauty is an architecture that transcends us. The true creator, the true architect, is the one whose work transcends him. Stefan Zweig explains this so well in "The Secret of Artistic Creation": "There is no greater delight or satisfaction than recognizing that man too can create imperishable values and that eternally we remain united to the Eternal through our supreme effort on earth: through art."[16] Zweig, like Saint Augustine, links beauty with the Supreme Being.

Moreover, that beauty that transcends us is not something unachievable or simply reserved for a few geniuses. I always try to convince my students that to achieve beauty is a possibility. It is possible to achieve works that are caressed by the "sound of a gentle breeze"[17] with which the Divine Presence was confirmed in the sacred scriptures and which in architectural creation is the sign that beauty is present.

In The First Book of the Kings (19:11–12) we read: "Then he [Elias] was told, 'Go out and stand on the mountain before Yahweh'. Then Yahweh himself went by. There came a mighty wind, so strong it tore the mountains and shattered the rocks before Yahweh. But Yahweh was not in the wind. After the wind came an earthquake. But Yahweh was not in the earthquake. After the earthquake came a fire. But Yahweh was not in the fire. And after the fire there came the sound of a gentle breeze." And there in that gentle breeze was the Lord.[18]

16 "The Secret of Artistic Creation" (Das Geheimnis des künstlerischen Schaffens) is the title of a lecture given by Stefan Zweig in Buenos Aires in 1938 and later collected in a book entitled *Tiempo y mundo. Impresiones y ensayos 1904–1940* (Time and the World. Impressions and Essays 1904–1940).

17 *The Jerusalem Bible*, The First Book of the Kings, 19:12, 447. New York, NY: Doubleday & Company, Inc., 1966. Available at: https://archive.org/details/thejerusalembible1966/page/n5/mode/2up (accessed September 2025).

18 Ibid., The First Book of the Kings, 19:11–12, pp. 446–447.

So it is that same gentle breeze, the *sibilus aurae tenuis* as Saint Jerome writes in the *Vulgate*, that we architects yearn for our works of architecture, and what all creators long for. It is a clear sign that there is beauty in our works when they are worthwhile.

UTILITAS, FIRMITAS, VENUSTAS

How could architects not understand that the truth of the idea generated by the fulfillment of function and construction is essential if we are to achieve beauty in architecture? As Vitruvius famously stated: reaching *Venustas* demanded the prior and exact fulfillment of *Utilitas* and *Firmitas*.

Utilitas

"When it is said that Architecture must be functional, it stops being functional because it only attends to one of the many functions it has," Oíza wisely stated.[19]

19 Alberto Campo Baeza heard the phrase spoken directly by Oíza [Editor's note].

Osip Mandel'štam, at the beginning of his superb "Conversation on Dante," says, referring to poetry: "Where a work can be measured by the yardstick of narration, the sheets have not been used, that is to say, (if I may be allowed the expression) Poetry has not spent the night there."[20] So, in this very pedagogical way, Mandelstam explains the crux of the question in artistic creation. The narrative elements must never be central, nor should they be in architecture. The *Utilitas* demanded by Vitruvius as a primary condition, the function, must be fulfilled and well accomplished. But architecture is something more, much more, than merely the perfect fulfillment of function. Function in architecture is the narrative.

20 Mandel'štam, Osip (2003). Discorso su Dante (Conversation on Dante). In: Osip Mandel'štam, *Sulla poesia* (On Poetry), 121. Milan: Bompiani.

When Bernini reveals the white marble of the ever-so-beautiful Proserpina kidnapped by Neptune, above and beyond the description of the scene and beyond the loveliness of the sculpture, the essence of what he is doing here is demonstrating his capacity to make the hard Carrara marble appear soft, tender. He manages to dominate the material, to bend and tame it; something so much more universal than simply representing a scene. The strong hand of Neptune grips Proserpina's delicate thigh and this is what is most interesting about this sculpture, how he manages to make what is hard appear soft. Once again the creator is conveying a universal theme that goes far beyond the mere narration of a story, something more than just a sculpture. In each and every one of his architectures Bernini seeks and finds something more than the mere perfect fulfillment of a function or the mere perfect construction. He seeks and finds beauty.

Gian Lorenzo Bernini, The Rape of Proserpina, 1622.

Pantheon, Rome, Italy, 112–124 CE. Architas / Wikimedia Commons / CC BY-SA 4.0 https://upload.wikimedia.org/wikipedia/commons/d/dc/Pantheon_%28Rome%29_-_Dome.jpg

Firmitas

And if in order to achieve beauty in architecture the timely fulfillment of function, *Utilitas*, is important, no less important is its good construction, *Firmitas*.

Viollet-le-Duc in his *Entretiens sur l'architecture* defended the construction, *Firmitas*, as the fundamental basis of architecture. He called for the judicious and adequate expression of materials in order to attain beauty in architecture. Beauty emanated from a well-conceived and well-constructed structure. "Any form that does not adapt to the structure must be repudiated."[21] It is the structure which, as I have repeated so many times, in addition to bearing the load and transmitting it to the ground, establishes the order of space; that establishment of the order of space, which is a central theme in architecture.

Venustas

And, finally, of course, after the precise fulfillment of *Utilitas* and *Firmitas*, as prescribed by Vitruvius, necessarily comes *Venustas*, beauty.

THE PANTHEON, THE ALHAMBRA, THE BARCELONA PAVILION

Let us now take a look at some buildings that in the history of architecture have clearly materialized the ineffable beauty that we are discussing here.

Few buildings in history have the quality of making us lose the notion of time like the Pantheon in Rome. Not only does it fulfill its universal function to perfection, not only is it extremely well constructed, but it is also of undeniable beauty. All the great creators have acknowledged that on visiting it. Suffice it to quote Henry James describing the memorable scene of Count Valerio kneeling inside the Pantheon illuminated from above by the light of the moon.[22] The scene is quite beautiful. In that marvelous story, *The Last of the Valerii*, the Count states: "This is the best place in Rome… It's worth fifty St Peters'."[23]

The Pantheon in Rome is an extraordinary container of beauty, of total beauty. If we stand with our backs against the wall inside the Pantheon, we feel that the space still fits inside our visual angle and therefore, inside our heads. Its 43 m in diameter make possible the

21 "Toute forme qui n'est pas indiquée par la structure doit être repoussée," in Eugène Viollet-Le-Duc (1863). *Entretiens sur l'architecture*, 305. Paris: A. Morel et Co. Available at: https://http://books.google.it/books?id=DtoDAAAAYAAJ&printsec=frontcover#v=snippet&q=Toute%20forme%20qui%20ne&f=false (accessed September 2025).

22 The scene to which Alberto Campo Baeza refers is described in James, Henry (1923). *The Last of the Valerii*, 26. London: Macmillan and Co. Available at: https://archive.org/details/in.ernet.dli.2015.179522/page/n11/mode/2up (accessed September 2025)

23 Ibid., p. 27.

Alberto Campo Baeza, Andalucia's Museum of Memory, Granada, Spain, 2005–2010. © Javier Callejas, Courtesy of Estudio Alberto Campo Baeza

Alberto Campo Baeza, International Book Fair (FIL), Guadalajara, Mexico, 2017. © César Béjar, Courtesy of Estudio Alberto Campo Baeza

miracle that is the result of the application of precise measurements by Agrippa's architect, Apollodorus of Damascus, to whom it is attributed. The same dimensions were wisely used by Pedro Machuca in the courtyard of the Palace of Charles V in the Alhambra many years later. And the very same dimensions I myself, having discovered the secret, used in the white elliptical patio of my Granada museum.[24]

In terms of *Utilitas*, the Roman temple is universal, so universal that it still remains a space for the future. There is no other architecture in Rome so future-oriented.

And in terms of *Firmitas*, it is so firm, so well constructed that it always emerged unscathed from the onslaughts it suffered. After its construction by Agrippa, it suffered such a great fire that Hadrian had to reconstruct it. And even Domitian and Trajan were involved in it. And nothing happened, as Douglas Adams said of buildings destroyed and built again: "It is always the same building."[25] And indeed the Pantheon, its beauty, is an idea, a built idea, precise in its dimensions and in its proportions and in its light. An enduring and eternal beauty. It is always the same building.

And if we were to speak of the light in the Pantheon, we might never finish. Suffice a reference to Chillida embracing the column of light that entered through the oculus, who described the sensation: "The illuminated air was lighter than the rest of the room."[26] Perhaps what he felt, what he touched, was the breath of that "gentle breeze."[27]

Another paragon of Beauty is yet another architecture that was constructed, destroyed, and reconstructed so many times while still remaining "always the same building": the Alhambra in Granada. Built by Yusuf I, reconstructed by Mohamed V, and restored by Leopoldo Torres Balbás in the last century. What could I at this stage add to what has been said about the Alhambra? We have to go back to the lyrical passages that those vizier-poets of the emirs of Granada recorded on its walls. Ibn Zamrak puts the words into the mouth of the Alhambra itself, in the decoration of the fountain in Daraxa's garden, such lovely words as these: "And he has granted me the highest degree of beauty, so that my shape causes the admiration of the sages" and without the least hesitation he continues: "for never have any eyes seen a greater thing than myself, neither in the East nor in the West and in no time has any king, neither abroad nor in Arabia." And we would never finish if we were to continue with the beautiful inscriptions of the Alhambra. Beauty speaking about beauty itself.

24 Alberto Campo Baeza refers to the Museum of the Memory of Andalusia, completed in 2010. Link to the project: https://www.campobaeza.com/andalucias-museum-memory (accessed March 2025).

25 Adams, Douglas and Carwardine, Mark (1990). *Last Chance to See*, 148–149. London: Pan Books.

26 Unidentified bibliographic reference [Editor's note].

27 *The Jerusalem Bible*, op. cit. The First Book of the Kings, 19:12, p. 447.

Then there are the words dedicated by Barragán: "Having made my way through a narrow and dark tunnel of the Alhambra, I was delivered to the serene, still, solitary and delightful courtyard of the myrtles of this ancient palace. It contained what a well-crafted garden ought to contain: nothing less than the entire universe. I have never forgotten that memorable experience and it is not by chance that from the first garden I did in 1941, all those that have followed humbly attempt to echo the immense lesson of the wisdom of the Alhambra of Granada."[28]

28 Unidentified bibliographic reference [Editor's note].

Of course, if we are to discuss contemporary architectures full of beauty, capable of resisting time, physical destruction, and their reconstruction, then we must speak of the Barcelona Pavilion of Mies van der Rohe, which appears to have been built only yesterday. Or tomorrow.

The Barcelona Pavilion is not only a synthesis of the principal conceptual achievements of modern architecture, but, in addition, a prodigy of beauty. A simple podium in Roman travertine, at just the right height to transport us into another world. A light slab for a roof, perfectly tensed, and supported by cruciform pillars – like dancers *en pointe* – which, on account of their form and brilliance seem to vanish. Exquisite walls of extraordinary onyx that serve as an epigraph to time with abstract signs moving with the freedom that the continuous space affords. And all with the precise measurements and proportions: nothing over here, nothing over there, and the miracle takes place. Architecture that has conquered beauty forever.

These three examples of architecture are capable of resisting time and reconstruction while always remaining "the same building." Not only that, in all of them, time stands still. In all of them, past, present, and future are there, suspended: time suspended for beauty to emerge. In all of them, we observe what Michael Bockemül expressed so well when referring to Rembrandt: "He converts the conceptual understanding of the canvas into its visual perception."[29] These three works of architecture convert so well their conceptual understanding into visual perception.

29 Bockemühl, Michael (2005). *Rembrandt*, 11. Cologne: Taschen.

The three architectures cited here corroborate to what extent architecture is a built idea whose beauty remains forever, it is indestructible.

MIES VAN DER ROHE, LE CORBUSIER, WRIGHT

But I could not end this discourse without mentioning, albeit very briefly, the words of some of the great masters of contemporary

architecture, Mies van der Rohe, Le Corbusier, and Frank Lloyd Wright, who, of course, constantly alluded to beauty as the ultimate goal of architecture.

Mies

Mies van der Rohe spoke prolifically about beauty. In a well-known text of his entitled, "Beautiful and Practical Buildings! Stop This Cold Functionality," he tells us: "What appears totally evident to me is that with our changed requirements and with the new means made available by technology we will arrive at a new type of beauty. That we will ever again befriend 'beauty per se', however, I find unlikely."[30] And emulating Plato and Saint Augustine, he repeats: "Beauty is the radiance of truth!"[31]

And he goes on to ask: "And what finally is beauty? Certainly nothing that can be calculated or measured. It is always something imponderable, something that lies in between things. Beauty in architecture, just as necessary and just as desirable as in formers times, can only be attained if in building we have more than the immediate purpose in mind."[32] How could we not agree with him?

Le Corbusier

And Le Corbusier was not to be outdone in his defense of beauty: "The architect, by his arrangement of forms, realizes an order which is a pure creation of his spirit. Through forms and shapes, he affects our sense to an intense degree and provokes plastic emotions. Through the relationships which he creates he wakes in us profound echoes, he gives us the measure of an order which we feel to be in accordance with that of our world, he determines the various movements of our heart and our understanding. And it is then that we experience the sense of beauty."[33]

Frank Lloyd Wright

And of Frank Lloyd Wright so many things could be said concerning beauty. But let us here just echo the sentences of the "Opening Message" of the book *Architecture: Man in Possession of His Earth*.[34] In it he tells us: "Science may produce a civilization but not a culture. Man's life under science alone stays sterile ... But man's great gift lies in his vision. Owing to over-reliance on science, too seldom is this vision turned inward toward the beauty of himself: man's own spiritual-haven. When vision does come into his being and as the mind of

30
Mies van der Rohe, Ludwig (1930). Beautiful and Practical Buildings! Stop This Cold Functionality. In: Pizzigoni, Vittorio and Sabatino, Michelangelo (ed.) (2024). *Mies in His Own Words. Complete Writings, Speeches, and Interviews 1922–1969*, 86. Berlin: DOM publishers.

31
Ibid. [In the Italian version of Mies van der Rohe' essay, "radiance" is translated into "splendore" (splendor in English). Editor's note].

32
Ibid., p. 87.

33
Le Corbusier (1986). *Towards a New Architecture*, 1. New York: Dover Publications. Available at: https://monoskop.org/images/b/bf/Corbusier_Le_Towards_a_New_Architecture_no_OCR.pdf (accessed September 2025).

34
Wright, Frank Lloyd and Wright, Iovanna Lloyd (1962). *Architecture: Man in Possession of His Earth*. Garden City, NY, Doubleday & Company, Inc.

➔
Mies van der Rohe, Barcelona Pavilion, Barcelona, Spain, 1929 (rebuilt 1983–1986). Alexander Hüls / Flickr / CC BY-SA 2.0 https://www.flickr.com/photos/lexlog/38325193134

man takes hold of his destiny, beauty becomes a vital experience of great consequence to him."[35] And he goes on to say: "Man seems to be dependent upon inspiration from a higher source. Neither by heredity nor by instinct does man succeed in the life-beautiful."[36] And he continues: "Not until the spirit of man becomes conscious of *need* fot the benison of beauty *in his way of being* in order to sustain his soul and uplift his spirit as well as comfort and protect his body, does man himself seem to share the instinct for beauty with subordinate orders and forms of life. So man's building is largely the mere craft of the carpenter with his square. By using his multifarious sciences man is furnished and circumscribed until he awakens to the vision of the intrinsic truth of form. Then beauty comes to his rescue and we have architecture – the mother-art of humankind. As a consequence, we also see sculpture, painting and music."[37] And he finishes with the very explicit statement: "As man-the savage-emerges from the natural cave to build one of his own, origins of the history of architecture are lost in perspective. As he civilized himself, he adorned these artificial caves as he set them upon the ground out under the sun. Soon after carne buildings from the mind of man himself. He created space in which to live; not only protected from the elements but protected from his fellow man as well. But that was not enough to live content, now civilized, he meant to make these cave-buildings beautiful. Then was architecture born."[38]

35 Ibid., p. 11.

36 Ibid., p. 10.

37 Ibid., pp. 10–11 [Italics in original, Editor's note].

38 Ibid., p. 11.

MELNIKOV, BARRAGÁN, SHAKESPEARE

However, following this incursion into the idea of beauty in Mies, Le Corbusier, and Wright, for very personal reasons, I cannot leave out three other figures: two architects and a poet.

Melnikov

Konstantin Melnikov is the Russian architect and contemporary of those masters who best defines that beauty that some of us architects strive for: a bare, radical, essential beauty: "Having become my own boss, I begged architecture in turn to take off her marble dress, remove her make-up and reveal herself as she is, naked, like a young and graceful goddess; and, as corresponds to true beauty, renounce being agreeable and obliging."[39]

39 Unidentified bibliographic reference [Editor's note].

Barragán

And for similar reasons, once again I turn to the words of Barragán. The universal Mexican maestro expresses himself clearly in relation to beauty in his Pritzker acceptance speech in 1982:

"Mr. Jay Pritzker stated in an announcement to the press with excessive generosity what I consider essential to that ideology: that I had been chosen as the recipient of this prize for having devoted myself to architecture 'as a sublime act of poetic imagination.' Consequently, I am only a symbol for all those who have been touched by Beauty. It is alarming that publications devoted to architecture have banished from their pages the words Beauty, Inspiration, Magic, Spellbound, Enchantment, as well as the concepts of Serenity, Silence, Intimacy, and Amazement. All these have nestled in my soul, and though I am fully aware that I have not done them complete justice in my work, they have never ceased to be my guiding lights."[40]

40 Barragán's acceptance speech is available at: https://www.pritzkerprize.com/sites/default/files/file_fields/field_files_inline/1980_Acceptance_Speech.pdf (accessed September 2025).

Shakespeare

I have searched the poets for explicit references to beauty. And I have returned once again to Shakespeare, using a well-known bilingual edition. And when I found that the word beauty did not appear, as in that prestigious edition in Spanish only "beautiful" or "lovely" figured, I returned to the original English and there is hardly a sonnet in which the word beauty does not appear, that the traitorous translator did not dare to translate as beauty. Are they so afraid of the term beauty? How could Shakespeare not speak of beauty? He starts his first sonnet with "That thereby Beauty's rose might never die."[41] And he starts his sonnet 54, with "O how much more doth Beauty beauteous seem."[42] The term Beauty literally invades Shakespeare's texts with its weapons. No wonder. Just as all of us would like beauty to invade our works.

41 Shakespeare, William (1974). Sonnet 1. In: Shakespeare, William, *Sonnets*. Available at: https://folger-main-site-assets.s3.amazonaws.com/uploads/2022/11/shakespeares-sonnets_PDF_FolgerShakespeare.pdf (accessed September 2025).

42 Ibid., Sonnet 54.

HUNGER FOR BEAUTY

After all these observations, one ought to consider if beauty is or is not necessary, if it is or is not useful. Nuccio Ordine, in his brilliant essay on *The Usefulness of the Useless*,[43] defends the need for useless beauty. Of course, we could defend the contrary: that beauty is useful to satisfy the hunger pangs of the soul, the hunger for beauty that is in everyone. Of course, beauty is useful, indispensable. Man hungers for beauty. *Venustas*, compatible and complementary to the usefulness of function and good construction, is what really interests us.

Einstein summed it up rather well: "The ideals which have lighted me on my way and time after time given me new courage to face life cheerfully, have been Truth, Goodness and Beauty."[44]

43 Ordine, Nuccio (2017). *The Usefulness of the Useless*. Philadelphia, PA: Paul Dry Books.

44 Einstein, Albert (1941). *The World as I See It*, 2. London: John Lane, the Bodley Head. Available at: https://ia801500.us.archive.org/21/items/in.ernet.dli.2015.127962/2015.127962.The-World-As-I-See-It.pdf (accessed September 2025).

BEAUTY, FREEDOM, MEMORY

Is not memory the deep and inexhaustible well for recognizing where beauty appears? How could someone devoid of memory recognize the fact that something, especially architecture, is part of beauty?

How could an architect be blown away by a Mies van der Rohe if he had not previously known of Palladio, or the Pantheon in Rome, or the Greek temples?

How could a painter admire Rothko without having adored Velázquez and Goya?

Today, fully immersed as we are in the third millennium, we are in no doubt about the depth of beauty in the paintings of Rothko or in the architecture of Mies van der Rohe. It is clear that the concept of beauty has not only opened its doors, but with the guiding hand of understanding, it will always remain open.

And evidently all this is largely true of architecture. Nonetheless, it may be as difficult for society to understand Rothko well as to really understand Mies van der Rohe. One of the merits of the masters of modern architecture has been managing to convince society that beauty was to be found in their works, that they were the bearers of beauty. Le Corbusier, Mies van der Rohe, and Frank Lloyd Wright knew this very well and tried to do so and almost succeeded.

In short, to capture beauty in architecture, and to be able to demonstrate it as such to society – beauty!

FINALE

In my architecture I have pursued beauty vigorously. I have sought beauty with tireless dedication. I have chased after beauty desperately. I have searched and still search and will continue to search for beauty unto death or until I kill her. To kill her with love when I find her because I have put my heart and soul into the endeavor.

The search for beauty always involves the search for freedom. Seeking in architecture the freedom arising from the radicalism of reason, in accordance with the desirable dream, always leads to truth resulting in beauty. The English poet Keats said it perfectly in the well-known lines of his "Ode on a Grecian Urn": "Beauty is truth, truth beauty, – that is all / Ye know on earth, and all ye need to know."[45]

45 John Keats, "Ode on a Grecian Urn." Available at: www.poetryfoundation.org/poems/44477 (accessed September 2025).

LIGHT 2

Architectura Sine Luce Nulla Architectura Est

ON THE MATERIAL NATURE OF LIGHT: ON LIGHT AS MATTER AND MATERIAL

"God said, 'Let there be light', and there was light. God saw that light was good, and God divided light from darkness. God called light 'day', and darkness he called 'night'. Evening came and morning came: the first day."[1]

1 *The Jerusalem Bible*, Genesis 1:1–5, 15. New York, NY: Doubleday & Company, Inc., 1966. Available at: https://archive.org/details/thejerusalembible1966/page/n5/mode/2up (accessed September 2025).

When an architect finally discovers that light is the central theme of architecture, it is then that he or she begins to understand and starts to become a real architect.

Light is not some vague or diffuse thing to be taken for granted just because it is always there. The sun does not rise for everyone, every single day, for nothing.

Yes, although we may no longer subscribe to corpuscular theory, light is nonetheless something specific, precise, continuous, material. It is the most measurable and quantifiable matter, something physicists are well aware of, but the fact seems to pass many architects by.

Light, like gravity, is unavoidable. And it is fortunate that this is so, since the history of architecture is defined by these two primeval realities: light and gravity. Architects should always carry with them a compass to measure the direction and angle of light and a photometer to measure the quantity of light, just as they carry a tape measure, a spirit level, and a plumb line.

If the struggle to master gravity continues to be a dialogue, from which the material construction of architecture is born, it is with the addition of the search for light, and the corresponding discourse, that this dialoueg reaches the most sublime levels. It is then that one discovers the essential truth that only light and light alone can

Eight Meditations on Architecture, First Edition. Alberto Campo Baeza. Edited by Matteo Zambelli.

➔
Pantheon, Rome, Italy, 112–124 CE.
shohei/Adobe Stock
https://www.flickr.com/photos/atibordee/13995519705

➔
Pierre Chareau, Maison de Verre, Paris, France 1928–1931.
BM / Flickr
https://www.flickr.com/photos/147316538@N02/35469790606/in/photostream/

truly overcome and conquer gravity. So, when the architect manages to trap sunlight, thus penetrating the space formed by structures of greater or lesser mass which need to be rooted to the ground to transmit the primitive strength of gravity, it is that very light that breaks the spell, making the space float, levitate, and soar. The Hagia Sophia, the Pantheon, and Ronchamp are tangible proofs of this wondrous reality – of the triumph of light over gravity.

Light has as much material substance in architecture as stone. We tend to think and write that builders in the Gothic period accomplished veritable marvels with stone, making architecture work to its utmost to attain more light. Strictly speaking, we should be saying that what Gothic architects did was to work with light as matter, as another material. Since they knew that the sun shines diagonally, they stretched their windows, raising them up to trap those diagonal, nearly vertical, rays. They foresaw the possibilities available to us today. Rather than organizing stone to trap light, Gothic architecture can be seen as a desire to organize light, material light, in order to create spatial tension.

We know that matter cannot be created or destroyed, it can only be transformed. That is why, instead of the term "modern materials," it would be more accurate to say "materials used in a modern sense." In this way, we can include centuries of thought which we can then enjoy sifting through. As always, when all is said and done, it's just a simple question of reasoning and thought. Thus was stone, plain old stone, transformed into the most modern of materials in the hands of Mies van der Rohe. Steel and sheet glass were not born out of nothing. These two materials, which have revolutionized architecture, have always been there, latent. Today, the conception of new ideas enables them to produce spatial miracles.

Might we not then think that the secret lies in a profound understanding of light as matter, as a material, as a modern material? Could it be that the moment in the history of architecture has arrived, that tremendously exciting moment when we finally confront light? *"Let there be light!" And there was light.* The first material created, the most eternal and universal of materials is thus identified as the central material with which we can build and create space. Space in its most modern sense. So the architect once again recognizes himself as a creator, as a master of the world of light.

"The radiance and glow of the stone, themselves shining only by grace of the sun, first bring the light of day, the expanse of the sky, and the darkness of night, to appear in relief. The secure towering-up of the temple makes visible the invisible space of air."[2]

2 Martin Heidegger, "The Origin of the Work of Art," 26. Available at: https://www.academia.edu/2083177/The_Origin_of_the_Work_of_Art_by_Martin_Heidegger?auto=download (accessed March 2025).

SINE LUCE NULLA!

On Light as the Central Theme of Architecture

When I propose the axiom *"Architectura sine luce nulla architectura est,"* I mean that no architecture is possible without light. For without light, an indispensable material would be missing.

If I were asked to give three prescriptions for the destruction of architecture, I would suggest: (1) covering over the central opening in the Pantheon dome, (2) walling up the glass block façade of La Maison de Verre, and (3) closing the openings which illuminate the priory of La Tourette.

If, so as to protect the Pantheon from the elements, the new mayor of Rome decided to cover over its crowning oculus of nearly 9 meters in diameter, a lot of things might or might not happen. Its skillful construction would not change, nor would its perfect composition; its universal function would not cease to exist; nor would its context, ancient Rome, notice (at least not on the first night). All that would happen is that the most wonderful snare that man has ever laid for the sun, to which that heavenly king joyously returned day after day, would be eliminated. The sun would burst into tears and so would architecture (because, after all, they are rather more than just friends).

If Doctor Dalsace's grandson had walled up the façade of La Maison de Verre for security reasons, a lot of things might happen. Or they might not. Its construction would remain untouched. Its composition would remain intact. With good electric lighting, it would continue to function without a problem. The immediate environment, the city of Paris, wouldn't know anything about it, even after the first night, given La Maison de Verre's private, not easily accessible location. All that would happen is that a most wonderful container of clear, diffuse light would be destroyed, a container that achieved its splendor thanks to the subtle and wonderful mechanism of the glass block, which surreptitiously allows light to pass through, transforming it into pure glory. Darkness would fall on the house, and architecture would be plunged into utter despondency.

If a new Dominican monk at La Tourette, zealously seeking a way to improve concentration levels, were to cover up the cracks and holes in the monastery chapel, many things would happen, or stop happening. Its robust construction would not change. Its composition

➔
Isidore of Miletus and Anthemius of Tralles, Hagia Sophia Grand Mosque, Istanbul, Turkey, 537.
Wolfgang Guelcker / MISSION MEDIA LLC / CC-BY 3.0
https://www.catalystplanet.com/travel-and-social-action-stories/hagia-sophia-istanbuls-oldest-church-building

➔
Mies van der Rohe, Tugendhat House, Brno, Czech Republic, 1928–1930.
Timothy Brown / Flickr / CC BY 2.0
https://www.flickr.com/photos/atelier_flir/3049514881

➔
Le Corbusier, Chapelle Notre-Dame du Haut, Ronchamp, France, 1950–1955.
Jean-Pierre Dalbéra / Flickr / CC BY 2.0
https://www.flickr.com/photos/dalbera/28945962492/in/photostream/

would remain untouched. Its sublime functions would continue, although they might become more "concentrated" in the candle-light. No one in the surrounding area would know, or it would at least take a long time for word to get out. Only the alarming stillness of the roosting pigeons would eventually alert the local country folk to the sacrilege that had been perpetrated there. The overly concentrated space would have darkened and the monks would find to their amazement that the luminous Gregorian chant was sticking in their throats. The monastery, and the architecture along with it, would have entered into a long, dark night.

Covering over the central opening in the Pantheon dome, walling up the Maison de Verre glass block façade, and filling the openings in La Tourette Chapel would signify an end to architecture, and history too. And the sun would refuse to come out again. Whatever for? The fact is that architecture without light is nothing; it is less than nothing.

"Spring is coming. I want to see the light!"[3] – and he sent his daughter-in-law Otilia to open the windows before closing his eyes forever – are Goethe's last words before his death.

3 According to the testimony of the disciple Johann Peter Eckermann, who was present at the time of Goethe's death on 22 March 1832. In the Wikipedia entry "Last words" - https://it.wikiquote.org/wiki/Ultime_parole (accessed March 2025) - it is reported that Goethe's last words would have been "Open the other shutter too, to let in a little more light" (*Macht doch den zweiten Fensterladen auch auf, damit mehr Licht hereinkomme*). However, over the years the version that has become more widespread is "'More light!"' (*Mehr Licht!*), cited in Purdy, Daniel (2011). *Goethe Yearbook 18*, vol. 18, 107. Rochester, NY: Camden House, Inc. According to Giuseppe Fumagalli, this is an example of how "translation takes pleasure in embellishing the phrases of great men," in Fumagalli, Giuseppe (1921). *Chi l'ha detto?* (Who Said That?), 285, 294, Milan: Hoepli.

LIGHT TABLES

On how Light Is Quantifiable and Qualifiable

Gian Lorenzo, a magician of light if ever there was one, drew up his own tables to measure light accurately, which were very similar to those now used to calculate structures, Meticulous and precise. The master knew that, like all matter, light can be measured and classified; it can be scientifically controlled.

What a pity that on Bernini's return from a tiring and fruitless trip to Paris in an attempt to build the Louvre, his young, absent-minded son Paolo lost his tables. On 20 October 1665, Bernini was quite relieved to be leaving the city of light, which had treated him so badly, but discovered to his horror that he did not have his tables, which were more valuable to him than the Law itself. He searched for them in vain. Chantelou, the punctilious, reliable chronicler of the trip to France, made no mention of the unfortunate incident in his felicitous narrative.

It is reported that many years later Le Corbusier managed to acquire some of the key pages of that valuable manuscript in a second-hand

bookshop in Paris, and knew how to use them cleverly. And he too was able to control light with great precision.

However, while capable of stirring our emotions and making us tremble in our innermost being, light is more than a feeling.

Light is quantifiable and qualifiable, whether with Bernini's tables or those of Le Corbusier. Or with a compass, solar cards, and photometer, Or with scale models or the most perfect computer programs now available. It is possible to control, tame, and dominate light.

The mechanisms, the snares with which architecture traps light, with their well-defined dimensions and proportions, are the cause of that spatial tension, the inimitable beauty of works that constitute the best history of architecture.

To change the small diameter of the skylights in the baths of the Alhambra, either reducing or enlarging them, or to change the height of the horizontal upper plane of the "continuum" that is Farnsworth House, by enlarging it or decreasing it, would be a sure recipe for destroying two brilliant pieces of our culture.

That is because continuous space, with Farnsworth House as its archetype, is also a question of light. The break in tension produced by doubling its interior height would not be so much an error of compositional dimension as a break with the clear and exact amount of light, of transparency, which permits space to accurately speak of continuity, achieved with such great effort by the Modern Movement. It took Mies van der Rohe many long years to build such an esteemed piece. To achieve the difficult continuity of continuous space, it must be controlled, its dimensions and proportions mastered so that light can efficiently sweep through them.

Thus one can affirm that light is quantifiable and qualifiable, controllable. With man as a yardstick; for, in the end, it is for him, for mankind, that we create architecture.

"This temple [the Pantheon], both open and mysteriously enclosed, was conceived as a solar quadrant. The hours would make their round on that caissoned ceiling, so carefully polished by Greek artisans; the disk of daylight would rest suspended there like a shield of gold; rain would form its clear pool on the pavement below; prayers would rise like smoke toward that void where we place the gods."[4]

4
Yourcenar, Marguerite (1955). *Memoirs of Hadrian*, 176. London: Secker & Warburg. Available at: https://archive.org/details/in.ernet.dli.2015.125737/page/n181/mode/2up?q=rain (accessed September 2025).

TRIAL BY FIRE

On Different Types of Light

We have already discussed the seductive quality of the Maison de Verre thanks to light, and how dark it would be without it. With everything else intact (construction, composition, function, and context), it would nevertheless be nothing without light, less than nothing. But, can you imagine if Doctor Dalsace's grandson, tired of so many visits and finding the light we have described as divine to be a trifle dim, decided to replace the great glass block wall with a technological and transparent curtain wall made of the biggest and flattest sheet glass he could find on the market? Many things would happen then, perhaps too many. Among other things, all the ugliness of the Parisian courtyard where it is located would be invited inside the defused space.

To avoid this, anticipating the disastrous results, it might occur to him to use the Gothic windows taken from the demolition of the nearby St. Denis church. Things would take on another hue, or rather, other colors. The invasion of angels with trumpets and biblical figures would block out the view of the bare courtyard and would transform the well-known space into a pure celestial glory of a thousand colors.

So this very same space, with identical dimensions, construction, use and context, has appeared in our imagination in various forms: dark at first, then very light, and finally gloriously colored; three different spaces and one true one, the original: merely by changing one material, light. Merely by changing its quantity and quality.

The architect of the Maison de Verre, Pierre Chareau, used light as a material, knowing that it had to be given a physical definition. To say the word light in the same way as one might say the word stone is to say almost nothing; it is only the beginning. Of course, most architects never move beyond this first stage of definition, which accounts for the results they achieve.

There are many kinds of light and we shall discuss some of them now; whatever its direction, horizontal light, vertical light, or diagonal light. Whatever its quality, solid light or diffuse light.

In the old days, when people needed to take light from above, what I call vertical light, they could not, because if they made openings in

the roof, water, wind, cold, and snow could enter. It was not a question of risking death just to obtain light. Only the immortal gods in the Pantheon dared to harness it. And in their honor, Hadrian commissioned that lofty architecture to anticipate the achievement of vertical light.

Thus, throughout the history of architecture, light has always been horizontal, taken horizontally, piercing the vertical plane – the wall – as was logical. Since the sun's rays fall diagonally upon us, a great part of the history of architecture can be read as an attempt to transform horizontal, or diagonal, light into light that might appear to be vertical.

This is what was achieved in Gothic architecture, which should not be understood simply as the desire to obtain a greater quantity of light, but fundamentally to achieve light that was qualitatively more vertical, in this case, diagonal.

Similarly, during the Baroque period, architects tried to twist light with ingenious mechanisms in order to convert horizontal light into a light that would appear as vertical light, and sometimes was by reflection. By taking one more step and achieving greater verticality than in Gothic structures. The magnificent transparent Baroque light achieved by Narciso Tomé in the beautiful Toledo cathedral is a masterful lesson in this very achievement.

The type of light – horizontal, vertical, or diagonal – depends on the position of the sun in relation to the planes that make up the spaces tensed by that light. Horizontal light is produced by the sun's rays as they penetrate through holes in the walls. Vertical light is produced when the sun enters through holes in the upper horizontal plane. Diagonal light is produced when the sun passes through both the vertical and horizontal planes.

This means that the possibility of vertical light entering climate-controlled spaces was not achievable until the advent of large-scale flat glazing. Thanks to the option of constructing the upper horizontal plane, which is drilled and glazed, it has become possible to introduce this vertical light. This is one of the keys to the Modern Movement, to contemporary architecture, in its understanding of light. These are the skylights in the upper horizontal plane, now a regular feature of contemporary architecture.

I don't know if the architects of the Alhambra Baths were aware of the wonder they had produced when they made those star-shaped openings in their domes. These were used not only to illuminate an area that demanded a certain degree of discretion, but also basically served as a natural outlet for the steam from the baths. However, above all, they were, perhaps without knowing it, allowing the entry of solid light that would slice through the air and steam like a knife. It is fascinating to spend some time in those rooms and watch the sunlight move and change as it streams in. It would be even more exciting to bathe there. Even now, it is still possible to see spaces of this kind in certain Turkish baths dating from Constantinople, where the intersection of solid light and steam makes the material nature of this white light all the more palpable.

I don't know either whether or not Le Corbusier, who was to later use solid light with such effect, was aware when he constructed the unequaled Ozenfant studio that what he was really constructing was a treatise on diffuse light. The ingenious construction of the small, glazed saw-tooth roof produced a material plane of diffuse light across a continuous translucent roof. Then, in alignment with the angle of large panes of glass, and with the necessary arrangement of lines, he created that amazing trihedron of diffuse light which has not yet received due consideration from contemporary architecture. That diffuse light which reaches its maximum state in the previously mentioned Maison de Verre.

Obviously that particular solid light can only be taken in when the architecture is oriented toward the south so as to receive the perfectly apportioned light that is cast upon it. It is this dramatic southern, solid, cast light, when properly handled, that produces the most spectacular effects capable of taking our breath away.

In the same way, diffuse light is normally taken in by orienting the architecture toward the north to obtain a serene and peaceful, reflected, diffuse light, the light that produces restful, calming effects.

Bearing all this in mind, we understand that we can search for and use the various qualities offered by light, depending upon its orientation in space and time. We can, therefore, tell the difference between the clear, blue morning light, when we look toward the east,

Alberto Campo Baeza, Sketch of Turégano House, Pozuelo de Alarcón, Madrid, Spain, 1986–1988.

Alberto Campo Baeza, Turégano House, Pozuelo de Alarcón, Madrid, Spain, 1986–1988.
© Hisao Suzuki, Courtesy Estudio Alberto Campo Baeza

Alberto Campo Baeza, Caja Granada Headquarters, Granada, Spain, 1992–2001.

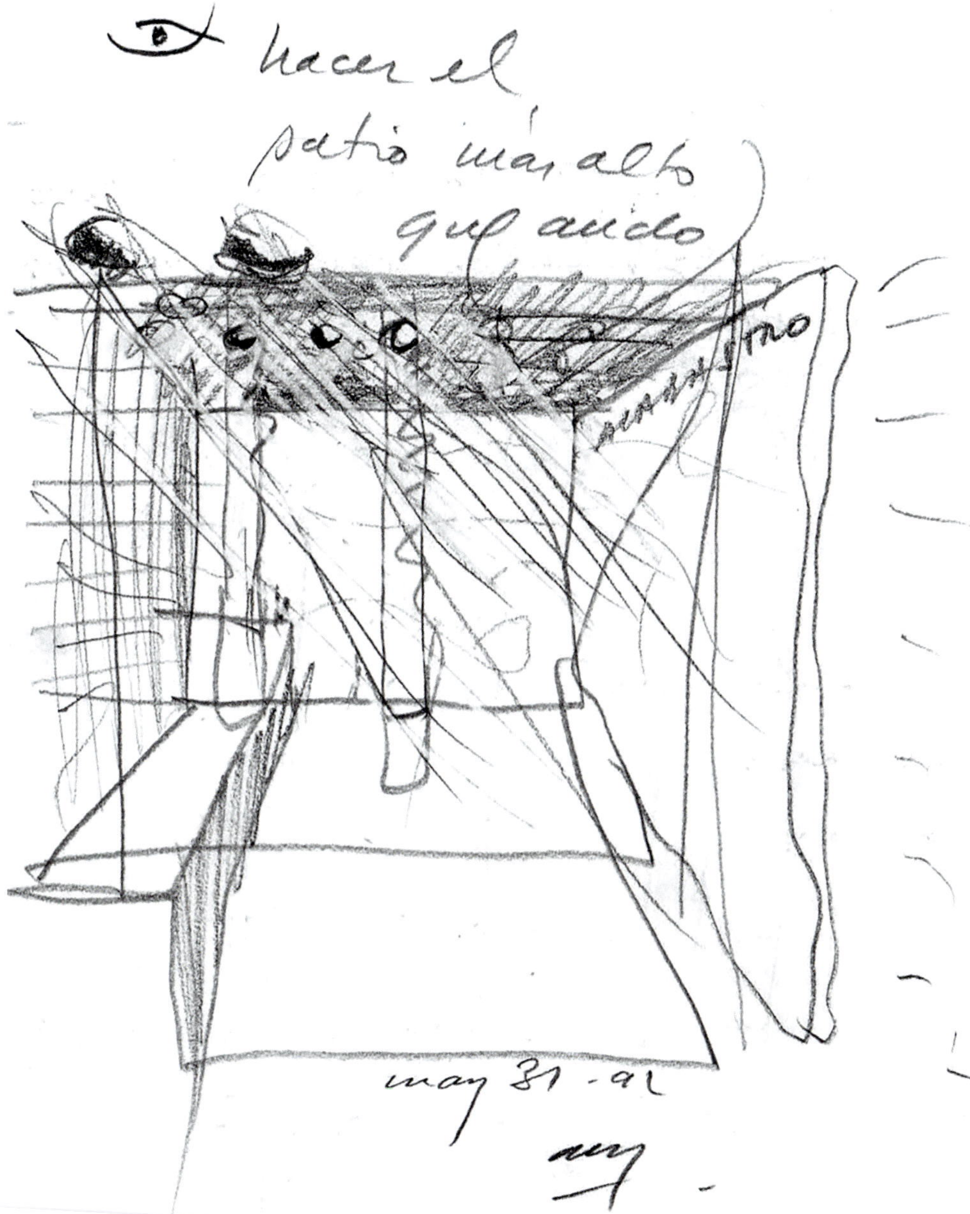

Alberto Campo Baeza, Sketch of Caja Granada Headquarters, Granada, Spain, 1992–2001.
© Alberto Campo Baeza

Alberto Campo Baeza, Model of Porta Milano, Milan, Italy, 2009.
Courtesy of Estudio Alberto Campo Baeza

Alberto Campo Baeza, Sketch of Porta Milano, Milan, Italy, 2009.

➔ North light: Alberto Campo Baeza, Multi-Sport Pavilion UFV, Madrid, Spain, 2012–2017. © Javier Callejas, Courtesy Estudio Alberto Campo Baeza

➔ West light: Alberto Campo Baeza, Caja Granada Headquarters, Granada, Spain, 1992–2001. © Roland Halbe, Courtesy Estudio Alberto Campo Baeza

East light: Alberto Campo Baeza, Casa Gaspar, Vejer de la Frontera, Cadiz, Spain, 1990–1992. © Hisao Suzuki, Courtesy Estudio Alberto Campo Baeza

South light: Alberto Campo Baeza, Caja Granada Headquarters, Granada, Spain, 1992–2001 © Hisao Suzuki, Courtesy Estudio Alberto Campo Baeza

and the warm, golden light of dusk when we look toward the west, knowing that both types of light are basically horizontal.

In this way, we could continue to delve into concepts and nuances relating to light in architecture, such as transparency, backlighting, shadow or darkness, luminosity and color.

And we should also mention that characteristic of light as matter in constant movement, following the solar rhythms marked out periodically by Nature. With man and for man, this light gives its life to the service of true architecture.

"And rising one morning, with the rosy dawn, he went before the sun and spoke thus unto it:

Thou great star! What would be thy happiness if thou hadst not those for whom thou shinest?"[5]

5 Friedrich W. Nietzsche (1917). *Thus Spake Zarathrustra*, 3. New York: The Modern Library. Available at: https://archive.org/details/thusspakezarathu00niet/page/n1/mode/2up (accessed September 2025)

WITH MANY LIGHTS AT THE SAME TIME

On the Combination of Different Types of Light Within a Single Space

Just as Edison would later invent electric light (how difficult it still is to use it wisely!), Gian Lorenzo, the greatest master of light, invented something equally simple; the work of genius known as "*luce alla bernina.*" Using various sources of visible light, he first created an environment with diffuse, homogeneous light, generally from the north, with which he illuminated and gave clarity to a space. Then, after centering it geometrically in relation to the shapes – bang! – he would step in at a specific point, hiding the source from the spectator's eyes, producing a funnel of solid light – "*luce gettata*" – making it the protagonist of the space. The contrast or counterpoint between the two types of light, creating a furious tension in the space, produced a first-rate architectural effect: solid light in visible movement dancing over an invisible, diffuse light in calm stillness.

The Greek architects Anthemius of Tralles and Isidorus of Miletus did the same thing without the aid of the Neapolitan's universal tables.[6] The great miracle of their Hagia Sophia, more in terms of light than size, is its fabulous dome. The sun throws its rays in diverging directions, and due to their distance from the ground, they

6 The author refers to Bernini's tables [Editor's note].

arrive as if they were parallel. So what is happening in the interior of Hagia Sophia, which receives light through all its high windows as if lit by many different suns? What is happening when the rays of light converge inside, producing those incredible effects? The simple secret is found in the exact dimensions and thickness of the windows, which infuse reflected light with nearly as much strength as direct solid light, and the effect is there for all to see. The secret formula of the miracle is the canny combination of both sources of light, direct and indirect.

Light, like wine, as well as having many varieties, shades and nuances, does not favor excess. The combination of various types of light to excess, just like wine, reverses the possible quality of the result.

The appropriate combination of different types of light, when one knows them, offers infinite possibilities in architecture. Bernini and Le Corbusier knew that well, as did Anthemius of Tralles, Alvar Aalto, Hadrian, and even Tadao Ando.

FINALE

On How Light Is the Theme

Finally, is not light the *raison d'être* of architecture? Is not the history of architecture the search for comprehension and domination of light?

Is not the Romanesque a dialogue between the shade of the walls and the solid light which penetrates its interior like a knife?

Is not the Gothic an exaltation of light that ignites unbelievable spaces with rising flames?

Is not the Baroque an alchemy of light in which the wise addition of diffuse light breaks through solid light, making it possible to create indescribable vibrations within its spaces?

Finally, is not the Modern Movement after breaking down the walls, a flood of light that we are still trying to control? Is not the contemporary period the time when, finally, we have all available means to dominate light?

Deep reflection about light and its infinite possibilities must be the central focus of the architecture of the future. While Paxton's intuitions and Soane's successes were a prelude to Le Corbusier's discoveries and Tadao Ando's experiments, there is still a long and rich road to follow. With light at the heart of it all.

If I am able through my work to make people feel the rhythms set by nature, harmonizing spaces with light, tempering them with the passage of the sun, then I believe that what we call architecture is all worthwhile.

➔
Alberto Campo Baeza, Caja Granada Headquarters, Granada, Spain, 1992–2001. © Duccio Malagamba, Courtesy Estudio Alberto Campo Baeza

3 TIME

The Suspension of Time

ON TIME. ON THE INEFFABLE DETENTION OF TIME

"Burnt Norton" is the first of the *Four Quartets*, one of T.S. Eliot's key works. In its first six lines, the word "time" appears seven times with surprising reiteration:

"Time present and time past/Are both perhaps present in time future,/And time future contained in time past./If all time is eternally present/All time is unredeemable."[1]

And Benedetto Croce seems to sum it up even more concisely: "Every true history is contemporary history," it is the past seen through the eyes of the present.[2]

This time that poets and philosophers express so well, the time of Eliot and Croce, is the time that architectural creation wants to capture. Because this time is the central theme of architecture.

In this text, I would like to analyze why some architectural spaces are able to stir up such an inner commotion within us. Although it may seem an abstract concept or theme more properly pertaining to poetry or philosophy, this concept of suspension of time occurs with an especially real and palpable force only in architecture. After all, architecture is the only artistic creation that surrounds us, that we enter into, and that we move around in. When we stand before or inside certain architectural spaces, time seems to stop, suspend itself, and become almost tangible.

There is no denying the profound emotion – the suspension of time – one feels on entering the Roman Pantheon. There time stands still and we are moved. I still shed tears every time I go back. I often mention to people the deal I've made with my students for many years now. When they visit the Pantheon, they have to send me

1 Eliot, T. S. (1943). Quartet No. 1: Burnt Norton. In Eliot, T.S. *Four Quartets*. The poem is available at: http://www.davidgorman.com/4quartets/1-norton.htm (accessed September 2025).

2 Croce, Benedetto (1922). *Theory & History of Historiography*, 12. London: George Harrap & Co. Ltd. Available at: https://archive.org/details/theoryhistoryofh00croc/page/12/mode/2up (accessed September 2025).

Eight Meditations on Architecture, First Edition. Alberto Campo Baeza. Edited by Matteo Zambelli.

Visit to the Pantheon with ETH students, Rome, Italy, 1998.
© Alberto Campo Baeza.

a postcard, a "*cartolina illustrata*" with a picture of the inside, telling me whether or not they cried. All of those who have written have cried. I've amassed a good collection by now.

I will never forget how, when my building for the Caja Granada[3] Headquarters had just been inaugurated, one of the people who worked there recalled having wept on entering the central space for the first time. Right there, at that very instant, time stood still. I must confess that, years later, every time I return there and enter that space, my heart still skips a beat, and even more so if the sun, up to its usual tricks, alights upon and strolls over its alabaster walls.

3 The Caja General de Ahorros de Granada headquarters was completed in 2001. Project link: https://www.campobaeza.com/caja-granada (accessed March 2025).

Architects must deepen their understanding of the architectural mechanisms that make these results possible. I'm still trying to reach that perennially elusive beauty that every artistic creation seeks to embody. And this is what architecture is all about.

It might be helpful to consider how architecture, in comparison to other art forms, is the only one whose creations are capable of physically enveloping man, its protagonist. The experience of being able to stand inside a work of art in flesh and bone pertains solely to architecture, and is impossible to produce in the other arts.

If a space built with gravity, with materials possessing an unavoidable gravitational weight is tensed by light – light which itself builds time – so that we are moved through the physical, beyond the physical, then we can properly say that we have attained architecture. Architecture happens when we succeed in stopping time in the constructed space: when it seems that time itself is suspended.

Time is a central theme of architecture: time that is structured by light; capable of stopping our hearts or tying them in a knot, much more than the forms of a passing style or the exquisite adornments of the best construction. *Utilitas* and *Firmitas* only acquire their full meaning when *Venustas*, Beauty, is attained.

Time in Architecture can be analyzed from many perspectives and that is what we are about to explore.

THE TIME OF *UTILITAS*. FUNCTION

There is a time that refers to the capacity of ensuring that the function for which the building was erected will endure. A time relative to function: use, utility, *Utilitas,* of making a building carry out the functions for which it was commissioned and, moreover, of being adaptable to different functions over the long haul. When I was a student, we learned this in terms of the "architecture of cases" versus the "architecture of boxes."

The case meets the requested function exactly, but it cannot be used for anything else. A knife sheath cannot be used for a spoon and vice versa. If the question is changed, the answer is no longer valid. This tends to happen when, in addition to the specific nature of the function, the dimensions are bound within certain settled parameters. A social housing building, even if it is resolved to the last millimeter, will most certainly not serve for any other purpose.

➔
Alberto Campo Baeza, Caja Granada Headquarters, Granada, Spain, 1992–2001. © Duccio Malagamba, Courtesy Estudio Alberto Campo Baeza

The box, in contrast, can admit many different functions over time. Obviously, the larger the size of the space, the greater the number of different functions it can allow. Boxes endure the test of time better than cases do.

Time is kinder to boxes than cases. And kinder still to large boxes rather than smaller ones. Berthold Lubetkin was right when he proudly proclaimed that he did no more than build boxes, shoe-boxes in concrete. Boxes, little boxes, big boxes.

THE TIME OF *FIRMITAS*. CONSTRUCTION

There is another time that speaks of physical duration, of the effective combination of materials that culminates in the most perfect construction of architecture. *Firmitas* means firmness, strength, and a well-constructed building will be able to last many years and remain on solid footing for a long time. All of the great masters of the past have been, furthermore, great builders.

I am particularly interested in the duration of the foundations of some buildings throughout history. The ruins, the worthwhile ones, are the traces of the architecture that was built there. And in them you can clearly read the architect's idea. They provide the ground plan of that architecture that has been able to remain in time.

THE TIME OF *VENUSTAS*. BEAUTY

The time of *Venustas* is that which can be suspended, that stops when we encounter beauty. It is the most difficult to control, but for that reason it is what most interests us.

All great writers on architecture have sought to come up with a few universal rules that would not only serve to transmit certain forms or styles, but also emit a beauty capable of moving men deeply on viewing their works.

It is a difficult enterprise. Just as happens with many excellent cookbooks in which nothing is spared to provide every last detail and consideration regarding a recipe, the exquisite dish still requires a skilled and passionate chef. No recipe can guarantee the quality of the cooking. The same thing is true in architecture; one needs a good head, a good hand, and one has to have a talent for it.

THE TIME OF MEMORY. PERMANENCE

Another thing is the time that the building is capable of remaining in men's memory: a built work's resistance to oblivion, or, in other words, the thing that secures its trajectory into architectural history, which has little to do with current fashion or passing fame. Those of us who are no longer children have seen lofty names and works that mean nothing today. The phenomenon, controlled and exaggerated by the press, still works at full strength. Many of the names that make up today's architectural "A-List" are sure to disappear tomorrow, their fame short-lived. They will never remain in men's memory.

But there are other, quieter sorts of architecture that are much more eloquent and capable of transcending our tendency to ephemerality. Above and beyond fashion and vanity, our aim should be to erect more profound architecture for history. Such architecture has a different rhythm, and belongs to truth and beauty in the fullest sense.

The time of memory – of permanence – is the "difficult desire for duration" (*le dur désir de durer*[4]) which Paul Éluard spoke of poetically and which is so profoundly rooted in the will of every creator: the will to transcend. Picasso put it so eloquently: "I am tired of being modern. Now I want to be immortal."[5]

And it is memory that enables us with the passage of time to value more highly those works of architecture that are truly worthwhile. In that wonderful book, *The War of Time* by Alejo Carpentier,[6] time passes simultaneously backwards and forwards. Carpentier manipulates time in such a way that only the novel, imagination guided by memory, can achieve; so it is that on his death, Don Marcial at the feet of Ceres, starts going back in time, living his life backwards to his birth. Sentences such as "the furniture was growing taller"[7] and "when the furniture had grown a little taller still"[8] and then: "but now time passed more quickly"[9] are Carpentier's tricks of the trade to explain this backward progression of time.

Does not something similar occur when we return after a long period of time to some of the best artistic creations and suddenly we understand them perfectly? Not only that, they seem even better than they did before. So it is that, like Don Marcial in *The War of Time*, I read the poems of Horace and Virgil with so much more pleasure than I did when obliged to read them as a child. I used to learn and now I learn too. And I enjoy. And here and now, just like that, time appears to stand still.

4

There are two books that have the phrase "Le dur désir de durer" in their title: Éluard, Paul and Chagall, Marc (1950). *Le dur désir de durer*. Paris: Bordas, and Paul Éluard and Man Ray (1960). *Le dur désir de durer: Le temps déborde*. Paris: Seghers.

5

"Estoy cansado de ser moderno. Quiero ser eterno" [Editor's note].

6

Carpentier, Alejo (1970). *The War of Time*. London: Gollancz.

7

Ibid., Chapter 8.

8

Ibid., Chapter 10.

9

Ibid., Chapter 12.

In a very special way this is what occurs with architecture. On my most recent visit to the Pantheon, time stood still when that stream of light traveled across the deep coffers of its bare dome at something other than physical speed and I felt it with much greater intensity than on the first occasion many moons ago. Thus, we architects must remind ourselves that the possibility of stopping time, of halting the sun as Joshua did, is something that we are capable of, just as we are capable of creating something that transcends us.

HISTORY

There are many buildings in History with that special capability of causing us to lose our sense of time.

The Roman Pantheon is the example *par excellence.* Well built, and a perfect embodiment of the universal function endowed to it by its creator, the Pantheon is also overwhelmingly beautiful. All of the great creators have understood that when they have been inside. Suffice it to quote Henry James when he recounts the memorable scene of Count Valerii[10], with his hands behind him, inside the Pantheon as the sun struggled through the heavy clouds above with the rainwater making the light from on high material. Exquisite. Or Piranesi's engravings of the Pantheon that should be in the libraries of all architects.

10 The scene referred to by Alberto Campo Baeza is described in James, Henry (1923). *The Last of the Valeri*, 25. London: Macmillan and Co., United. Available at: https://archive.org/details/in.ernet.dli.2015.179522/page/n11/mode/2up (accessed September 2025).

And if I were to give just one example of contemporary architecture, it would be Mies van der Rohe's Farnsworth House. A small, white, sublime piece, capable of giving continuity not only to space but also to the history of architecture. It belongs, with its radical beauty, to an architecture without time, capable of generating, like the Pantheon, the desired suspension of time.

THE BLUE-EYED ROTHKO

Every time I enter the Olnick Spanu family home in Manhattan my heart skips a beat: there in front of me, I see a painting by Rothko, my favorite painter, in an unusual size and color. Its small dimensions and blue and green tones completely blow me away. A good friend of mine, with whom I often discuss this painting, tells me it is "the blue-eyed Rothko." He's right. I can testify that there, in front of this wonderful painting, time stops, it disappears.

It happens that painting, like architecture, shares this special capacity to carry us away and suspend time. I'll never forget my first visit to London when, with Sáenz de Oíza, my beloved teacher and Spanish master, we stood in front of Velázquez's *Venus of the Mirror* in the

National Gallery. Time, space, desire – everything – disappeared. In that brief infinite lapse we stood as if in divine rapture.

MUSIC CAPABLE OF STOPPING TIME

Peter Phillips, director of The Tallis Scholars, in an interview he gave in early spring 2011, before performing Tomás Luis de Victoria's *Requiem* in New York, spoke of "suspended time."

In that interview, the words flowed from his mouth as if in a cascade: intensity, sobriety, profundity, precision, simplicity, clarity, but above all, suspension, referring to time. When asked where his musicians had sounded best, he replied: the Sydney Opera House by the master Jørn Utzon. It could not have been otherwise. Utzon's sublime architecture welcoming Victoria's marvelous music.

The concert, devoted entirely to Tomás Luis de Victoria, and commemorating the fourth centenary of the Spanish composer's death, was long, but I would say that for all of us who filled the packed church of St. Mary the Virgin in 46th Street, everything happened in a second. Time stopped there, in the way that only beauty can make possible.

SORT OF DISAPPEAR: CINEMA

And while we could survey all artistic creations and discover that the crux of the matter is always the same, namely reaching man's heart through his head, I am going to limit myself to a couple of examples of how film, the seventh art, is also capable of stopping time.

An unforgettable scene comes to mind: the white plastic bag floating in the air in the film *American Beauty* – something so elemental magically transformed by the work and grace of a young director, Sam Mendes, into a masterful piece. Given the supreme beauty of something so simple, we all cry with Wes Benly and Thora Birch. There, time disappears and our heart dissolves in five infinite minutes.

Of course, Billy Elliot expresses it still more clearly in that "sort of disappear" that he repeats twice when the panel asks him what it is that he feels when he dances. With a stroke of genius, Stephen Daldry summed up something as abstract as suspended time in artistic creation so precisely in that short phrase!

THE SECRET OF ARTISTIC CREATION

Architecture, painting, literature, music, and film are, in fact, no more than the creative works of human beings which redeem us and make this life worth living.

➜ Alberto Campo Baeza, Sketch of the Tomb, "Il cielo in terra" (Heaven on Earth), San Doná di Piave, Venice, Italy, 2017–2019. © Alberto Campo Baeza

➜ Alberto Campo Baeza, Tomb, "Il cielo in terra" (Heaven on Earth), San Doná di Piave, Venice, Italy, 2017–2019. © Javier Callejas, Courtesy Estudio Alberto Campo Baeza

MESTRE
10 ottobre 2016

Edgar Allan Poe, in his *Philosophy of Composition*, captured this suspension of time so well: "I kept steadily in view the design of rendering the work universally appreciable. I should be carried too far out of my immediate topic were I to demonstrate a point upon which I have repeatedly insisted: that beauty is the sole legitimate province of the poem."[11]

"Truth, in fact, demands a precision, and passion, a homeliness (the truly passionate will comprehend me) which are absolutely antagonistic to that beauty which, I maintain, is the excitement, or pleasurable elevation, of the soul."[12]

That "pleasurable elevation of the soul" is precisely the suspension of time that we are referring to here.

Our works go on to transcend material and limited life. Stefan Zweig, in that essential text I have quoted so very often, *The Secret of Artistic Creation*, manifests this with such force: "There is no greater pleasure or satisfaction than recognizing that man is also capable of creating everlasting values."[13]

Works that are worthwhile transcend us; they transcend their creators and no longer belong to us. They already belong to the memory of men.

Paul A.M. Dirac, 1933 Nobel Laureate and one of the great physicists of our time, proclaimed, "Beauty and truth go together in theoretical physics."[14] Could today's architects, instead of musing on vanities, concur with the poets, philosophers, and physicists in the primacy of the pursuit of truth, and attempt to actualize this all-too-possible miracle of the suspension of time?

Le Corbusier, in simpler language, spoke of "*d' espace indicible*" (unspeakable space),[15] and on other occasions, of how the most useful buildings were those that fulfilled the desires of the heart. The master was so very right.

And as we started with one poet, T.S. Eliot, we will conclude with another, William Blake. In his "Auguries of Innocence," he proposes: "To see a world in a grain of sand, / And a heaven in a wild flower, / Hold infinity in the palm of your hand,/ And eternity in an hour."[16]

Eternity, suspended time, is what we would like to achieve with our architecture.

11 Poe, Edgar Allan (1907). *The Raven and The Philosophy of Composition*, 23. San Francisco: Paul Elder. Available at: https://archive.org/details/in.ernet.dli.2015.179522/page/n11/mode/2up (accessed September 2025).

12 Ibid., p. 24.

13 "The Secret of Artistic Creation" (Das Geheimnis des künstlerischen Schaffens) is the title of a lecture given by Stefan Zweig in Buenos Aires in 1938 and later collected in a book entitled *Tiempo y mundo. Impresiones y ensayos (1904–1940)* (Time and the world: Impressions and essays).

14 Dirac's sentence was quoted by Prigogine as, he says, he almost remembered it. Prigogine, Ilya (1996). *The End of Certainties: Time, Chaos and the Laws of Nature*, 163. New York, NY: The Free Press. Available at: https://archive.org/details/endofcertaintyti0000prig/page/162/mode/2up?q=beauty (accessed September 2025).

15 See Wogenscky, André (2006). *Le Corbusier's Hands*. Cambridge, MA: MIT Press.

16 William Blake, in his poem, "Auguries of Innocence." Available at: https://www.poetryfoundation.org/poems/43650/auguries-of-innocence (accessed July 2025).

MEMORY 4

Aula Ingenti Memoriae

"Memory is the faculty of the mind that stores and remembers the past." That is how it is defined by the Spanish Royal Academy. Memory is a necessary tool, essential for every creator, and especially for every architect.

Memory is the main tool with which reason and, by extension, the human being works. With memory, man can do everything, or almost everything. Without memory we can do nothing, and less than nothing. And architects less still. Like a needle without thread.

OUR MUCH-MALIGNED MEMORY

In order to write about memory, about the memory of an architect, I have decided to start from memory, from my own memory. In the words of Quintilian, man's most powerful and effective tool.[1]

In its day, in the chapter of my book, *Principia Architectonica*, entitled "Mnemosine vs Mimesis,"[2] I already highlighted several themes relating to memory that now appear here in greater detail.

I see clearly that in our time, the age of computers, with the capacity that these artifacts have to accumulate vast quantities of information, it is more necessary than ever to have a tool capable of ordering all that information and, after studying it, producing what we understand by learning, and then making it effective in order to reach the knowledge of wisdom. That marvelous tool is memory. Greater, much greater, than the hard disk of computers. Memory, helped by reason, is infinitely superior to any other instrument.

For this reflection on memory, I have resorted to texts as evocative as T.S. Eliot's *What Is a Classic?* And I've turned to my old friend Saint Augustine, because if there is anyone who has written copiously

1

Quintilian (2002). *The Orator's Education*. Cambridge, MA: The Harvard University Press. Quintilian writes about memory, in particular, in Book XI, Chapter II: "Memory."

2

Campo Baeza, Alberto. Mnemosine vs Mimesis. Available at: https://oa.upm.es/32759/1/MNEMOSYNE-VS-MIMESIS_COMPLET.pdf (accessed July 2025).

Eight Meditations on Architecture, First Edition. Alberto Campo Baeza. Edited by Matteo Zambelli.

and very well and very clearly about memory, it is he, especially in Book X of his *Confessions.*

The clear distinction that T.S. Eliot makes between information, knowledge, and wisdom, describes to perfection the value of memory in obtaining the coveted goal of wisdom. In *What Is a Classic?* he writes: "In our age, when men seem more than ever prone to confuse wisdom with knowledge, and knowledge with information."[3]

3 Eliot, T. S. ([1944] 1950). *What Is a Classic?* 30. London: Faber and Faber. Available at: http://bracchiumforte.com/PDFs/tseliot.pdf (accessed September 2025).

I still remember how, when I was a child at school, we used memory as a very effective learning tool. "Let from its dream the soul awaken,/And reason mark with open eyes/The scene unfolding,/ How lightly life away is taken,/How cometh Death in stealthy guise,/ What swiftness hath the flight of pleasure/ That, once attained, seems nothing more/Than respite cold;/How fain is memory to measure/Each latter day inferior/To those of old."[4] I write by heart these verses by Jorge Manrique that I learned at school, and I am almost frightened by the accuracy of my memory. What can one say about the beauty of these couplets? With each passing day, they seem more beautiful to me.

4 Manrique, Jorge (2005). *Elegia di Jorge Manrique alla morte del padre* (Jorge Manrique's Elegy on the Death of His Father), 35. Venice: Marsilio Editori.

And yet in these past few years, memory has become maligned. They say that we used to learn like parrots, and that an education based on memory was inadequate. How wrong they are. Memory, together with reason, is more than just a useful tool; it is essential for intellectual life, and for the life of the architect.

I tell my students repeatedly that reason is the first and most important tool with which an architect works. And I am also telling them today that by this I mean reason assisted by memory.

MEMORY CONNECTS

I have written more than once that, after such a long time together on my bookshelves, my books speak to each other. This is also true of the ideas stored in our memory. They relate to each other in a mysterious way, and new ideas emerge from them.

In 1770, Mozart listened to Allegri's *Miserere* and on his return home he promptly transcribed it from memory, not to copy it but to draw inspiration from it.

In 1655, Rembrandt traced the edge of the Lithostrotos with a ruler in his etching of the presentation of *Jesus by Pilate.* And Picasso in

Rembrandt, Christ Presented to the People, 1655.
Penta Springs Limited / Alamy Stock Photo
https://www.alamy.com/stock-image-christ-presented-to-the-people-1655-drypoint-eighth-state-of-eight-162509274.html

his *Ecce Homo,* where he paints the same theme as Rembrandt, the *Lithostrotos,* drew on his memory and copied it, and he performed the same operation using his ruler to achieve a perfect horizontal line. All very architectural. Both knew that the horizontal plane at eye level becomes a perfect horizontal line.

Mies van der Rohe visited the Athens Acropolis in 1950, and since then applied the theory of the flat horizontal plane that, at eye level, becomes a line. And he ended up raising that horizontal plane aloft, floating, in his Farnsworth House, and in so many of his other works.

Alvaro Siza is a pure reminder of Alvar Aalto in his early works, in his beautiful Boa Nova Tea House in Matosinhos. And his restoration of the Chiado district in Lisbon is a clear memory of Rome.

Picasso, Ecce homo, 1970.
Album / Alamy Foto Stock
https://www.alamy.it/ecce-homo-dopo-rembrandt-museo-musee-picasso-parigi-image515378366.html

And, where would Barragán be, as he himself pointed out, without his memory of the Alhambra?

And one wonders how could even Le Corbusier have designed his Ville Savoye without his long stay at Eileen Gray's E1027 in Roquebrune-Cap-Martin?

For all of these architects, memory plays a crucial role. Furthermore, memory purifies. Of the best architects, we remember above all their finest works. The less important ones we tend to forget.

ON INTELLECTUAL ENJOYMENT AND MEMORY

On intellectual enjoyment I have written: "I know well that all this is largely due to memory. As the years go by, our memory fills up in such a way that relationships often occur between things and events, which becomes a reliable source of this intellectual pleasure."[5] And, like a well, this memory needs to be replenished with the water of knowledge, which requires time and deep study. That devotion to study, considered an obligation in our youth, becomes a pleasure in later life.

Saint Augustine speaks of the enormous space of memory, the *aula ingenti memoriae.* Memory that is not only able to accumulate new knowledge but, better still, to bring it all together. Who has not been surprised on recognizing common themes or ideas in authors that would seem to have nothing in common? To recall is to travel to the heart,[6] to put the heart back into someone or something that happened.

And Saint Augustine is so clear when he speaks of memory that we have only to transcribe his wise words: "And I enter the fields and spacious halls of memory, where are stored as treasures the countless images that have been brought into them from all manner of things by the senses . . . Men go forth to marvel at the heights of mountains and the huge waves of the sea, the broad flow of the rivers, the vastness of the ocean, the orbits of the stars, and yet they neglect to marvel at themselves. Nor do they wonder how it is that, when I spoke of all these things, I was not looking at them with my eyes – and yet I could not have spoken about them had it not been that I was actually seeing within, in my memory, those mountains and waves and rivers and stars which I have seen, and that ocean which I believe in – and with the same vast spaces between them as when I saw them outside me."[7]

5
Alberto Campo Baeza, Intellectual enjoyment. On intellectual enjoyment in architecture. Available at: https://www.campobaeza.com/wp-content/uploads/2019/09/2019-Sharpening-the-scalpel-10-On-intellectual-enjoyment-in-architecture.pdf (accessed July 2025).

6
The Spanish verb "recordar," which means "recall," comes from the Latin "recŏrdari." "Recŏrdari" is composed by the prefix "re-" and the noun "cor, cordis," which means "heart," because Latins thought that the heart was the seat of memory. This explains why Alberto Campo Baeza refers to the heart in the sentence [Editor's note].

7
Augustine, Saint (1945). *The Confessions of St. Augustine*, Book 10, Chapter VIII. "Of the nature and the amazing power of memory," 218. New York, NY: Sheed and Ward. Available at: https://archive.org/details/in.ernet.dli.2015.157225/page/n5/mode/2up (accessed September 2025).

↑ Alvar Aalto, Maison Louis Carré, Bazoches-sur-Guyonne, France, 1956–1963.
Florent Darrault / Wikimedia Commons / CC BY-SA 2.0
https://en.wikipedia.org/wiki/Maison_Louis_Carr%C3%A9#/media/File:Maison_Louis_Carre.jpg

↑ Álvaro Siza, Boa Nova Casa de Chá Restaurant, Leça da Palmeira, Portugal, 1963.
Vitor Oliveira / Wikimedia Commons / CC BY-SA 2.0
https://upload.wikimedia.org/wikipedia/commons/6/66/Casa_de_Ch%C3%A1_da_Boa_Nova_-_Le%C3%A7a_da_Palmeira_-_Portugal_%2831042152470%29.jpg

Eileen Gray, House E-1027, Roquebrune-Cap-Martin, France, 1926–1929.
Olivier Martin Gambier/ARTEDIA/VIEW / Alamy Foto Stock
https://www.alamy.it/foto-immagine-esterno-dell-edificio-modernista-eileen-grays-house-e-1027-roquebrune-cap-martin-francia-architetto-eileen-gray-1929-103382111.html?imageid=C49A424B-8B30-4857-BBE4-29CAEBE958C3&p=382816&pn=1&searchId=0b43aeaf0f05c6bf59b5a3ac5fa726fc&searchtype=0

Le Corbusier, Villa Savoye, Poissy, France, 1928–1931.
Lstrike / Wikimedia Commons / CC BY-SA 3.0 DE
https://de.wikipedia.org/wiki/Datei:Villa_Savoye_2015.jpg

THE POWER OF THE SOUL

We humans have memory, understanding, and will. That is what we learned as children. This was referred to in scholasticism as the powers of the soul. And it is easy to understand how memory, aided by understanding, reason, and will, is what makes creative work possible and in a very special way, the work of architects.

A sage is someone who not only accumulates information in his memory, but after suitably processing it, makes these data his own as knowledge and retains them. And then he uses them appropriately and efficiently. And the place where that data and knowledge are stored, processed, and used is memory.

An architect, a good architect, a wise architect stores information and knowledge in his memory so that, when suitably processed, he can design with rigor.

Memory is capable of recording and storing what is worthwhile from history, from the general history of humanity, and from the history of architecture. Memory has the capacity to supply that distilled, processed information to architects, so that we do not invent gunpowder.

Taking a leap forward requires the momentum we receive when, with one foot in the air, the other leans firmly on the ground, on memory, and so we finally attain knowledge, wisdom.

To dream – and to design is to dream – one has to first accumulate the material with which to build those dreams.

THE BELLY OF AN ARCHITECT

The Belly of an Architect was a gorgeous film by Peter Greenaway, starring Brian Dennehy in the role of the architect Stowrley Kracklite, set around the Pantheon in Rome.

And Saint Augustine, in Book X of his *Confessions*, with its profound pedagogical significance, describes memory as "the belly of the soul,"[8] where everything is digested (Rainer Sorgel uses the term, ruminated), in order to feed man, the soul of man.

8 Ibid., p. 219.

It may well be that Francis Bacon, the philosopher, had read Saint Augustine's text, when he spoke of books in his essays and in particular in his essay "Of Studies": "Some books are to be tasted, others to be swallowed, and some few to be chewed and digested."[9] How could a philosopher like Bacon, who sometimes seems so distant, hit the nail on the head with such precision?

9 Bacon, Francis (1625). Of Studies. Available at: https://www.psy.gla.ac.uk/~steve/best/BaconJohnson.pdf (accessed September 2025).

THE MEMORY OF THE HOUSE

I was asked at the Venice Biennale 2012 to focus on *common ground*, which I immediately understood to be memory. Since I was asked to center on the house, I decided to investigate the memory of the house.

An architect is a house. This is the name under which I developed one of my last academic courses at the ETSAM in Madrid. And I used it again for that small pavilion within that biennial: An architect is a house.

What and how is the memory of the house? What is an architect's *common ground* when he creates a house? I must confess that every time I build a new house, all the great houses in the history of architecture parade through my memory. Not to copy them, but, assisted by memory, to take a step forward and attempt to do something different and better.

From Adam's house in Paradise, as Joseph Ryckwert[10] described and studied it for us, to the prehistoric caves. And Abbot Laugier's primitive hut. But also Palladio's Villa Rotonda and Adolph Loos's Villa Moller. And Soane's house in Lincoln's Inn Fields in London. And so many others.

10 The author is referring to the book, Ryckwert, Joseph (1981). *On Adam's House in Paradise: The Idea of the Primitive Hut in Architectural History*. Cambridge, MA: MIT Press [Editor's note].

The houses that one thinks of are sometimes the ones that architects built for themselves. Even if occasionally, as in the case of Mies van der Rohe's client, Mrs. Farnsworth, the client's name may figure in the title.

And to order and center that work, I link the houses of the history of architecture to the four elements of Greek philosophy: earth, air, water, and fire. These, when translated into dwellings, can be the cave and the hut, the boat, and the ruin.

Alberto Campo Baeza, House of the Infinite, Cadiz, Spain, 2014.

The cave, which first Semper and then Frampton identified with the stereotomic, embodies our dwelling on earth. Heavy architecture speaks of man's dominion over the earth. We identify it with earth as the pre-Socratic element that best suits it.

The cabin, to which Semper and Frampton assigned the attribute of tectonic, addresses the concept of a change of place, the possibility of deciding where man wishes to settle. In short, it speaks of freedom. And air will be the pre-Socratic element that we link it to.

The boat, the raft, immediately reminds us not only of Noah's ark where the inhabitants of the Earth survived the Universal Flood, but also of Le Corbusier's Ville Savoye, or Mies van der Rohe's Farnsworth House, because both houses float and sail. I myself, in my House of the Infinite,[11] presented the upper horizontal stone plane as the deck of a grounded ship facing the Atlantic Ocean, facing the infinite sea.

11 "The House of the Infinite" was completed in Cadiz in 2014. Project link: https://www.campobaeza.com/house-infinite (accessed March 2025).

FROM TRACES TO RUINS

Ruins are the material, indelible traces, and the memory of the architecture that stood there once upon a time. These traces are the embodiment of the architects' ideas with exact measurements. They are, let me say, the memory of what was there.

When archeologists discover, analyze, and value a ruin, they rarely speak of architecture. Yet it is architecture, the most fundamental element of it, which appears there. The most basic thing about the creation of architects, its traces, is what causes ruins to exert such a power of fascination over us. What attracts us to ruins is the intensity of those few basic, radical elements of architectural creation.

What is the mysterious power that so directly connects the beginning and the end of a creation? Ruins display the very essence of architecture: the structure. Because when we talk about architectural ruins or traces, what we are talking about is the structure that establishes the order of space, which is central to architecture, the most essential thing that has been able to resist time. Just like the skeleton in the human body, ruins, traces, are the memory of that architecture that strongly evokes the spaces that had been built there.

FINALE

To conclude, I will return once more to Saint Augustine who ventured to speak of architects in Chapter 12 of Book X of the

Confessions entitled, "On the Recollection of Things Mathematical." "I have seen the lines drawn by architects, some of them as fine as a spider's web; but the truths are different, they are not the images of such things as the eye of my body has shown me. To know them is to recognize them interiorly without any concept of any kind of body whatsoever."[12]

12 Saint Augustine, op. cit., Book 10, Chapter XII, "On the Recollection of Things Mathematical," p. 223.

How I would have liked to have talked with a man with such a keen intellect as the Bishop of Hippo about the plans of architects drawn, as he tells us, with lines as delicate and subtle as a spider's thread. Precise lines and detailed plans, essential elements in the creation of architectural works that constitute the memory of architecture.

I will conclude with a quotation from the Franciscan friar, Diego de Valadés (1533–1582), author of the work *Rhetorica christiana*,[13] published in 1579 in Perugia, in which I dare to introduce the terms architects and architecture, *architecti* and *architecturae,* instead of

13 Diego de Valadés' book, *Rhetorica christiana*, is available at: https://books.google.it/books?id=aqM9AAAAcAAJ&printsec=frontcover&redir_esc=y#v=onepage&q=Memoria%20autem%20plurimus&f=false (accessed March 2025).

Luis Barragán, Cuadra San Cristóbal, Los Clubes, Atizapán de Zaragoza, Mexico, 1966–1968.

https://www.flickr.com/photos/esparta/3573608700/in/photostream/

oratori and *rhetoricae*, since memory is a necessary tool for all architects: “Memoria est firma animi, rerum, et verborum et dispositionis perceptio. Est haec maxime architecti necessaria. Nec sine causa thesaurus inventorum atque ómnium partium architecturae custos.”

“Memory is the firm retention in the mind of the matter, words and arrangement. It is extremely necessary to the architect. And not without cause is it the treasure of discoveries and the guardian of all parts of architecture.”[14]

And so Cicero concludes, and with him so do we: “So that there is truth in what Solon says in a certain bit of verse, already mentioned, that, as he grew old, he learned many things every day; and surely there can be no greater pleasure than the pleasures of the mind.”[15]

14
The original Latin phrase is: “Memoria est firma animi, rerum, et verborum, et dispositionis perceptio. Est haec maxime oratori necessaria. Nec sine causa thesaurus inventorum, atque omnium partium rhetorice custos appellantur” (Valadés, ibid., p. 87). With the substitution mentioned by Alberto Campo Baeza, it becomes: “Memoria est firma animi, rerum, et verborum, et dispositionis perceptio. Est haec maxime *architecti* necessaria. Nec sine causa thesaurus inventorum, atque omnium partium *architecturae* custos appellantur.” Diego de Valadés' phrase “Memoria est firma animi, rerum, et verborum, et dispositionis perceptio” (Memory is the firm retention in the mind of the matter, words, and arrangement) is, in fact, a quotation from Cicero Marcus, Tullius (1964), *Rhetorica ad Herennium*, Book First, II:3, 7. London: William Heinemann Ltd; Cambridge, MA: Harvard University Press. Available at: https://archive.org/details/adcherenniumdera00capluoft/page/n67/mode/2up?view=theater (accessed September 2025) [Editor's note].

15
Cicero, Marcus Tullius (1971). *De Senectute, de Amicitia, de Divinatione*, vol. XIV:50, 61, 63. Cambridge, MA: Harvard University Press. Available at: https://archive.org/details/cicero-in-28-volumes.-vol.-20-loeb-154/page/60/mode/2up?view=theater (accessed September 2025).

➔
The Alhambra, Granada, Spain, 976.
Tuxyso / Wikimedia Commons / CC BY-SA 3.0
https://en.m.wikipedia.org/wiki/File:Patio_de_los_Arrayanes_Alhambra_02_2014.jpg

5 UNIVERSALITY

On Surrender and Universality

T.S. ELIOT, ORTEGA, AND SOTA

All creative work, including architecture, requires a degree of individual surrender, of depersonalization, if one is to achieve greater universality. So we are told by our protagonists: a poet, a philosopher, and an architect.

And well might you ask: What is the connection between a poet, a philosopher, and an architect? What has T.S. Eliot to do with Ortega y Gasset, and with Alejandro de la Sota?

T.S. Eliot was an American by birth who became a British citizen and writes poetry like the angels. Ortega is a clear and transparent Heideggerian. And Sota is a laconic, Bachian Spanish architect.

The three could well have known one another because they are contemporaries. Had this happened, they would have been surprised to learn how much the poet, the philosopher, and the architect had in common. If we were to ascribe a single adjective to each of them, one could call T.S. Eliot transparent, Ortega clear, and Sota laconic.

And all three coincide in their respective genres – poetry, philosophy, and architecture – in the demand for a certain sobriety of expression, a certain surrender of the individual, as a prerequisite for attaining the universality that every creator longs for.

T.S. Eliot

In his essays, *What Is a Classic?*[1] and *Tradition and the Individual Talent?*,[2] T.S. Eliot stoutly defends the need for the extinction of personality in his work in the interest of greater universality. The first wonderful text is a speech he delivered in 1944 as the first

1 Eliot, T. S. (1950). *What Is a Classic?* London: Faber and Faber.

2 T.S. Eliot, "Tradition and the Individual Talent?" (1920). Available at: https://www.sas.upenn.edu/~cavitch/pdf-library/Eliot_Tradition_1919.pdf (accessed September 2025).

Eight Meditations on Architecture, First Edition. Alberto Campo Baeza. Edited by Matteo Zambelli.

President of the Virgil Society of London. The second text dates from 1919, and in it we find many of the arguments that had previously appeared in the former. "When an author appears, in his love of the elaborate structure, to have lost the ability to say anything simply; when his addiction to pattern becomes such that he says things elaborately which should properly be said simply, and thus limits his range of expression, the process of complexity ceases to be quite healthy, and the writer is losing touch with the spoken language."[3]

3
T.S. Eliot, *What Is a Classic?*, op. cit., p. 16.

Try exchanging the words "author" and "writer" with the word "architect."

"There comes a time when a new simplicity, even a relative crudity, may be the only alternative."

"Now, to some extent, the sacrifice of some potentialities in order to realize others is a condition of artistic creation, as it is a condition of life in general."[4]

4
Ibid., p. 16.

"In short, without the constant application of the classical measure, we tend to become provincial."[5]

5
Ibid., p. 17.

T.S. Eliot uses the term *provincial.* I don't know if in English the term *provincial*, has the same pejorative connotations as the word *provinciano* in Spanish. But the poet's idea in his search for the universal is very clear.

"A distortion of values, which confounds the contingent with the essential, the ephemeral with the permanent."

"But my concern here is only with the corrective to provincialism in literature."[6]

6
Ibid., pp. 29–30.

"The progress of an artist is a continual self-sacrifice, a continual extinction of personality.

There remains to define this process of depersonalisation and its relation to the sense of tradition. It is in this depersonalisation that art may be said to approach the condition of science."[7]

7
Eliot, "Tradition and the Individual Talent?," op cit., p. 55.

These quotes come from the beautiful edition of T.S. Eliot's two texts, translated by Juan Carlos Rodríguez and edited by the National Autonomous University of Mexico in 2013 under the title: *Lo clásico*

y el talento individual. (The Classical and Individual Talent). It is an edition well worth acquiring. Lying next to it on my table is another little gem: the original edition in English of *What Is a Classic?* edited by Faber & Faber in London in 1950.

Ortega

In an essay *En torno al Coloquio de Darmstadt,* written in 1951, Ortega said:

> "In effect, style has a very peculiar role in architecture, which it doesn't have in other arts, even in the purer arts. Paradoxical though it may seem, that is how it is. In other arts style is merely a question of the artist: he decides – with all his being and with a level of decision-making that runs deeper than his will and consequently acquires an aspect of

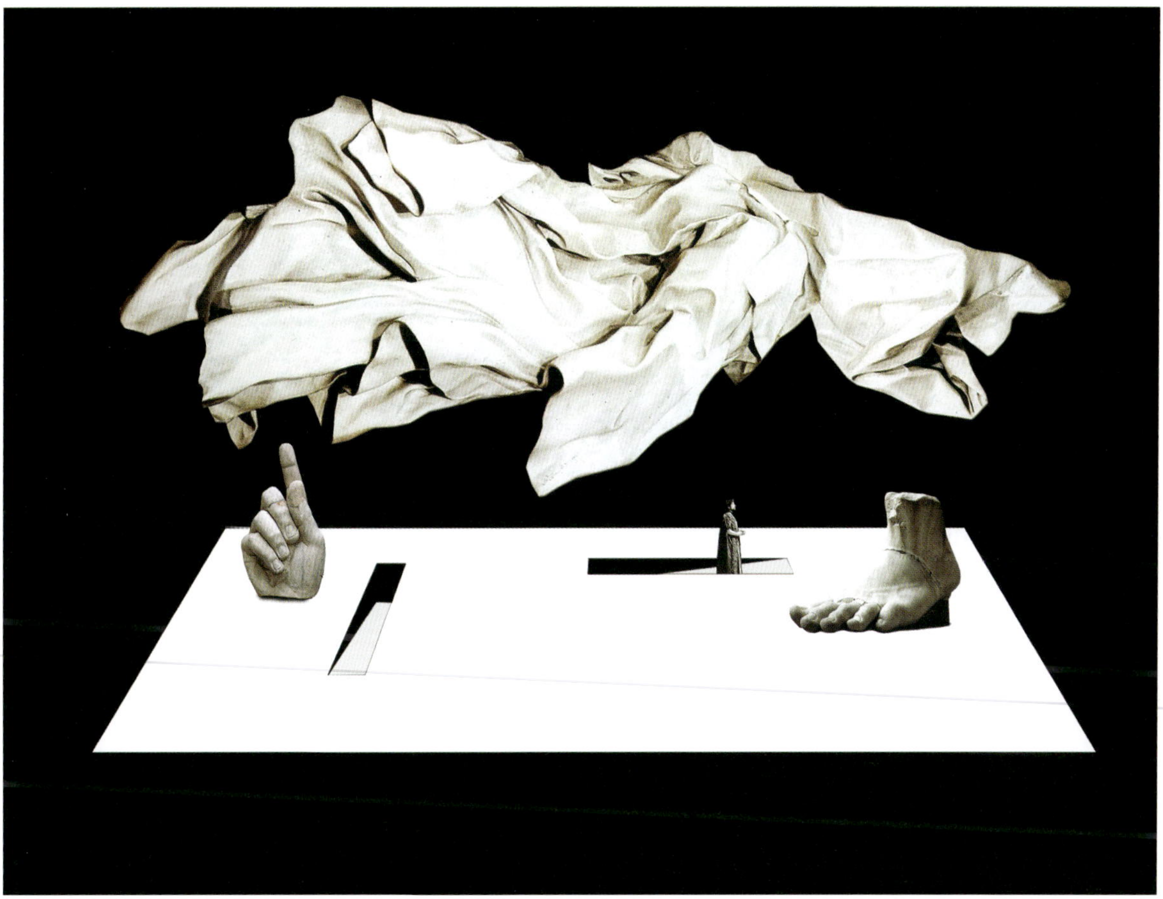

Alberto Campo Baeza, Scenography for Greek Theatre of Syracuse, Syracuse, Italy, 2015. Courtesy of Estudio Alberto Campo Baeza

> necessity rather than free will – for himself and unto himself. His style does not and cannot depend on anyone else but himself. But the same is not true of architecture. If an architect produces a project with an admirable personal style, he is not, strictly speaking, a good architect."[8]

8

Ortega y Gasset, José (2011). Intorno al colloquio di Darmstadt, 1951 (About the Darmstadt Colloquium). In: *Meditazione sulla tecnica e altri saggi su scienza e filosofia* (Meditation on Technique and Other Essays on Science and Philosophy) (ed. José Ortega y Gasset), 110. Milan: Mimesis Edizioni, Kindle edition.

In 1951, an architectural congress was held in Darmstadt which was attended by Heidegger and Ortega. And surprisingly Ortega dares to directly criticize that style of personal architecture, *provincial* in Eliot's terms, with such clarity. It reminds me of the work of an extraordinary architect like Gaudí, and how his excessive personality takes from the universality that we find in maestros like Mies Van der Rohe or Le Corbusier.

And Ortega goes on to say:

> "The architect finds himself in a relationship with his art, very different from the bond formed between other artists and their respective works. The reason for this is obvious: architecture is not, cannot be, must not be an exclusively individual art. It is a collective art. The genuine architect is an entire people, which provides the means of construction, its purpose and its unity. Imagine a city built by 'amazing', but dedicated architects, each out for himself, and his own individual style. Each one of these buildings could be magnificent and yet the overall effect would be bizarre and intolerable. In such a scenario, far too much emphasis would be given to an aspect of all art which has not been sufficiently remedied; its capricious element. Its capriciousness would manifest itself naked, cynical, indecent, intolerable. We would not be able to see the building as part of the sovereign objectivity of a great mineral body, but displaying, on the contrary, the impertinent profile of someone who is doing whatever he feels like."[9]

9

Ibid., p. 110.

It would seem that Ortega's words could have been uttered today regarding much of the arbitrary, capricious architecture that we see being built right now.

Sota

"One tires of seeing beauty and the grace of things (perhaps they are the same) being pursued with added embellishments, knowing the secret is not there. My unforgettable friend Josep Antoni Coderch used to say that ultimate beauty is like a beautiful bald head (Nefertiti, for example), from which one had pulled out each and every hair, lock by lock, with the pain of ripping them out, one by one. Painfully we must tear from our works the hairs which impede us from achieving their simple, simple end."[10]

10

de la Sota, Alejandro (1990). *Alejandro de la Sota*, 74. Madrid: Pronaos Editorial.

These expressive sentiments from the Spanish architect Alejandro de la Sota are the closing words from the book on his work that define so well the views on architecture and life itself of this true maestro, who began each day playing a Bach sonata.

Sota's architecture has that extreme elegance of the precise gesture, of the exact phrase, that so accurately touches silence. The silence of his work and his personality is gifted with the difficult capacity to fascinate. So close to poetry, to poetic breath, to hushed music.

Sota's architecture is encapsulated in the Gymnasium of the Maravillas School in Madrid. This superb building is impressive in its extraordinarily terse, pithy, absolute simplicity. So much so that for non-architects it goes unnoticed and it may be hard for the layman to understand the beauty contained in it. For the same reason that it is not easy to understand Mark Rothko's painting. This simplicity of the most logical architecture led Sota to say: "I believe that not making architecture is a way of making it."[11] And when asked about the Gymnasium of the Maravillas School, he simply replied: "It solved a problem."

11 Ibid.

A little more and we could hear Sota saying that "Architecture is not a turning loose of emotion but an escape from emotion,"[12] which is what T.S. Eliot wrote about poetry.

12 Ibid.

How could we fail to recognize an identical universal breath in our three creators? As the years go by, I must acknowledge the great intellectual enjoyment produced by the interaction of these characters and these issues in one's memory. How great and profitable is the passage of time!

NOTE

And, just when I thought this text had concluded, Gombrich appears. Well, it's not as if Ernst H. Gombrich, whose wonderful text *The Preference for the Primitive*[13] I have been acquainted with for such a long time and is on my desk, has just appeared out of the blue. Simply that I periodically reread a selection of very special texts that I keep together on a shelf of favorites. I have written many times of the enormous intellectual enjoyment of returning over the years to one's sources.

13 Gombrich, Ernst H. (2006). *The Preference for the Primitive: Episodes in the History of Western Taste and Art.* London: Phaidon. Available at: https://archive.org/details/preferenceforpri0000gomb/page/6/mode/2up (accessed September 2025).

The book opens with a quotation from Cicero, *De Oratore*, III. 25.98, that says everything: "However, though they captivate us at first

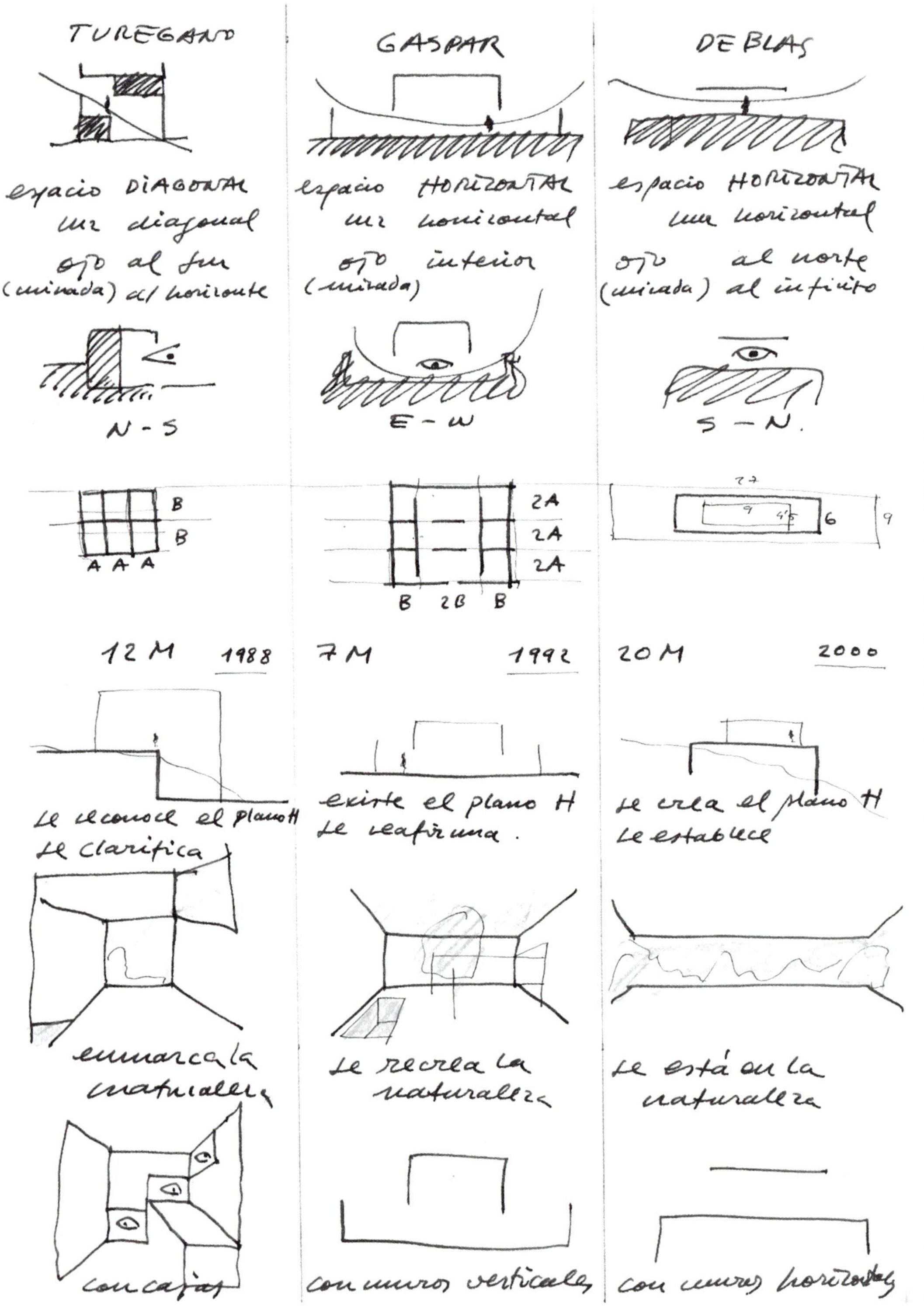

Alberto Campo Baeza, Sketches of Turegano House, Gaspar House, and de Blas House

sight, [they] do not afford any lasting pleasure; whereas we are strongly attracted by rough and faded colouring in the paintings of antiquity."[14]

14 Ibid., p. 7.

And Gombrich remarks: "The more the artist knows how to flatter the senses, the more he will mobilize defences against this flattery."[15]

15 Ibid., p. 27.

In the end, this preference for the primitive is a clear expression of the need to surrender excessive individuality in order to attain universality.

Or, as my old friend, the Russian architect Konstantin Mel'nikov said:

> "Having become my own boss, I entreated Architecture to throw off her gown of marble, remove her make-up and reveal herself as she really is: like a goddess, naked, graceful and young. And to renounce being agreeable and compliant, as befits true beauty."[16]

16 Unidentified bibliographic reference [Editor's note].

➔ Alberto Campo Baeza, Gaspar House, Vejer de la Frontera, Cadiz, Spain, 1990–1992.

6 WISDOM

On the Wisdom of the Architect

[Wisdom] is the reflection of eternal light.

—Sapienza 7:26[1]

For within her [wisdom] is a spirit intelligent, holy, unique, manifold, subtle, active, incisive, unsullied, lucid, invulnerable, benevolent, sharp, irresistible, beneficent, loving to man, steadfast, dependable, unperturbed, almighty, all-surveying, penetrating all intelligent, pure and most subtle spirits; for Wisdom is quicker to move than any motion; she is so pure, she pervades and permeates all things.

She is a breath of the power of God, pure emanation of the glory of the Almighty; hence nothing impure can find a way into her. She is a reflection of the eternal light, untarnished mirror of God's active power, image of his goodness.

Although alone, she can do all; herself unchanging, she makes all things new. In each generation she passes into holy souls, she makes them friends of God! and prophets; for God loves only the man who lives with Wisdom. She is indeed more splendid than the sun, she outshines all the constellations; compared with light, she takes first place, for light must yield to night, but over Wisdom evil can never triumph.

—Sapienza 7:22–30[2]

T.S. Eliot makes an accurate distinction between information, knowledge, and wisdom. First, in his poem, Choruses from "The Rock,"[3] written in 1934, and later in his landmark study, *What Is a Classic?*,[4] the text of the keynote address before the Virgil Society in London on October 16, 1944.

In "Chorus I" in Choruses from "The Rock," he writes: "Where is the wisdom we have lost in knowledge?/Where is the knowledge we have lost in information?"[5]

And in *What Is a Classic?*, he writes: "In our age, when men seem more than ever prone to confuse wisdom with knowledge, and knowledge with information."[6]

1 *The Jerusalem Bible*, Wisdom, 7:26, 1015. New York, NY: Doubleday & Company, Inc., 1966. Available at: https://archive.org/details/thejerusalembible1966/page/n5/mode/2up (accessed September 2025).

2 Ibid., pp. 1515–1516.

3 T.S. Eliot, "Choruses from 'The Rock.'" Available at: https://www.poetrynook.com/poem/choruses-%C3%B4%C3%A7%C2%A3the-rock%C3%B4%C3%A7%C3%B8 (accessed September 2025)

4 Eliot, T. S. ([1944] 1950). *What Is a Classic?* London: Faber and Faber. Available at: http://bracchiumforte.com/PDFs/tseliot.pdf (accessed September 2025).

5 Eliot, "Choruses from 'The Rock,'" op. cit.

6 Eliot, *What Is a Classic?*, op. cit., p. 30.

Eight Meditations on Architecture, First Edition. Alberto Campo Baeza. Edited by Matteo Zambelli.

I am an increasingly fervent admirer of T.S. Eliot. Maybe for the same reasons that Octavio Paz gives us in his acceptance speech for the T.S. Eliot Prize: "The magnet that attracted me was the excellence of the poem, the rigor of its construction, its depth of vision, the variety of its parts and the admirable unity of the whole."

Besides being a wonderful poet and a wise one at that, T.S. Eliot was a true sage. Because I must confess – a daring confession indeed – that what I, who only know that I know nothing, would like is to become a wise architect, as my teachers were. And when talking to my students about beauty, in the same way that I tell them that they, as architects, can also achieve that beauty which is not reserved for exceptional beings, I also tell them that they can become wise, that they can attain wisdom. Let me explain.

Being equipped with all the information is very good, because if we filter it and order it judiciously, we can achieve knowledge. "That is a very knowledgeable person," we sometimes say. But that is not enough. Because afterwards, if you are unable to process that knowledge, it is of no use. But if we "cook" it, if we develop it for a specific purpose, it becomes activated, it becomes truly useful. Which is what the wise do.

I am convinced that, like beauty, wisdom is not reserved for a mere few. All the wise men and women I have met have turned out in person to be normal, simple, and direct; in a word, humble.

INFORMATION

Today we have more sources of information than ever thanks to IT resources. I have never known where those thousands of people are who produce and order and put such a quantity of information at our disposal. Google and its like are admirable. They provide and make available to us comprehensive and orderly information that makes some people think that libraries are no longer essential, although this can never and should never be so. But if the Library of Alexandria was on fire, all that would be required to remedy the disaster is for someone to have had the precaution and patience to store all that digitalized information that occupies so little physical space.

I remember my last sabbatical year at Columbia University in New York. Every day I spent a long time studying, in its marvelous Avery Library, which is where the School of Architecture is located. I was the only one who had books on my desk and who wrote by hand, hastily filling up my notebooks. The others were buried in

their computers, in sepulchral silence, isolated by their headphones and illuminated by the divine light of their screens. I never saw anyone get up to consult a single book or write anything by hand.

And all that overwhelming information is now available to the millions of users, people who more often than not waste their time with nonsense on their iPads, iPhones, and iPods.

Because information is still simply information. If it is not processed, it remains like an inert material. It might help to turn someone into a scholar. On the scale of being informed, knowing, and understanding, they remain on the first steps of the ladder leading to wisdom.

KNOWLEDGE

But if information is processed, ordered, and developed, one gets to the next stage, which is knowledge.

Whenever I'm writing a text, the first thing I do is prepare a script. Of course, before that, I have to find a good excuse to tackle a particular topic. In this case, it was reading the wonderful text of T.S. Eliot's *What Is a Classic?*, which quite by chance I happened to receive as a gift twice in the same week, in a delightful little edition by the National Autonomous University of Mexico[7] in 2013. And to crown it all, in today's post I received from Germany a second-hand copy of *What Is a Classic?* by T.S. Eliot in English, in the Faber & Faber fourth edition, May MCML, printed in Great Britain by R. Mac Lehose and Company Limited, The University Press Glasgow. A real gem.

7 The essay is contained in Eliot, T. S. (2013). *Lo clásico y el talento individual* (ed. Juan Carlos Rodríguez). Mexico City: National Autonomous University of Mexico.

When we take on board a considerable amount of information and store it in our memory, it can later be studied and related to a topic, with the result that we attain a certain amount of knowledge of the subject in question – what we have always understood as studying a subject.

And so I view a school, in my case, a school of architecture, as an instrument not only for the transmission of information but also for its development. It is an instrument for the creation of knowledge, and for its transmission. Like coffee beans that need to be selected, roasted, ground, and filtered with hot water in order to achieve that final delicious potion. And, perhaps, having tasted that splendid coffee, the neurons awake and even lead one on to wisdom.

I have been studying the *Meditations* by Marcus Aurelius[8] (121–180 CE) for several years, written in Greek by this stoic emperor. I have acquired

8 Aurelius, Marcus (1964). *Meditations*. London: Penguin.

44 different editions in several languages, and it goes without saying the enormous enjoyment it gives me every time I go back to them. But I assure you that I still "know nothing" about this amazing person, or about his work, although I have dared to publish something about him and the numerous editions of that wonderful text.

I remember as a child I always saw my father studying. And I used to wonder, with all that he knew, why was he still studying? My father was a surgeon and for a time Assistant Professor of Anatomy at the Faculty of Medicine in Valladolid. His career was brilliant. And he was a true sage who was an example to us all his life, never ceasing to study. And that is what I now try not to stop doing.

"Knowledge is science, the know-how provided by many data, combining induction and deduction, which does not tell me what it is, but what I can do. Science tells me what I can do, but not what I should do"[9] – the words of Emilio Lamo de Espinosa in a clear article on information, science, and wisdom. It is wisdom that deals with the ultimate meaning of our existence. Without wisdom, science is no more than an archive of instruments. And he concludes by saying: "We are swamped with information, with solid scientific knowledge, but almost completely starved of wisdom."[10]

WISDOM

According to T.S. Eliot, after information and knowledge comes wisdom. But what is it really to be wise? To know everything about everything? To know everything about something? Because once we know a great amount of things relating to a particular subject, we surely could take one step further, we should attain something more.

Maybe it would be something like a doctor's diagnosis. Having gathered all the patient information, which is then filtered by the doctor's knowledge, this should lead to an accurate diagnosis, capable of solving the problem.

In The First Book of Kings 3:7–9, we are told how the young King Solomon asks God for his listening ear and how God grants him the gift of Wisdom. "Now, Yahweh my God, you have made your servant king in succession to David my father. But I am a very young man, unskilled in leadership. Your servant finds himself in the midst of this people of yours that you have chosen, a people so many its number cannot be counted or reckoned."[11]

9 Emilio Lamo de Espinosa, "El conocimiento es la ciencia, un saber que, a partir de muchos datos, y combinando inducción y deducción, no me dice lo que es, sino lo que puedo hacer. La ciencia me dice lo que puedo hacer, pero no lo que debo hacer." In: Lamp de Espinosa, Emilio, Información, ciencia y sabiduría, *El País*, 23 January 2004. Available at: https://canal.ugr.es/prensa-y-comunicacion/medios-digitales/el-pais-universidad/informacion-ciencia-y-sabiduria-articulo-de-opinion-de-emilio-lamo-de-espinosa (accessed March 2025).

10 "Vivimos anegados de información, con sólidos conocimientos científicos, pero ayunos casi por completo de sabiduría," ibid.

11 *The Jerusalem Bible*, op. cit. The First Book of the Kings, 3:7–9, pp. 421–422.

God was pleased that Solomon had made that request, so he said to him: "Since you have asked for this and not asked for long life for yourself or riches or the lives of your enemies, but have asked for a discerning judgement for yourself, here and now I do what you ask. I give you a heart wise and shrewd as none before you has had and none will have after you. What you have not asked I shall give you too: such riches and glory as no other king ever had."[12]

12 Ibid., 3:11–13, p. 422.

That is why, when we speak of wisdom, we have to quote King Solomon, the wise Solomon. Wisdom as the capacity of discernment.

ON THE WISDOM OF ARCHITECTURE

Of course, some of you will say: what is an architect doing talking about wisdom? Why? What for? I am doing it because, among other reasons, I think that to make the best architecture possible, it is necessary to be wise. "He who knows only medicine doesn't know medicine,"[13] said the nineteenth-century Catalan physician José de Letamendi y Manjarrés. Well, he who knows only architecture, doesn't know architecture, say I.

13 Martínez Martín, Abel Fernando, El médico que sólo sabe medicina... In: "El diario de salud." Available at: https://eldiariodesalud.com/catedra/el-medico-que-solo-sabe-medicina (accessed March 2025).

I remember well my teachers, the architects who were my teachers at the School of Architecture of Madrid, who were truly wise. How discerning they were about architecture. They combined professorship with being extraordinary architects. They were true teachers. Their project critiques were classes where one talked about everything. Philosophy or History, Music or Poetry were all topics that emerged in the most natural way from their rich pool of wisdom. This was more than information and more than just knowledge. This was wisdom.

And those teachers were wise. Francisco Javier Sáenz de Oíza in his apocalyptic classes, Alejandro de la Sota in his quiet classes, Javier Carvajal in his precise classes, Julio Cano Lasso in his delightful classes, and Miguel Fisac in his classes without classes. All of them were true sages. They all had a capacity of discernment about architecture, and about life. Of each of them, it could be said that they were a fountain of wisdom. I would like to be like them.

So too were those egregious professors under whom I studied a selective course at the Faculty of Sciences, Madrid, in the 1960s, which I will never forget. Enrique Gutérrez Ríos, Salustio Alvarado, and José Javier Etayo Miqueo were true sages in such complex subjects as Chemistry, Biology, and Mathematics. They were so wise that not only had they acquired the knowledge of such topics, but they communicated it to us with crystalline clarity, with convincing conviction.

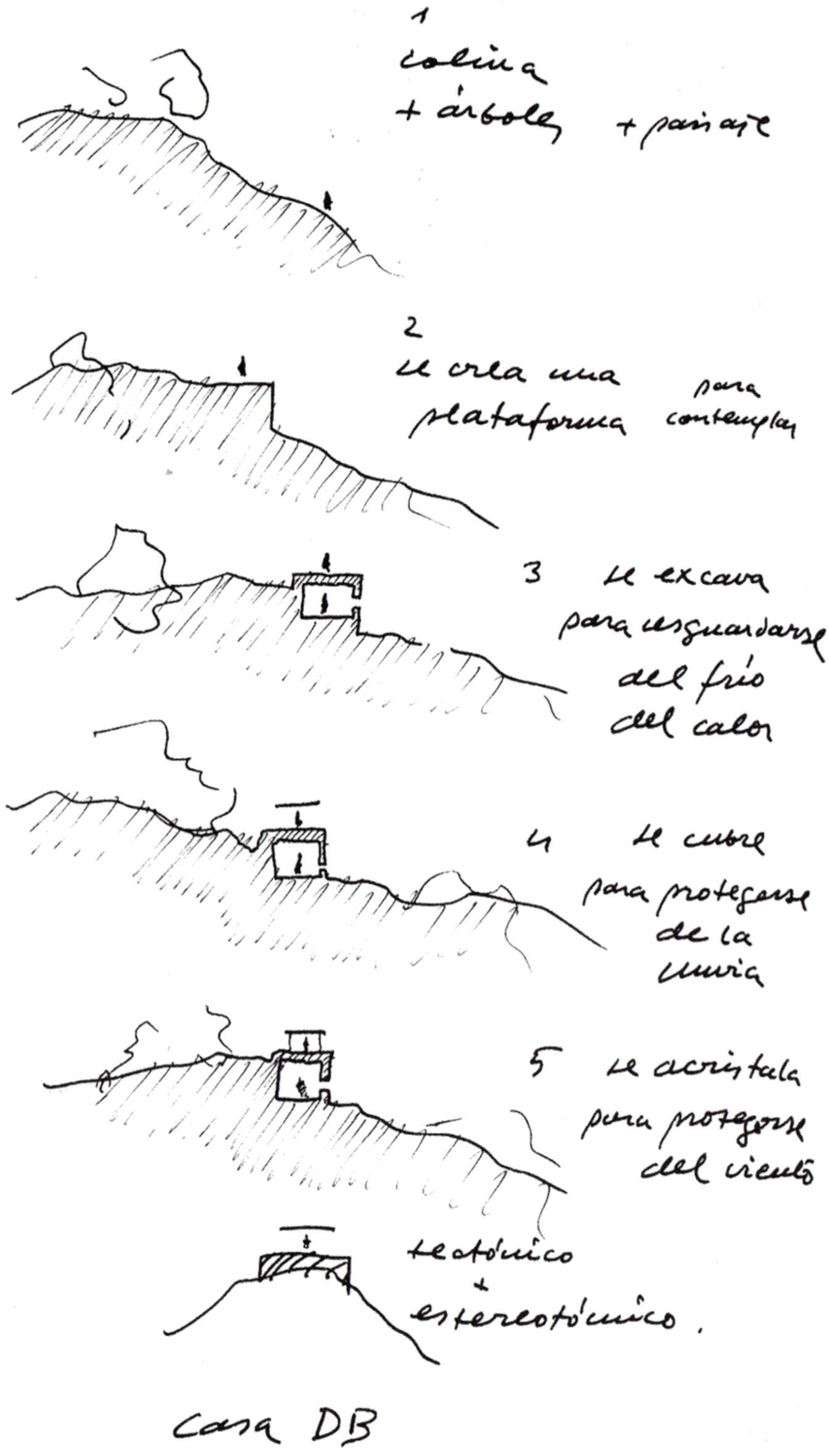

Alberto Campo Baeza, Sketches of de Blas House, Sevilla la Nueva, Madrid, Spain, 1999–2000.

14 The library in Orihuela was completed in 1992. Project link: https://www.campobaeza.com/es/public-library-orihuela (accessed March 2024).

Alberto Campo Baeza, de Blas House, Sevilla la Nueva, Madrid, Spain, 1999–2000. © Hisao Suzuki, Courtesy of Estudio Alberto Campo Baeza

I published a text on "Project Design Is Research," because I firmly believe that it is so. I would like that text, like this one, to be like depth charges. In that text I describe how, more than 30 years ago, I dared to present a project of mine under construction at the time, the Library of Orihuela,[14] as the Research Project for my candidature for the Chair of Design. And all the members of that generous tribunal, full of wisdom, with Oíza and Carvajal at the head, understood it perfectly and accepted it as a work of research.

WISDOM IN THE HISTORY OF ARCHITECTURE

How can we not understand that the History of Architecture, with capital letters, is full of architects who were sages?

Ictinos and Callicrates (both fifth century BCE), the Greek architects of the Parthenon of Athens were true sages. The Parthenon, and before it, the Acropolis, were creations out of time; they were of yesterday, today, and tomorrow. Not surprisingly, both Le Corbusier and Mies van der Rohe were photographed in front of those ruins, as a testimony to their timelessness, and in recognition of the roots of their architecture, which is ours.

And, was not Apollodorus of Damascus, architect of the Pantheon of Rome, a true sage? Definitely. The structural and building operation of this architectural marvel can only be the result of a privileged architect's head. Every time I go back to study and analyze the Roman Pantheon, I continue to learn.

And what can we say of Marcus Vitruvius Pollio with his *De Architectura*? How many times in word and deed have we not used your *Utilitas*, *Firmitas*, and *Venustas*?

Andrea Palladio was so wise, that, in addition to making first-class architecture, and writing the Four Books of Architecture, he has continued to influence architects to this day. And so it is that McKim, Mead and White designed the most representative buildings of Columbia University in New York in 1869.

When Michelangelo officiated as an architect in the Campidoglio, he showed how wise he was, making the world visible, making it emerge in that unequaled space. And to crown it all, there he placed our Marcus Aurelius on horseback in the center of the world, to make that spatial operation even more visible.

And so great was the wisdom of Sir John Soane that, to contradict the architect of the Pantheon, in proposing his lightness vis-à-vis the heaviness of the Roman dome, he makes the light of his suspended domes slide down the edges, causing them to float. If this is not wisdom, let God come and take a look for himself!

And Le Corbusier and Mies van der Rohe, what can we say of these two old sages? The two of them were proudly photographed on the Acropolis in front of the Parthenon, as if wanting to bear witness that they, the great modernists, have their feet, their roots, in history and in this way are revolutionizing the world and building new history.

And even Jørn Utzon, like an old druid, who withdrew with his wisdom to his house in Mallorca. We can still hear the echoes not only from his Sydney Opera House, or from Can Lis, but also from his "Platforms and Plateaux,"[15] a key text published in 1962 that has influenced so many architects.

CONCLUSION

In *The Banquet*, also known as *The Symposium*, Plato advised us: "It would be a happy state of affairs, Agathon, if wisdom were something that could flow between us through mere contact, from the one who is full to one who is empty, like water flowing along a strand of wool from a full cup to an empty one."[16]

If we are to do things in the best possible way in life, in all fields, including architecture, we should try to approach wisdom; we should try to be wise. This involves not only having all the information, developing it, and acquiring knowledge, but above all, on attaining that wisdom, employing study and discernment to make it the best, or better than the best.

And if we started out with T.S. Eliot as our guide, we're returning to him again. Because in a nutshell, this business of being wise is nothing more than being able to bring together present, past, and future time: what the poet proposes in "Burnt Norton," the first of his *Four Quartets*: "Time present and time past/are both perhaps present in time future/and time future contained in time past/If all time is eternally present/all time is unredeemable."[17]

ADDENDUM

Recently a rare gem fell into my hands, Aristotle's *Protrepticus*, translated into Spanish in 1983 by Alberto Buela in Argentina. In that

15

Utzon, Jørn, Platforms and Plateaux: Ideas of a Danish Architect. In: "Zodiac," no. 10 (1962), 114–117. Available at: https://www.transfer-arch.com/monograph/platforms-and-plateaus/ (accessed July 2025).

16

Plato (1985). *The Symposium*, 11. New York, NY: Concord Grove Press.

17

Eliot, T. S. (1988). Burnt Norton. In: *The Four Quartets* (ed. T. S. Eliot). London: Harcourt, Brace Jovanovich.

wonderful text, in its fragments, wisdom is spoken of with such clarity that I would recommend my readers and my students to exchange this text "On the Wisdom of the Architect" for that of the Greek philosopher. They would certainly benefit from it.

The Emperor Marcus Aurelius was inspired by Aristotle's *Protrepticus*[18] to write his *Meditations*,[19] and Cicero to write his *Hortensius*.[20] And Saint Augustine had explored the "Hortensius" before writing many of his admirable texts.

I cannot resist transcribing and sharing with you some fragments of that *Protrepticus* by Aristotle.

18 Aristotele (2000). *Protreptico: Esortazione alla filosofia* (Protrepticus. Exhortation to Philosophy). Turin: UTET Libreria srl.

19 Marcus Aurelius, *Meditations*, op. cit.

20 Cicero, Marcus Tullio. *Hortensius*. Available at: archive.org/stream/hortensius-fragments-english/

Fragment 38

"That wisdom is the greatest of all goods and the most useful of all things is evident from this: we all agree that the most virtuous among us, who is by nature the best, should be the one to lead. And that it is the law alone that directs and has authority, that which is the expression of wisdom and the manifestation of wise thought."[21]

21 Aristotle, op. cit., p. 25.

Fragment 53

"We ought, therefore, not to flee philosophy, if it is, as we think, the acquisition and use of wisdom, and wisdom is among the greatest goods; and if in pursuit of gain we run many risks by sailing to the pillars of Hercules, we should not shrink from labor or expense in the pursuit of wisdom."[22]

22 Ibid., p. 35.

Fragment 67

"Therefore, nothing is more desirable than wisdom, which we say is the capacity of the most important part within us, to judge disposition in relation to disposition."[23]

23 Ibid., p. 43.

Fragment 108

"Nothing, therefore, that is divine or blissful belongs to men, except that one thing worthy of attention, that is, that which is in us of intelligence and wisdom: for this one thing alone, among the things that are in us, seems to be immortal and this one alone divine."[24]

24 Ibid., p. 65.

ON DIVINE PROPORTION 7

Then moonlight will be bright as sunlight and sunlight itself be seven times brighter – like the light of seven days in one – on the day Yahweh dresses the wound of his people and heals the bruises his blows have left.

—Isaiah 30:26[1]

1 *The Jerusalem Bible*, Isaiah, 30:26, 1190. New York, NY: Doubleday & Company, Inc., 1966. Available at: https://archive.org/details/thejerusalembible1966/page/n5/mode/2up (accessed September 2025).

I've been reminded countless times that I keep repeating that the latest project on my desk will be the most beautiful. It has always been like that.

And at this stage in my life, I must admit once again that this is my intention. It is my hope that the tabernacle-altarpiece that the Vincentian Fathers have commissioned from me for the Basilica de la Milagrosa church in Madrid will be the most beautiful thing I have ever done, both for the client and in terms of the work itself.

At present, the main nave of the church is finished off with a smooth headwall, the result of recent renovation work.

The operation should be simple and logical, very simple and very logical. The idea is to make the altarpiece the focal point of this space: creating a focus of light that will be the center of attraction as soon as one sets foot inside.

Anyone entering the church should find themselves impelled to pray, not only because of their faith, but also because of that very special spatial form that compels them to do so, rather like the Poetry of St. John of the Cross, whose feast we celebrate today, December 14th.

We carved out a 1.20 m square in the center, at exactly the right height and the same width as the former stained-glass window. And we penetrated this bearing wall to insert a cube of 1.20 × 1.20 × 1.20 m full of shining light. The height of the rim of this cube will be such that

Eight Meditations on Architecture, First Edition. Alberto Campo Baeza. Edited by Matteo Zambelli.

it is at eye level from the entrance to the nave, but also when one is close, really close to this luminous cube.

And to get that wonderful light, we relied on present-day LEDS technology that resolves the task perfectly.

And in the center of that cube of radiant light, the golden cubic tabernacle measuring 0.75 × 0.75 × 0.75 m, floating at the height of the eyes of the faithful.

We made a number of scale-models and renderings so as to fine-tune the operation as much as possible.

As if we were creating Poetry, where the accuracy of the words and their perfect placement are paramount.

As if we were creating Music, the perfect tuning of this musical instrument of ours is essential for the divine music that will fill that space.

Despite its narrow layout and the surrounding tall buildings, in the summer evenings it will not be electric light but natural sunlight that will light up the glass cube. And then we can speak of yet another miracle, a miracle of light, within the church of Miracles.

Alberto Campo Baeza, Sketch of Lumen de Lumine – La Milagrosa Altarpiece, Madrid, Spain, 2023–2025.

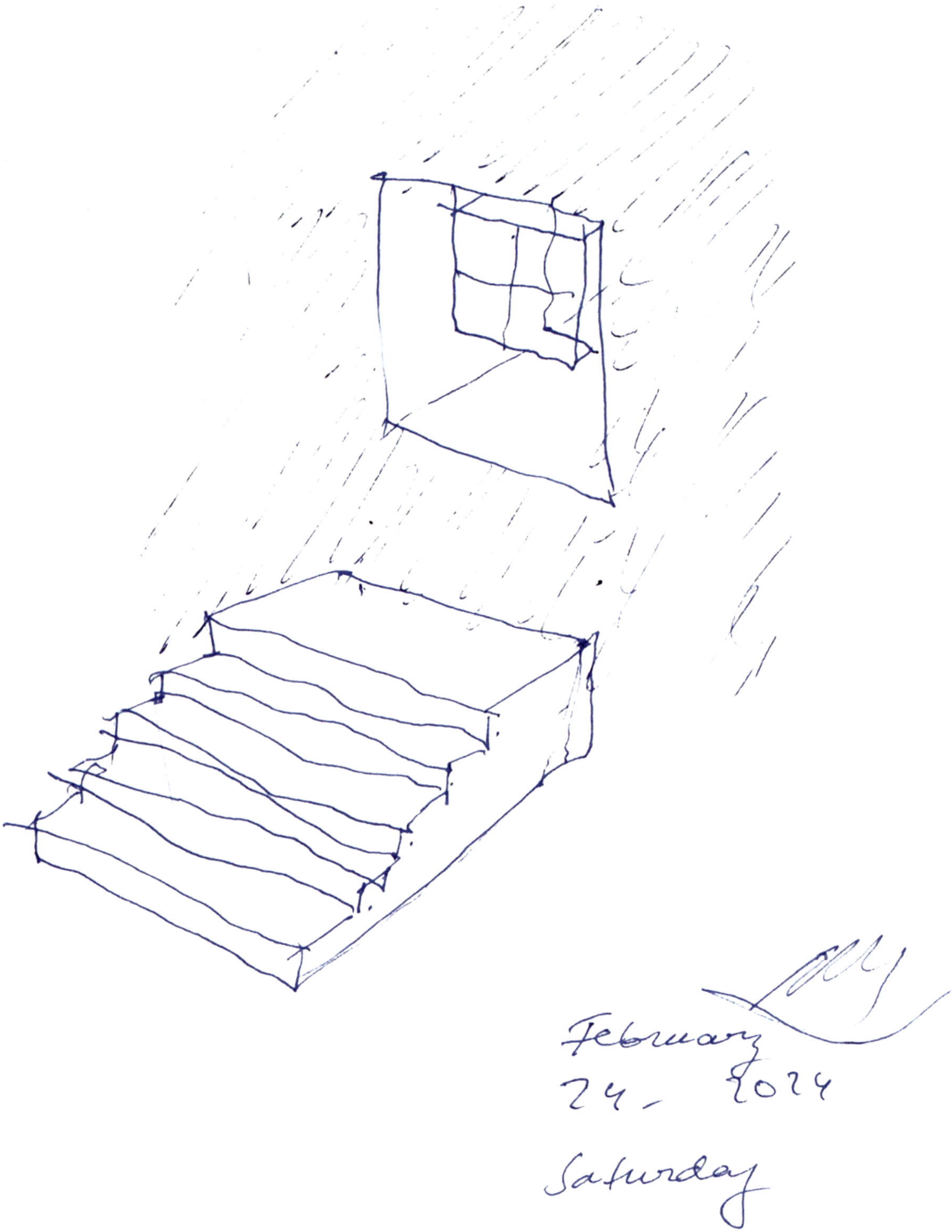
February
24, 2024
Saturday

Alberto Campo Baeza, Lumen de Lumine – La Milagrosa Altarpiece, Madrid, Spain, 2023–2025. © Javier Callejas, Courtesy of Estudio Alberto Campo Baeza

Alberto Campo Baeza, Lumen de Lumine – La Milagrosa Altarpiece, Madrid, Spain, 2023–2025. © Javier Callejas, Courtesy of Estudio Alberto Campo Baeza

8 ESSENTIALITY

More with Less

I propose an ESSENTIAL Architecture of IDEA, LIGHT and SPACE. Of a built IDEA, materialized in ESSENTIAL SPACES animated by the LIGHT.

An Architecture which has the IDEA as an origin, the LIGHT as a basic material, and in the ESSENTIAL SPACE the will to do MORE WITH LESS.

An IDEA being called to be built, an ESSENTIAL SPACE with the capacity to translate these ideas efficiently, and the LIGHT which put man in relation to those SPACES.

IDEA

The IDEAS which give origin to the Architecture are complex concepts. Complexity in Architecture is properly of the IDEA. An IDEA capable of synthesizing the very specific factors which come together in the architectural fact. CONTEXT, FUNCTION, COMPOSITION and CONSTRUCTION.

The CONTEXT bears relation to the place, to the Geography, to the History. To the "where." The UBI.

The FUNCTION is always in the origin of Architecture with its "for what."

The COMPOSITION which organizes the SPACE with its "geometric how." With the Dimension and the Proportion. With Scale.

The CONSTRUCTION which builds the SPACE with its "physical how." With the Frame, the Materials and the Technology. Driving the Gravity. With Material.

Eight Meditations on Architecture, First Edition. Alberto Campo Baeza. Edited by Matteo Zambelli.

The IDEA will be more correct when it better answers these: where?, for what?, and how?

LIGHT

LIGHT is an essential component of all possible understanding of the quality of the SPACE. Isn't the History of Architecture a history of different understandings of the LIGHT? Of searching for the LIGHT? Adriano, Bernini, Le Corbusier! Isn't the LIGHT the only way to transform the unbearable gravity of the material into lightness?

LIGHT is the basic material of Architecture. With the mysterious, but real, magical, capacity of putting the SPACE in tension for man. The capacity of producing the INTENSITY of the SPACE, which makes it efficient for man. With the capacity of giving QUALITY to this SPACE to make men feel.

SPACE

The SPACE shaped by Ihe form, which certainly translates Ihe IDEA and which put into tension by the LIGHT, is the material, palpable, tangible result of the Architeclure. The use of elementary forms aims to create, in the most direct way, the SPACE which I call ESSENTIAL. And after being put into tension by the LIGHT, it is capable of being understood by man. Rather than the elementary feature of the forms, the ESSENTIALITY of those SPACES. lt is the translation of IDEAS, with the most conceptual richness through only the precise number of elements that will make possible its better understanding. Something much more profound and more positive than a mere minimalism.

In the same way that Poetry uses words. Looking for the poetic halo in these SPACES for man. Trying to find the BEAUTY, the intelligent Beauty.

PRECISIONS I

About Essentiality

ESSENTIAL Architecture (Not Essentialist) is NOT MINIMALISM ESSENTIALITY.

➔ Alberto Campo Baeza, Cathedral Square, Almería, Spain, 1978–2000. © Hisao Suzuki, Courtesy of Estudio Alberto Campo Baeza

ESSENTIALITY

is NOT Essential ISM

is NOT an ISM

is NOT a Minimal ISM

is ESSENTIALITY

is Precision

is something more than only a question of Form

is a BUILT IDEA

is POETIC

is MORE WITH LESS

ESSENTIAL ARCHITECTURE

is NOT cold and cruel

is NOT perfectionist and untouchable

is NOT imposing and overwhelming

is NOT only to be photographed

is CLEAN and SIMPLE

is NATURAL and OPEN

is FREE and LIBERATING

is FOR LIVING

I would like my ARCHITECTURE to be as PRECISE as Bernini's, as luminous as NATURAL as Barragán's, architecture for man as "DES-HABILLÉ" as Le Corbusier's, as strong and powerful

NOT for the purpose of becoming famous but making man happy

NOT only for this time but forever

NOT to be photographed but to be lived in

PRECISIONS II

About the Perfect Perfectionist Work (Praise of IMPERFECTION)

I think, like Heidegger, that architectural spaces tensed up by the LIGHT are to be inhabited by man.

I think, like Barragán, that the creation of cleaner and more free spaces does not mean the creation of hard, cold, and untouchable ones. Architectural spaces are to be inhabited (they are not freezers).

I think, like Le Corbusier, that the creation of spaces for man calls for a level of imperfection (*deshabillé*) which underlines the power of architecture. Architectural spaces should house man not expel him. In this way, the Parthenon, the Hagia Sofia, or the Pantheon have all housed man in History (they are admirably corroded).

And even more than perfect and unpolluted houses I prefer:

the imperfect Ville Savoye by Le Corbusier

the uncurtained houses by Barragán

the huddled Villa Malaparte by Libera

Mel'nikov's own defective house in Moscow

Utzon's own corroded house in Palma.

And I discover in them that the History of Architecture is the History of IDEAS, of BUILT IDEAS, of magnificent imperfect works with magnificent LIGHT which provokes a magnificent life, Emotion in man and intelligent Beauty!

➔ Alberto Campo Baeza, Magazzino II (Warehouse II), Robert Olnick Pavilion, New York, United States, 2018–2023. © Javier Callejas, Courtesy of Estudio Alberto Campo Baeza

BIBLIOGRAPHY

Adams, Douglas and Carwardine, Mark (1990). *Last Chance to See.* London: Pan Books.

Aristotle (2000). *Protreptico: Esortazione alla filosofia* (Protrepticus. Exhortation to Philosophy). Turin: UTET Libreria srl.

Aurelius, Marcus (1964). *Meditations.* London: Penguin.

Bacon, Francis, "Of Studies" (1625). Available at: https://www.psy.gla.ac.uk/~steve/best/BaconJohnson.pdf (accessed September 2025).

Blake, William, (n.d.). "Auguries of Innocence." Available at: https://www.poetryfoundation.org/poems/43650/auguries-of-innocence (accessed July 2025).

Bockemühl, Michael (2005). *Rembrandt.* Cologne: Taschen.

Campo Baeza, Alberto (2015). The Built Idea. Beijing, China: Oscar Riera Ojeda Publishers.

Campo Baeza, Alberto, (n.d.). "Mnemosine vs Mimesis." Available at: https://oa.upm.es/32759/1/MNEMOSYNE-VS-MIMESIS_COMPLET.pdf (accessed July 2025)

Campo Baeza, Alberto, (n.d.). "Intellectual enjoyment. On intellectual enjoyment in architecture." Available at: https://www.campobaeza.com/wp-content/uploads/2019/09/2019-Sharpening-the-scalpel-10-On-intellectual-enjoyment-in-architecture.pdf (accessed July 2025).

Carpentier, Alejo (1970). *The War of Time.* London: Gollancz.

de Cervantes, Miguel *Adventures of Don Quixote de la Mancha.* New York: Thomas Y. Crowll & Co., no. 13 Astor Palace, n.d. Available at: https://upload.wikimedia.org/wikipedia/commons/2/2b/Adventures_of_Don_Quixote_de_la_Mancha_%28IA_cu31924027657075%29.pdf (accessed September 2025)

Chillida 1957–1997, Exhibition Catalogue, Madrid: Editorial Fibulas, Galería Antonio Machón, November–December 1999.

Cicero, Marcus Tullius (1971). *De Senectute, de Amicitia, de Divinatione.* Cambridge, MA: Harvard University Press.

Cicero, Marcus Tullius, (n.d.). *Hortensius.* Available at: archive.org/stream/hortensius-fragments-english/ (accessed September 2025).

Croce, Benedetto (1921). *Theory & History of Historiography.* London: George Harrap & Co. Ltd. Available at: https://archive.org/details/theoryhistoryofh00croc/page/12/mode/2up (accessed September 2025)

Eight Meditations on Architecture, First Edition. Alberto Campo Baeza. Edited by Matteo Zambelli.

de Espinosa, Emilio Lamo, "Información, ciencia y sabiduría," *El País*, 23 January 2004. Available at: https://canal.ugr.es/prensa-y-comunicacion/medios-digitales/el-pais-universidad/informacion-ciencia-y-sabiduria-articulo-de-opinion-de-emilio-lamo-de-espinosa (accessed March 2025).

de la Sota, Alejandro, *Alejandro de la Sota.* Madrid: Pronaos Editorial, 1990.

de Valadés Diego, (n.d.). *Rhetorica christiana.* Available at: https://books.google.it/books?id=aqM9AAAAcAAJ&printsec=frontcover&redir_esc=y#v=onepage&q=Memoria%20autem%20plurimus&f=false (accessed March 2025).

Einstein, Albert (1941). *The World as I See It.* London: John Lane, the Bodley Head. Available at: https://ia801500.us.archive.org/21/items/in.ernet.dli.2015.127962/2015.127962.The-World-As-I-See-It.pdf (accessed September 2025)

Eliot, T.S., "Tradition and the Individual Talent?" (1920). Available at: https://www.sas.upenn.edu/~cavitch/pdf-library/Eliot_Tradition_1919.pdf

Eliot, T. S. (1944). *What Is a Classic?* 1950. London: Faber and Faber.

Eliot, T. S. (1988). *Four Quartets.* London: Harcourt Brace Jovanovich.

Eliot, T.S., (n.d.). "Choruses from 'The Rock'." Available at: https://www.poetrynook.com/poem/choruses-%C3%B4%C3%A7%C2%A3the-rock%C3%B4%C3%A7%C3%B8 (accessed September 2025).

Eliot, T.S., (n.d.) "Burnt Norton." Available at: http://www.davidgorman.com/4quartets/1-norton.htm (accessed September 2025).

Éluard, Paul and Chagall, Marc (1950). *Le dur désir de durer.* Paris: Bordas.

Éluard, Paul and Ray, Man (1960). *Le dur désir de durer. Le temps déborde.* Paris: Seghers.

Fumagalli, Giuseppe (1921). *Chi l'ha detto?* (Who said That?) Milan: Hoepli.

Gombrich, Ernst H. (2006). *The Preference for the Primitive: Episodes in the History of Western Taste and Art.* London: Phaidon.

Heidegger, Martin, (n.d.). "The Origin of the Work of Art." Available at: https://www.academia.edu/2083177/The_Origin_of_the_Work_of_Art_by_Martin_Heidegger?auto=download (accessed March 2025).

James, Henry (1923). *The Last of the Valerii. Master Eustace. The Romance of Certain Old Clothes and Other Tales.* London: Macmillan and Co.

John Keats, (n.d.). "Ode on a Grecian Urn." Available at: www.poetryfoundation.org/poems/44477 (accessed September 2025).

Le Corbusier (1986). *Towards a New Architecture.* New York: Dover Publications.

Mandel'štam, Osip (2003). *Sulla poesia* (On Poetry). Milan: Bompiani.

Maritain, Jacques (1974). *Art and Scholasticism and The Frontiers of Poetry.* Notre Dame, IN: University of Notre Dame Press.

Manrique, Jorge (2005). *Elegia di Jorge Manrique alla morte del padre* (Jorge Manrique's elegy on the death of his father). Venice: Marsilio Editori.

Martínez Martín, Abel Fernando, (n.d.). "El médico que sólo sabe medicina..." In: "El diario de salud." Available at: https://eldiariodesalud.com/catedra/el-medico-que-solo-sabe-medicina (accessed March 2025).

Nietzsche, Friedrich W. (1917). *Thus Spake Zarathrustra.* New York: The Modern Library. Available at: https://archive.org/details/thusspakezarathu00niet/page/n1/mode/2up (accessed September 2025)

Ordine, Nuccio (2017). *The Usefulness of the Useless.* Philadelphia, PA: Paul Dry Books.

Ortega y Gasset, José (2011). "Intorno al colloquio di Darmstadt, 1951" (About the Darmstadt Colloquium). In: *José Ortega y Gasset, Meditazione sulla tecnica e altri saggi su scienza e filosofia* (Meditation on Technique and Other Essays on Science and Philosophy). Milan: Mimesis Edizioni.

Pizzigoni, Vittorio and Sabatino, Michelangelo (ed.) (2024). *Mies in His Own Words. Complete Writings, Speeches, and Interviews 1922–1969.* Berlin: DOM publishers.

Plato (1985). *The Symposium.* Translated from the Greek by Percy Bysshe Shelley. New York: Concord Grove Press.

Poe, Edgar Allan (1907). *The Raven and The Philosophy of Composition.* San Francisco: Paul Elder and Company. Available at: https://archive.org/details/in.ernet.dli.2015.179522/page/n11/mode/2up (accessed September 2025)

Prigogine, Ilya (1996). *The End of Certainties: Time, Chaos and the Laws of Nature.* New York: The Free Press.

Purdy, Daniel (2011). *Goethe Yearbook 18.* Rochester, NY: Camden House, Inc.

Quintilian (2002). *The Orator's Education* (Ten volumes). Cambridge, MA: Harvard University Press.

Ryckwert, Joseph (1981). *On Adam's House in Paradise: The Idea of the Primitive Hut in Architectural History.* Cambridge, MA: MIT Press.

Sáenz de Oíza, Francisco Javier, "El sueño del Paraíso." A&V, 31 August 1995. Available at: https://arquitecturaviva.com/articulos/el-sueno-del-paraiso (accessed March 2025).

Augustine, Saint (1943). *The Confessions of St. Augustine,* Translated and Annotated by J.G. Pilkington, M.A. New York: Liveright Publishing Corp. Available at: https://archive.org/details/confessionsofsta011875mbp/page/n129/mode/2up (accessed September 2025)

Saint Augustine, (n.d.). *On the Trinity.* Available at: https://www.monergism.com/thethreshold/sdg/augustine/On%20The%20Trinity%20-%20Augustine.pdf (accessed July 2025).

Shakespeare, William, (n.d.). *Sonnets.* Available at: https://folger-main-site-assets.s3.amazonaws.com/uploads/2022/11/shakespeares-sonnets_PDF_FolgerShakespeare.pdf (accessed September 2025).

The Jerusalem Bible. New York: Doubleday & Company, Inc., 1966.

Utzon, Jørn (1962). Platforms and Plateaux: Ideas of a Danish Architect. In: *Zodiac*," no. 10, 114–117. Available at: https://www.transfer-arch.com/monograph/platforms-and-plateaus/ (accessed July 2025)

Venier, Veniero (ed.) (1995). *"L'origine dell'opera d'arte" di Heidegger e il problema della verità*, (Heidegger's "The Origin of the Work of Art" and the problem of truth). Turin: Paravia. Available at: https://iris.unive.it/retrieve/e4239ddc-af63-7180-e053-3705fe0a3322/15%29%20Origine.pdf (accessed March 2025)

Viollet-Le-Duc, Eugène, (2007). *Entretiens sur l'architecture.* Paris: A. Morel et Co. Available at: http://books.google.it/books?id=DtoDAAAAYAAJ&printsec=froncover#v=snippet&q=Toute%20forme%20qui%20ne&f=false (last accessed March 2025).

Wogenscky, André (2006). *Le Corbusier's Hands.* Cambridge, MA: MIT Press.

Wright, Frank Lloyd Wright and Wright, Iovanna Lloyd (1962). *Architecture: Man in Possession of His Earth.* Garden City, NY: Doubleday & Company, Inc.

Yourcenar, Marguerite (1955). *Memoirs of Hadrian.* London: Secker & Warburg.

AFTERWORD

Western Light

Paolo Zermani

Alberto Campo Baeza and Juhani Pallasmaa discuss their reflections on architecture by ideally uniting two vertices of the continent, the south and the north, the two different lights on the horizon of the eye and the soul. It is on the contour of this common geographical and cultural space called Europe, defined by great distances and differences, that they meet and seem to have always spoken to each other.

It was almost evening when I began reading the reflections in the book and the sun was setting behind the Apennine hills that encircle the Po Valley. I imagined two other sunsets, set on different parallels and different times, tones, colors.

How can one see the same things from such distant vantage points?

What is the common root that sustains the sharing?

The first element to consider is certainly the relationship of the work of art with reality.

In his valuable booklet, *L'opera d'arte (The Work of Art)* from 1949, Romano Guardini emphasizes how "An essential property of the work of art is that it does not reside, at its most proper core, in reality."[1]

The philosopher emphasizes how "Real are its colors, the sounds that are heard, the materials with which buildings are constructed; however, all this is not peculiar to it. Its specificity consists in that interpenetration between the essence of man and the essence of the object . . . that emerges in the manifestation of expression. It is not

1 Guardini, Romano (1988). *L'opera d'arte*, 41. Brescia: Morcelliana.

Eight Meditations on Architecture, First Edition. Alberto Campo Baeza. Edited by Matteo Zambelli.

to be found in the realm of reality, but in that of representation - even if from here it tends to penetrate into the real, that is to say into malleable materials, and thus to objectivize itself. By this, we do not mean that only what is material is real; spirit is also real, indeed, it is real to an even greater degree than matter. An act of knowing is more real than a crystal or a tree; yet its content is not real: that which in knowing I have inwardly before me. This is represented, thought, which means, however, that it is not real. The same can be said of the work of art."[2]

2 Ibid.

Guardini exemplifies his argument by referring to the example of a cathedral: "Even the peculiar core of a cathedral is not real. Real are the stones, the entablatures, the static relationships. What the architect meant in the proper sense, however, is in fact something else: a space arranged in a certain way, full of life, indeed itself alive, a spatial essence that pulsates and breathes. Pillars that constitute ascending forces; arches as thrusts that continually fulfill themselves; vaulted ceilings that implement the closing work - and expressed in all this, a certain manifestation of what the 'House of God among men' means . . . All this has the character of an allusion through which the artist makes the viewer understand what he really intends to communicate and which is in itself in that unreal space that man is able to open up with his gaze and his representation so as to enter into a relationship of tension with reality."[3]

3 Ibid., pp. 42–43.

But there is also a second element that gives a reason for the sharing.

Given that there is a second structure, higher than reality, which characterizes the work of art and the work of its creators, and that it can only be fully accessed by lifting the latter from the weight of necessity and ordinariness, we can perhaps see in the thought of Campo Baeza and Pallasmaa, uniting and intertwining the one with the other, the highest fruit of a centuries-old canonical European thought, which is implanted in the bed of western events and from which it draws its roots and its shared determination.

This "surreal" condition of the work of art that soars in its own flight before returning to affect what belongs to the real world does not, however, arise by chance, but manifests itself as a consequence of a precise condition of the environment, a *humus* already consolidated by time.

Thus, it appears a Europe that bases its own measures of architecture on those of culture, in a disposition to continuous replanting, as opposed to mere regret as to the superficiality of much of the contemporary.

Secular flows are the anchors to avoid the catastrophe of a time without memory and without history, anchors that do not deny the changed distance of things and measures, but oppose them in order to force them to a meaning and not only to a purpose.

This is how the two summits of the continent, which we continue to believe must constitute, also from the point of view of architecture, a common home, are joined.

That, in the story of Western Europe, the light would gradually begin to fade had been announced in advance by Friedrich Nietzsche, Max Weber, Sigmund Freud, down to Oswald Spengler: the unfolding of the twentieth century confirmed a progressive decline of civilization.

But even we contemporaries continued to read the same books and were moved by the same authors, whether it was the great Greeks or Dante or the Russians, they themselves were also affected by European culture.

Joseph Brodsky wrote: "That generation – the generation born precisely at the time when the Auschwitz crematoria were working at full blast, when Stalin was at the zenith of his Godlike, absolute power, which seemed sponsored by Mother Nature herself – that generation came into the world, it appears, in order to continue what, theoretically, was supported to be interrupted in those crematoria and in the anonymous common graves of Stalin's archipelago."[4]

In a line that reaches from the Mediterranean to the Baltic, "We aspired precisely to the recreation the effect of culture's continuity, to the reconstruction of its forms and tropes, toward filling its few surviving, and often totally compromised, forms, with our own new, or appearing to us as new, contemporary content … because we were extremely animated by the idea of preserving the hereditary nobility of the forms of culture we knew, the forms that were equivalent, in our consciousness, to the forms of human dignity."[5]

4
Brodsky, Joseph (1987). Aesthetics and Language. In: Nobel Prize Literature Laureates (2007). Nobel lectures: from the literature laureates, 1986 to 2006, 265. New York, NY: The New Press. Available at: https://archive.org/details/nobellecturesfro00newy/page/264/mode/2up?q=auschwitz (accessed November 2025).

5
Ibid.

Belonging to this common story leads us to recognize ourselves.

The aptitude for observation of the Grand Tour traveler, even if starting from geographically opposite polarities, unites the gaze of Campo Baeza and Pallasmaa and finds a precise continuity of references that, starting from classicism and its central authors and arriving at the Modern, offers enrichment to the ancient through the twentieth-century filter.

Architecture, like the other arts, has been able to express in the last hundred years, despite the crisis of our civilization, an extraordinary season, because the sunset is not necessarily always a sunset of death.

Awareness of belonging to an identified cultural context still lays the foundations for a cultural proposal in which architecture can be the teacher of a new beginning, where the Modern responds to the Ancient, and vice versa, and where the elements in play - place, time, earth, light, silence - are composed to design space in a sequence that can be read in the two opposite directions: the balance in which, through the processual of measures, art is manifested and sublimated.

With Guardini, we have stated that the work of art is not in reality.

But it is again the German philosopher who explains, without contradicting himself, that the work of art enters reality through the set of recognizable elements that are perceivable to the sensibility of the men in charge of it.

From Italy, which is a paradigmatic site of the western European condition, the intellectual work of Campo Baeza and Pallasmaa cannot but be seen as the bearer of a line of continuity that originates from the classic, as Goethe saw it, then rightly related to the anguished eyes with which the classic can see us.

From our landscape now filled with interior and exterior ruins, the same ones observed by Joseph Brodsky, by Andrei Tarkovsky, by Guido Ceronetti, we know that architecture, in order to preserve and reproduce itself, must subject itself to severe discipline.

There is no doubt that "the immortal land of the dead" still contains, in the bowels of its tired body, the genes for potential fertility.

From here we can still see a field that, if plowed to the right depth and sown with care, can be united with other fields until it defines the outline of that great evolved and conscious western enclave we were talking about, the only real revolution our time can afford.

"This nature then" – Guardini reminds us again – "does not even seek extraordinary objects for its creativity. It shuns every striking manifestation and every explosive movement. It loves a clear presence, a controllable measure, what is humanly comprehensible, indeed even the things of everyday existence. But in the work the lines shine, the relationships are full of meaning and the whole is hovering in lightness."[6]

6

Guardini, Romano (2010). *Nello specchio dell'anima* (In the Mirror of the Soul), 25. Brescia: Morcelliana.

⬆ Alberto Campo Baeza, Tomb “Il cielo in terra” (Heaven on Earth), San Doná di Piave, Venice, Italy, 2017–2019. Source: © Javier Callejas, courtesy Estudio Alberto Campo Baeza.

➔ Pantheon, Rome, Italy, 112–124 CE. Source: Pexels: © Martino Grua (Public domain) https://www.pexels.com/ko-kr/photo/people-walking-under-dome-in-museum-4326183/

INDEX

A

Adams, Douglas, 171
Alhambra in Granada, 171–172, 224
Andalucia's Museum of Memory, 167–170
Anthemius of Tralles, 196
architecture
- complexity in, 250
- light, 179–197
- wisdom of, 238–243

Aristotle, 243, 244
Augustine, Saint, 161, 215, 218
Aurelius, Marcus, 236, 244

B

Bacon, Francis, 219
The Banquet (Plato), 161, 243
Barcelona Pavilion, 172
Barragán, Luis, 176–177, 255
beauty
- Alhambra, 171–172
- Barcelona Pavilion, 172
- capacity to transcend, 163–164
- freedom, 178
- hunger for, 177
- investigation, 161–162
- memory, 178
- Pantheon, 166–171
- poetic precision, 163
- purpose, 157–158
- reason, 158–159, 161
- *Venustas,* 166

The Belly of an Architect (film), 218
Bernini, Gian Lorenzo, 184, 196
Blake, William, 210
Boa Nova Casa de Chá Restaurant, 216
Bockemül, Michael, 172
Buela, Alberto, 243

C

Caja Granada Headquarters, Granada, Spain, 191, 194, 203
Carvajal, Javier, 158, 242
de Cervantes, Miguel, 158
Coderch, Josep Antoni, 229
Composition, 250
Confessions (Augustine), 218
Construction, 250
Context, 250
Cuadra San Cristóbal, Los Clubes, Atizapán de Zaragoza, Mexico, 223

D

de Valadés, Diego, 223
diagonal light, 187
Dirac, Paul A. M., 210
Don Quixote (de Cervantes), 158

E

Einstein, Albert, 177
Eliot, T. S., 211, 212, 226–228, 230, 234–237
En torno al Coloquio de Darmstadt (Ortega), 228
Entretiens sur l'architecture (Viollet-le-Duc), 166
essentiality, 250–251

F

Firmitas, 157, 204
Function, 250

Eight Meditations on Architecture, First Edition. Alberto Campo Baeza. Edited by Matteo Zambelli.

G
Gaspar House, Vejer de la Frontera, Cadiz, Spain, 232–233
Gombrich, Ernst H., 230
Goya, Francisco, 159
Greenaway, Peter, 218

H
Hagia Sophia, 182, 197
Heidegger, Martin, 255
House of the Infinite, Cadiz, Spain, 220–221

I
Ideas, 250–251
Isidorus of Miletus, 196

J
James, Henry, 166

L
The Last of the Valerii (James), 166
Le Corbusier, 173, 184–185, 210, 243, 255
de Letamendi y Manjarrés, José, 238
light, 251
  "alla Bernina", 196
  central theme of architecture, 183–184
  different types of, 186–196
  horizontal light, 187
  material nature of, 179–182
  quantifiable and qualifiable, 184–185
  within single space, 196–197
  vertical light, 187
Lumen de Lumine–La Milagrosa Altarpiece, Madrid, Spain, 246–248

M
Mandel'štam, Osip, 164
Maritain, Jacques, 161
Mel'nikov, Konstantin, 176, 232
memory
  architect, 218–219
  beauty, 178
  connects, 212–215
  house, 219–222
  on intellectual enjoyment, 215–217
  our much-maligned, 211–212
  power of soul, 218
  from traces to ruins, 222
Mies van der Rohe, Ludwig, 173, 180, 185, 213, 243
Model of Porta Milano, Milan, Italy, 192–193
modern materials, 180
Multi-Sport Pavilion UFV, Madrid, 194

O
on divine proportion, 245–249
Ordine, Nuccio, 177
Ortega y Gasset, José, 228–229

P
Palladio, Andrea, 242
Pantheon in Rome, 166–171
Phillips, Peter, 207
Philosophy of Composition (Poe), 210
Plato, 161
Poe, Edgar Allan, 210
poetic precision, 163
Pritzker, Jay, 176–177
Protrepticus (Aristotle), 243, 244
provincial, 227

R
The Rape of Proserpina, 165
Rhetorica christiana (de Valadés), 223
Rodríguez, Juan Carlos, 227
Ryckwert, Joseph, 219

S
Sáenz de Oíza, Francisco Javier, 157, 158, 164, 206, 238
scenography, 228
The Secret of Artistic Creation (Zweig), 210
Shakespeare, William, 177
Siza, Álvaro, 162, 213
Soane, John, 243
de la Sota, Alejandro, 229–230
Space, 251
The Symposium (Plato), 243

T
time
  blue-eyed Rothko, 206–207
  Firmitas, 204
  history, 206
  ineffable detention, 200–203

memory, 205–206
music, 207
secret of artistic creation, 207–210
Utilitas, 203–204
Venustas, 204
Turégano House, Pozuelo de Alarcón, Madrid, Spain, 190

U

The Usefulness of the Useless (Ordine), 177
Utilitas, 157, 203–204
Utzon, Jørn, 243

V

Venice Biennale, 219
Venustas, 157, 158, 204
Villa Savoye, Poissy, France, 217
Viollet-le-Duc, Eugène, 166
Vitruvius, Marcus Pollio, 242

W

What Is a Classic? (Eliot), 211
wisdom, 237–238
of architecture, 238–243
information, 235–236
knowledge, 236–237
Wright, Frank Lloyd, 173–176

Z

Zambrano, María, 163
Zubiri, Xavier, 162
Zweig, Stefan, 163, 210